BRITISH
VANS & PICK UPS
1945-1965
including camper vans

BRITISH VANS & PICK UPS
1945-1965
including camper vans

By Rinsey Mills

Herridge & Sons

Published in 2013 by Herridge & Sons Ltd
Lower Forda, Shebbear
Beaworthy, Devon EX21 5SY

© Copyright Rinsey Mills 2013

ISBN 978-1-906133-31-3
Printed in Hong Kong

Contents

INTRODUCTION

Ford's policy of catering for every niche in the market saw its English operation at Trafford Park, Manchester, offering vans such as this 1927 version on the standard Model T chassis.

Several years ago I came up with the idea for a book on British lorries, based around period sales literature and authored by me. My publisher and I agreed that if there was sufficient interest a companion volume should be produced – especially as I had already gathered a good deal of similar material relating to light commercials.

Happily, the initial work and its format was enthusiastically received, so we decided to go ahead with the second, sticking to the same formula. It should have appeared much earlier than now, but prior commitments conspired against me; so I do hope those of you who have enquired as to the possibility of such a thing will not be disappointed with the outcome.

The bones of the story are by necessity along the same lines, insomuch that in 1945 Britain had emerged victorious but severely debilitated from nearly six years of war. Industry and life as a whole had to return to some semblance of normality as soon as possible, so the availability of commercial transportation, large and small, would be essential – limited petrol supplies notwithstanding.

Light commercials of every type were the blood vessels of the country's factories, tradesmen and shopkeepers, so their manufacture had to recommence – not only for home consumption but also to earn desperately needed export revenue.

For the most part, pre-war models were put back into production, both for speed and simply because they would do the job. But by the early 1950s these machines were gradually replaced by more modern designs such as the medium-capacity forward-

"Yes! — send it, please"

THE better the class of your trade, the more you are expected to "deliver the goods" and the higher mounts the cost of service.

The Ford Enclosed Light Van costs but £140 complete. It is a quality production, ideally suitable for taking care of merchandise requiring complete protection during transit. Mounted on the standard Ford Light Chassis. Cab entirely enclosed—two doors, with sliding plate glass windows. One-piece windscreen. Electric lighting and starter. Four balloon tyres and spare rim. Sliding doors behind driver. Body dimensions (interior):—50in. long, 53¾in. wide, 48in. high.

THE ENCLOSED LIGHT VAN

£140 net

(At Works, Manchester)

It's war time and Great Britain's future Queen, Princess Elizabeth, takes five beside one of Austin's 10hp Tilly pick-ups with a K2 ambulance in the background.

control, which eventually featured in every major maker's catalogue. This format proved particularly suitable for a variety of conversions – perhaps most notably into camper vans for the expanding leisure market.

Our period takes us from the tiny Morris Eight of the 1940s (which would struggle to cope with much more than 5cwt of potatoes and 45mph) to the Transit of 1965, which carried three times the amount, drove like a car and did over 70 on the clock with ease.

From post-war austerity to the swinging sixties, Britain's small commercials underwent a great transformation and were also part and parcel of the social changes that took place.

Nowadays, nearly 50 years after the last of the vehicles featured in this book first took to the road, you'd be unlikely to see more than a handful in daily use, and the only manufacturer to have escaped extinction is Ford. A series of manoeuvres undertaken in the '50s and '60s had given the American parent company sole ownership of first its European and then British operations, the two becoming Ford Europe in 1967; to this day, although they have minority ownership, old Henry's descendants and relations still have a controlling interest in the whole thing.

As for the rest, the reasons they met with their doom were numerous – a melange of ineptitude, complacency, bad management, labour costs, meddlesome politicians, and simply prevailing economic situations being foremost.

This is not the place for you to read about that entire sad saga, however, but rather to indulge in a little nostalgia.

Like our lorry book, it is not intended to be encyclopaedic but I believe you will find the majority of makes and models well represented. The sales material I have drawn upon ranges from little more than flyers produced by local printers to glossy brochures published by companies specialising in such work,

By the mid-'30s Austin was sufficiently into light commercials – with a Seven, Ten and Twelve – that the firm offered to design signwriting for you..

and the artwork ranges from beautifully executed to crude or – sometimes amusingly – naive. By the end of our period, photography was playing an increasing role in advertising, and like the vehicles themselves an age was passing by – both were becoming increasingly efficient but at the same time bland.

Almost all the material I have used came to me from the collection of my late friend Peter Richley, whilst Chris Baber and Hermann Egges kindly helped me to fill one or two gaps.

Rinsey Mills
July 2013

Some motorcycle manufacturers got in on the light commercial market too. The first James vans were made from 1929 – Heath Robinson devices with feeble single-cylinder engines that were superseded by this slightly more conventional version with a big vee-twin engine.

AUSTIN

There was little or no material difference between pre- and post-war Austin Eight and Ten vans. They and their saloon siblings were built upon a box-section chassis frame with integral floor pans. The sills created additional box-sections when the body was fitted; the whole formed a very rigid structure.

Austin Motor Company's first serious foray into light commercial production had begun towards the end of the 1920s when it offered a van version of its diminutive Seven, as well as a modified tourer (which incorporated a tailgate) that was marketed as the Milk Delivery.

During the next decade an increasing amount of Austins were made as vans, but whichever the model they were strictly based on the firm's equivalent car chassis, albeit equipped with stronger springs and lower gear ratios as well as, in the case of some,

distinctive disc wheels.

In 1939 a new Austin range of 8-to-12hp cars was announced that owed their looks, complete with so-called alligator bonnets, to Buick across the Atlantic. Most were saloons so similar in appearance that size alone denoted the model, although Eights and Tens could be supplied as open tourers or vans. They had hardly reached the showrooms, however, when the Second World War was declared, and by mid-1940 when matters became really serious, Austin's manufacturing capability was concentrated on the war effort.

Thenceforth private car output all but ceased and the bulk of road vehicle production took the form of tens of thousands of military lorries, as well as over 13,000 K2 heavy ambulances. There was a need for light vehicles among the forces as well, and this was catered for by a military version of the Eight tourer and – perhaps more famously – by the immortal Ten, also known as the Tilly; some 30,000 of these light pick-ups served on the home front and beyond.

Peace saw recommencement of the immediate pre-war range of saloons and vans, as well as the introduction of the Sixteen, which was basically a Twelve with an overhead-valve, four-cylinder, 2.2-litre engine.

The public had to wait until the autumn of 1947 for the first entirely new post-war Austins, when they were treated to the grand 4-litre Sheerline and its sister the Princess, whilst for the bread-and-butter mass market came the A40. The four-door Devon saloon and what would turn out to be the less popular two-door Dorset were followed by a 10cwt van and pick-up.

Export was the watchword at the time and – surprisingly, in retrospect – the A40 proved to sell well in the United States, whilst the 2.6-litre A90 Atlantic that was launched a year later (and had been specially designed for the American market) was a disappointment; its tenuous claim to fame, however, being that of donor aunt to Donald Healey's forthcoming collaboration with Austin. Also at the '48 motor show was the A40's big brother the A70; before long it was made in pick-up form but Austin didn't bother with a van.

With negotiations already under way that would result in the formation of the British Motor Corporation the following year, Austin's last new model as an

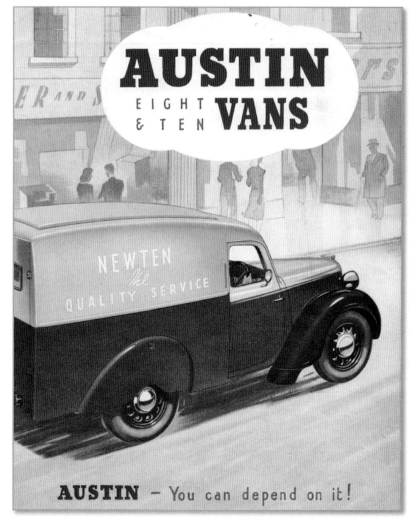

independent was unveiled at the 1951 motor show – the diminutive A30 Seven four-door saloon, its first unit-construction vehicle. Anyone who wanted a two-door would have to wait a couple of years, and it would not be until 1954 that Austin considered it worthwhile to make van and Countryman versions; yet nearly 30,000 were sold before the larger 948cc A35 was launched in the autumn of 1956.

As well as a van there was an A35 pick-up, which, if nothing else, proved that someone with enough clout to make it happen had a sense of humour. In reality it was all but useless for its stated purpose, and to make matters worse the powers that be classified it as a car – which meant it was liable for purchase tax. It is a credit to marketing that Austin managed to sell nearly 500 of the things by the time it was dropped in '57, but this ensured a rarity that, combined with its undoubted quirkiness, has made it sought after today. Vans, on the other hand, were made for a further nine years after A35 saloons had stepped down to give way for the Mini, and were finally discontinued in 1968.

Another new arrival in 1956 was BMC's joint Venture, the forward-control Austin 152 Omni – or, badged as a Morris, the J2 (as it is probably better known). Available as a van, pick-up, minibus or chassis cab, from the outset it was manufactured at Nuffield Metal Products in Birmingham. Whether Austin or Morris, it had a 1498cc B-series engine to begin with and a 1622cc version from 1961 until discontinuation in 1967.

Austin's A40 Devon had been superseded by the A40 Somerset in 1952, and it in turn by the unit-construction A40/A50 Cambridge in 1954. The Devon-styled van and pick-ups had run on until 1956 and would shortly be replaced by the equivalent Cambridge style, which appeared in 1957 as the A55 – featuring minor restyling rather than an increase in engine size, as it retained the A50's 1498cc B-series unit.

In 1959 Cambridge saloons were brought up to date with a Pininfarina-designed body but the light commercials never underwent the transformation and were unchanged until 1962, when they were given a little more chrome; a year later the larger 1622cc engine was added, which sufficed until they were euthanized when well in their dotage during 1973.

The A- and B-series engines brought to the table by Austin when BMC was formed proved to be of considerable significance, as in various forms and states of tune they were to power the majority of the corporation's vehicles for very many years.

The A started off in the A30 with 803cc, and during its life was made in nine capacities up to 1275cc; the B began with 1200cc in the 1954 Austin Cambridge and progressed through five capacities, and a twin-overhead-camshaft version, to 1786cc. In one form or other the B was to be used until 1980, whilst the A was still current until the early '90s.

A light commercial exception to this, however, was Austin's version of the Morris LD range, which featured the 2.2 motor that had started off life in the Austin Sixteen.

The year 1956 was also when Alec Issigonis commenced working for BMC, after the corporation's chairman Leonard Lord persuaded the man responsible for the post-war Morris Minor to take charge of the engineering design department at Longbridge. Upon the formation of the conglomerate, Issigonis had left Morris and taken up a post at Alvis, but found the firm lacked the resolve to develop the advanced vehicles he'd been asked to design – so the call to, in effect, re-join an organisation that did was welcome.

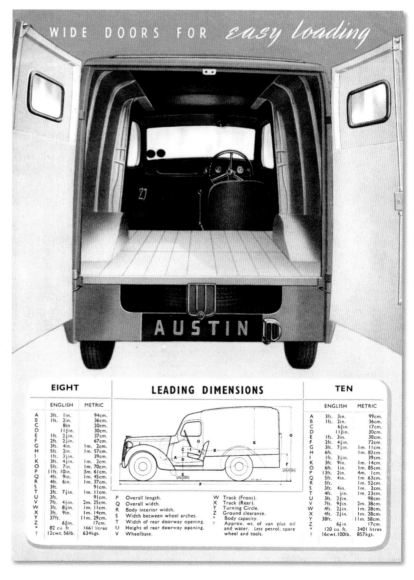

WIDE DOORS FOR *easy loading*

AUSTIN

This is the Eight, which had a wheelbase of 7ft 4½in, while the Ten's was 7ft 9in. The Eight's 900cc sidevalve engine produced 24bhp, whereas the Ten's 1125cc sidevalve unit boasted 32bhp. Both had four-speed gearboxes and Girling brakes.

Hardly had Issigonis embarked upon his new work than what became known as the Suez Crisis kicked off, and oil supplies were threatened to the extent that Great Britain suffered several months of petrol rationing. Lord's reaction was to shelve what had been done so far and instruct Issigonis and his team to come up with a new economy car that could be put into production as soon as possible. A saloon car, no

more than 10ft long, that would truly be – to borrow that much hackneyed term – deceptively spacious, economic to manufacture and operate, and use the existing A-series engine.

Within the confines of his brief the engine fitment would have been nigh on impossible had not Issigonis, who was a great proponent of front-wheel drive, come up with the gearbox-in-sump arrangement allied to driven front wheels.

The rest, as they say, is history. And by the summer of 1958 an advanced prototype had been driven and okayed by Lord, who gave the new model's go-ahead – in some respects this was a second beginning, but a year later and after numerous revisions the Mini went into production at both Longbridge and Cowley, as the Austin Seven and the Morris Mini-Minor.

Although originally envisualised simply as a saloon, other possibilities had become apparent and a van version of the Mini was launched early in 1960, with a pick-up joining it the following year. The Mini car's history of success cannot be related here, but suffice to say that by the time that both van and pick-up were discontinued in 1982, over half-a-million of the former and some 60,000 of the latter had been produced.

Austin's other new commercial for 1960 was the J4 10/12cwt forward-control and, although historically overshadowed by its diminutive relation, if one counts its 1974 transformation into the Sherpa and subsequent incarnations, it outlasted the Mini pick-ups and vans.

Sadly, their manufacturer had just a few more years of relative normality – even expansion in the face of declining home-market sales – before becoming enmeshed in a turmoil that would lead to its demise.

By the end of 1966 BMC had not only taken over Pressed Steel (its main body supplier) but Jaguar Cars, as well undergoing a name change to British Motor Holdings. This did little to hide the fact that the industry was in decline, and the British Labour government reasoned (if governments can be said to be capable of such processes) that further mergers might save the day.

Under not a little pressure from the government, BMH combined with the Leyland Motor Corporation and became the British Leyland Motor Corporation early in 1968. Things didn't improve and in 1975, a year after the awful Edward Heath had been removed from power, Labour partially nationalised BLMC – which by that time comprised the majority of the British motor manufacturers and getting on for 50 per cent of the home market.

Now split into several divisions there were some

One has to wonder where Austin's publicity department envisualised this fruit, veg and florist shop might have been.

momentary highs but inexorably, by way of sell-offs, buyouts, mergers and simple failures the whole thing went downhill – a hill so long and tortuous it would be impossible to relate even a fraction of the story here.

Suffice to say that what remained of car manufacturing, after its more marketable brands had been hived off (with Mini now owned by BMW and both Jaguar and Land Rover by Tata Motors of India), carried on as the MG Rover Group until 2005 when the company went into administration. For a while it seemed that no one could be found to pick up the pieces – even the MG name – but during September equipment started to be shipped to the Nanjing Automobile Group in China. For a while it made a mildly-rehashed MG TF with assembly at Longbridge, but demand was at best poor and production lapsed in 2011.

The truck and commercial vehicle division merged with DAF in 1987 to become Leyland UK in Great Britain until DAF went to the wall in 1993, whereupon a management buyout of the Birmingham Freight Rover factory created LDV. In some products it was just possible to see lineage that stretched back to the Sherpa and even the J4 but, or maybe because of this, after 12 years LDV also failed; and after a period of different owners and broken promises the firm's assets ended up in the ownership of SAIC Motor (the Chinese state-owned automaker) in 2010.

No mention of the pick-up's weight-carrying capacity, but it was good for 10cwt or a little more.

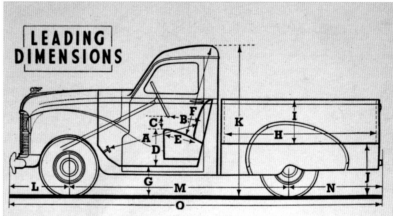

"Modern Business demands a modern van," read Austin's brochure for its new A40, at the same time drawing attention to how the, "strong box-section chassis, cross braced at the centre, forms a firm foundation for this fine, sturdy vehicle, while independent front suspension ensures stability and smooth riding." Austin was also rather pleased about the, "Concealed hinges and built-in concealed running boards," and the, "bonnet lock controlled from inside the cab."

LEADING DIMENSIONS			
		English	Metric
A —Pedal to seat squab	...	3' 2½"	0.97 m.
B —Steering wheel to seat squab	...	1' 2"	0.36 m.
C —Steering wheel to seat cushion	...	7½"	0.19 m.
D —Seat cushion height above floor	...	1' 0"	0.30 m.
E —Seat cushion depth	...	1' 3½"	0.39 m.
F —Height over seat	...	3' 2½"	0.97 m.
G —Cab floor to ground (unladen)	...	1' 4"	0.41 m.
H —Interior body length	...	5' 3½"	1.61 m.
I —Height of body sides	...	1' 5"	0.43 m.
J —Height, body floor to ground (unladen)	...	2' 4½"	0.72 m.
K —Overall height	...	5' 6¾"	1.70 m.
L —Length, front bumper to centre of front hub	...	2' 0½"	0.61 m.
M —Wheelbase	...	7' 8½"	2.35 m.
N —Length, tail lamp to centre of rear hub	...	3' 5"	1.04 m.
O —Overall length	...	13' 4"	4.07 m.
Overall length with tailboard down	...	14' 4"	4.37 m.
Overall width	...	5' 1½"	1.56 m.
Track front	...	4' 1½"	1.25 m.
Track rear	...	4' 2½"	1.27 m.
Interior body width	...	4' 3"	1.29 m.
Width between wheelarches	...	3' 3"	9.90 m.
Ground clearance	...	6¾"	0.17 m.
Turning circle	...	38' 0"	11.58 m.
Body capacity	...	30 cub. ft.	0.85 cu. m.
Approximate weight—less spare wheel, tools and petrol, plus oil and water	...	18 cwt. 18 lbs.	922.6 Kgs.

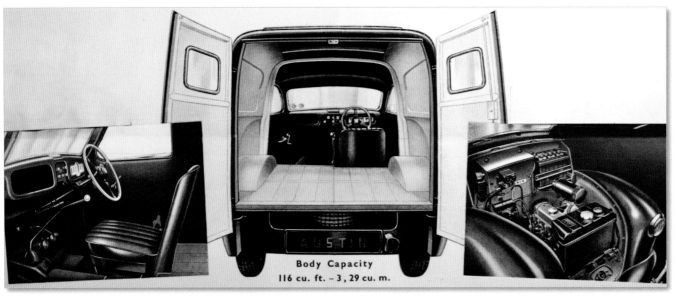

Body Capacity
116 cu. ft. - 3,29 cu. m.

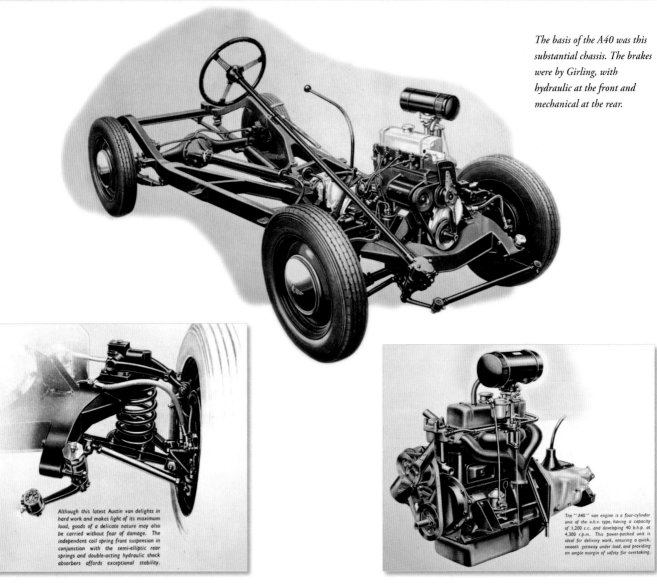

The basis of the A40 was this substantial chassis. The brakes were by Girling, with hydraulic at the front and mechanical at the rear.

Although this latest Austin van delights in hard work and makes light of its maximum load, goods of a delicate nature may also be carried without fear of damage. The independent coil spring front suspension in conjunction with the semi-elliptic rear springs and double-acting hydraulic shock absorbers affords exceptional stability.

The "A40" van engine is a four-cylinder unit of the o.h.v. type, having a capacity of 1,200 c.c. and developing 40 b.h.p. at 4,300 r.p.m. This power-packed unit is ideal for delivery work, ensuring a quick, smooth getaway under load, and providing an ample margin of safety for overtaking.

All you want to know
about the new AUSTIN 10CWT VAN

ENGINE.—Bore 2·578 in. (65·48 mm.); Stroke 3·5 in. (89 mm.); Capacity 73·17 cu. in. (1,200 c.c.); b.h.p. 40 at 4,300 r.p.m.; max. torque 59 lb. ft. at 3,000 r.p.m. Compression ratio 7·2 to 1.

Cylinders: Four cylinders cast integral with crankcase. Full length water jackets. Detachable cast iron head carrying overhead valve rocker gear.

Crankshaft: Forged steel crankshaft supported by three detachable "Thinwall" bearings.

Connecting Rods: Forged steel with detachable "Thinwall" big-end bearings.

Pistons: Split skirt pistons in aluminium alloy with anodized finish. One compression, one taper and one oil control ring fitted.

Camshaft: Forged steel supported by three "Thinwall" bearings. Cams of patented design for quiet operation. Drive by duplex roller chain from crankshaft with tensioner ring of synthetic rubber to ensure quiet chain operation.

Valves: Overhead valves operated by push-rods. Exhaust valves of heat- and corrosion-resisting steel. Inlet valves of silicon chrome alloy steel. Valve oil seals are fitted.

Lubrication: Pressure gear pump forces oil to all main, big-end, camshaft and overhead valve rocker-shaft bearings. Holes in the big-end bearings provide for jet lubrication of the cylinder walls and the front camshaft bearing provides a controlled feed of oil to the timing chain. Both main and big-end bearing oil feeds are of a patented design which ensures longer crankshaft life. A by-pass filter is fitted. Oil capacity 7½ pints (4·2 litres).

Cooling: Circulation by centrifugal type pump with thermostat control. Patented radiator to prevent loss of cooling water through expansion. Cooling system capacity 12½ pints (7 litres).

Ignition: Coil and battery ignition with automatic advance and retard and additional vacuum control.

Dynamo: 12-volt fan ventilated unit with compensated voltage control.

Starter: Lucas unit operated with manual control.

Fuel System: Fuel from a rear tank of 8¼ gallons (37 litres) capacity is fed by an AC mechanical pump to a Zenith downdraught carburetter with "T" type air cleaner. The rocker cover vent pipe is connected to the air cleaner and the aluminium alloy induction manifold incorporates a stainless steel hot spot.

Mountings: Flexible, inclined, "live" rubber mountings, front and rear, with integral torque reaction stops.

CLUTCH.—A flexible dry single-plate Borg and Beck clutch is employed with a spring cushion drive. The clutch pedal is isolated from the clutch housing by a special adjustable linkage. Clutch diameter 7¼ inches (18.4 cm.)

GEARBOX.—The gearbox has four forward speeds and reverse. The gear lever is centrally mounted and there is synchromesh engagement for second, third and top gears. The gearbox third motion shaft is extended in a special housing which provides additional bearings for propeller shaft load. Oil capacity 2½ pints (1·26 litres.)

TRANSMISSION.—Open propeller shaft with Hardy Spicer needle roller bearing universal joints. Lubrication nipples to each joint and to the sliding spline.

REAR AXLE.—Spiral bevel three-quarter floating in "banjo" type casing. The pinion is carried by pre-loaded taper roller bearings. Oil capacity 2¼ pints (1·54 litres).

OVERALL GEAR RATIOS.—6·14; 9·4; 14·95; 24·70; reverse 31·7.

ROAD SPEEDS AT 1,000 R.P.M.—Top, 12·94 m.p.h.; Third, 8·46 m.p.h.; Second, 5·31 m.p.h.; First, 3·22 m.p.h.

STEERING.—Special Cam gear steering with ratio of 14 to 1, and provision for taking up wear. Spring spoke 16 inch (41 cm.) diameter steering wheel with cellulose acetate covering. The tubular steering rods have Austin type ball joints with large hardened bearing surfaces and oil seals.

SUSPENSION.—Front: Independent coil springs. Wishbones mounted on rubber bushes with shoulders to take thrust loads. Control by double-acting hydraulic shock absorbers.

Rear: Long semi-elliptic reverse camber springs, underslung and fitted with zinc interleaves. The springs are mounted on silentbloc bushes and controlled by double acting hydraulic shock absorbers, interconnected by an anti-roll torsion bar.

BRAKES.—Girling hydraulic on the front wheels with Girling mechanical on the rear wheels. All lever bearings of the mechanical linkage are sealed against the entry of dirt. The handbrake is of the pistol-grip type and is mounted under the facia close to the steering column. The front brakes are of two-leading shoe design.

WHEELS and TYRES.—Pressed steel disc wheels with ventilation slots. Large chromium wheel caps. Spare wheel carried below floor at rear. Tyre size: 5·00 x 17.

FRAME.—Welded pressed steel frame with full length box section side members and box section front and rear cross members. The centre part of the frame is stiffened by cross bracing which ensures great torsional and diagonal stiffness.

ELECTRICAL.—12-volt battery of 51 ampere-hour capacity at 10 hour rate; built-in combined head- and side-lamps; left hand head-lamp has double filament bulb for dipping; foot controlled dip-switch; stop- and tail-lamp; interior roof lamp; direction indicators; horn; windscreen wiper.

INSTRUMENTS. — Oil and petrol gauges; ammeter; speedometer with trip and total readings; ignition warning lamp.

BODY. — Tradesman's enclosed light delivery van with unit construction for body and cab. Cab and body sides of metal construction with steel floor framing. Floor boards of hardwood, tongued and grooved; roof of fabric. Rear opening cab doors with concealed hinges, and built-in concealed running boards. Wide rear doors with opening restricted to prevent projection beyond width of van. Driver's seat covered in leather-cloth. Facia panel with glove box on left and controls in centre. Combined barrel-type ignition, front and rear door key. Toughened glass screen and windows. Passenger seat available at extra cost.

FINISH.—Painted in grey priming or in one of three standard colours: cream, green or blue.

"A40" VAN—LEADING DIMENSIONS

		English	Metric
Pedal to seat squab	A	3' 3"	0.99 m.
Steering wheel to squab	B	1' 3"	0.38 m.
Steering wheel to seat	C	6"	0.15 m.
Floor to seat	D	1' 1⅞"	0.35 m.
Seat cushion depth	E	1' 5"	0.43 m.
Height over seat	F	3' 1"	0.97 m.
Cab floor to ground (unladen)	G	1' 2"	0.35 m.
Length of body floor	H	6' 1"	1.86 m.
Body interior height	I	3' 7"	1.09 m.
Height of rear door	J	3' 2"	0.96 m.
Overall height (unladen)	K	6' 0"	1.83 m.
Body floor to ground (unladen)	L	2' 3½"	0.70 m.
Centre front wheel to bumper	M	2' 0"	0.62 m.
Wheelbase	N	7' 8½"	2.35 m.
Centre rear wheel to door handle	O	3' 4"	1.03 m.
Overall length		13' 1½"	4.00 m.
Overall width		5' 4"	1.64 m.
Track, front		4' 1½"	1.25 m.
Track, rear		4' 2½"	1.28 m.
Width (maximum) between panels		5' 2"	1.58 m.
Width between wheel arches		3' 3½"	1.01 m.
Width of rear door opening		4' 2"	1.27 m.
Turning circle		38' 0"	11.40 m.
Ground clearance		6½"	0.17 m.
Body capacity		116 cu. ft.	3.29 cu. m.
Approximate weight, less spare wheel, tools and petrol : plus oil and water		16 cwt. 78 lb.	847 kgs.

LEADING DIMENSIONS

PRICE at works : *in grey primer* £315, *in standard colour* £325

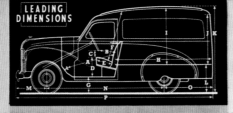

THE A40 10-CWT. VAN has 116 cu. ft. of goods space in its smartly styled, strongly built body. It has tongued and grooved hardwood flooring, a 40 b.h.p. O.H.V. engine, and is ideally suited to tradesmen.

DIMENSIONS : Overall length 13 ft. 1½ in.; overall width 5 ft. 4½ in.; overall height (unladen) 6 ft. 1½ in.; length of body floor 6 ft. 1½ in.; body interior width (max.) 5 ft. 2½ in.; body interior height 3 ft. 7 in.

THE A40 'COUNTRYMAN' seats six passengers plus goods. The rear seat can be folded into the floor to give the full half-ton capacity—and still leave ample room for the driver and two passengers.

DIMENSIONS : Overall length 13 ft. 1½ in.; overall width 5 ft. 4½ in.; overall height (unladen) 5 ft. 1½ in.

THE A40 'PICK-UP' is an open truck with a strong cross-braced frame and a sturdy body that easily takes a 10-cwt. load. The tailboard can be lowered to provide extra space.

DIMENSIONS : Overall length (tailboard raised) 13 ft. 4 in.; overall width 5 ft. 4½ in.; overall height 5 ft. 4½ in.; interior body length 5 ft. 3½ in.; interior body width (max.) 4 ft. 3 in.

THE A70 'COUNTRYMAN' provides seating for six passengers plus goods. The rear seat folds into the floor to make space for a comprehensive load. It has a 68 b.h.p. engine and steering column gear control.

DIMENSIONS : Overall length 13 ft. 7 in.; overall width 5 ft. 8½ in.; overall height 5 ft. 8 in.; length of body floor 4 ft. 7½ in.; interior body width (max.) 4 ft. 3½ in.

THE A70 'PICK-UP' takes a 15-cwt. load with ease. There is room for three in the cab and the sturdy body has hardwood flooring with metal wearing strips. The tailboard can be lowered on chains.

DIMENSIONS : Overall length (tailboard raised) 13 ft. 8½ in.; overall width 5 ft. 7 in.; overall height 5 ft. 8½ in.; interior body length 5 ft. 3½ in.; interior body width (max.) 4 ft. 8½ in.

The entire light commercial range for 1949, including the delicious "woodie" A70 Countryman. This model was contracted out to Papworth Industries, a series of workshops for convalescence and rehabilitation allied to the Papworth, Cambridgeshire, TB hospital. At first they were based upon A70 Hampshire saloons supplied by the makers, then later on the A70 Hereford.

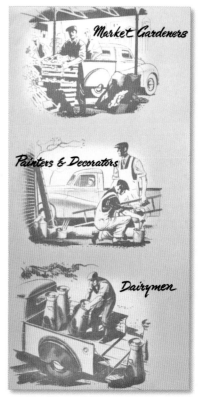

Market Gardeners

Painters & Decorators

Dairymen

Back for the next load – quicker . . .

AUSTIN A70 "Pick-up"

The first of the A70 pick-ups was a commercial version of the A70 Hampshire – Longbridge did not make a van.

Austin A70s, whether saloon or pick-up, had a column gear-change from the outset. This was very much in vogue at the time and allowed three-abreast seating. Centrally-placed instrumentation facilitated manufacture in either right- or left-hand drive.

A LIGHT OPEN TRUCK of 15-cwt. capacity, the Austin A70 Pick-Up has been specially developed to provide quick, economical and unfailing transport for those whose livelihood depends on the efficient delivery of goods and materials. Sturdily constructed, powerful and smooth in operation, the A70 Pick-Up can be relied on to give service first, service fast and dependable service always.

PRICES AT WORKS:

In Grey Priming **£505**
(Plus £87 2s. 9d. Purchase Tax)

In Standard Colour ... **£515**
(Plus £87 2s. 9d. Purchase Tax)

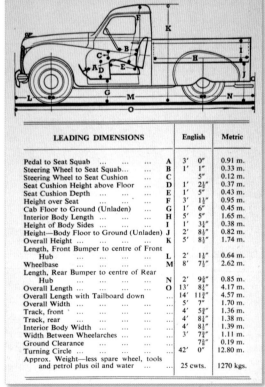

Front suspension and brakes were a more substantial version of the A40 design, complete with Luvax shock absorbers operating through the upper suspension arms.

LEADING DIMENSIONS		English	Metric
Pedal to Seat Squab	A	3' 0"	0.91 m.
Steering Wheel to Seat Squab... ...	B	1' 1"	0.33 m.
Steering Wheel to Seat Cushion ...	C	5"	0.12 m.
Seat Cushion Height above Floor ...	D	1' 2½"	0.37 m.
Seat Cushion Depth	E	1' 5"	0.43 m.
Height over Seat	F	3' 1½"	0.95 m.
Cab Floor to Ground (Unladen) ...	G	1' 6"	0.45 m.
Interior Body Length	H	5' 5"	1.65 m.
Height of Body Sides	I	1' 3¼"	0.38 m.
Height—Body Floor to Ground (Unladen)	J	2' 8½"	0.82 m.
Overall Height	K	5' 8½"	1.74 m.
Length, Front Bumper to centre of Front Hub	L	2' 1½"	0.64 m.
Wheelbase	M	8' 7½"	2.62 m.
Length, Rear Bumper to centre of Rear Hub	N	2' 9¾"	0.85 m.
Overall Length	O	13' 8½"	4.17 m.
Overall Length with Tailboard down ...		14' 11¾"	4.57 m.
Overall Width		5' 7"	1.70 m.
Track, front		4' 5¾"	1.36 m.
Track, rear		4' 8½"	1.38 m.
Interior Body Width		4' 8½"	1.39 m.
Width Between Wheelarches		3' 7¾"	1.11 m.
Ground Clearance		7½"	0.19 m.
Turning Circle		42' 0"	12.80 m.
Approx. Weight—less spare wheel, tools and petrol plus oil and water ...		25 cwts.	1270 kgs.

It's 1952 and this is one of Austin's first export brochures as part of the newly-formed British Motor Corporation. The A40 Devon had been discontinued but its light commercial variants – the van, pick-up and Countryman – were manufactured until 1956.

A40 commercials, including the Countryman, had this plainer radiator grille from mid-1951, and at the same time the van's roof became pressed steel with three wide ribs to prevent drumming. Until that point Austin's small vans had been fitted with fabric roofs due to post-war steel shortages. Quarterlights for the front windows had been introduced on the A40 Devon for the 1950 model year, with commercials following after. The artist included these, but what about the trafficators?

Although a passenger seat was shown in this left-hand-drive version it was an optional extra for home and export vehicles. Capacity was unchanged at 116 cubic feet.

ADAPTABILITY is the key that is opening many doors for the A40 Countryman in numerous markets overseas. For here, incorporated within the one all-steel body, is a six-seater with generous space for luggage or a half-ton load carrier with comfortable accommodation for driver and mate. The conversion can be simply accomplished within the short space of a minute.

AUSTIN A40 Countryman
WITH ROBUST ALL-STEEL BODY

To counter Ford's popular Utilecon, Austin introduced its Countryman in the autumn of 1948. But for this 1952 export brochure the firm failed to update all the illustrations, as the roof should be ribbed like the van's.

Wood-grain dash and simplified layout with large, round, black-faced speedo, by now along with a redesigned steering wheel; more radical had been the change to a fashionable column gear-change in 1951. Export models were equipped with marginally higher gear ratios that resulted in 13.6mph per 1000rpm in top, as opposed to the home-market vehicles' 12.94mph. Also in '51, the Girling brakes had been uprated to hydraulics all round.

AUSTIN LIGHT COMMERCIALS
A40 *Pick-up*

Although this brochure was for the pick-up, the illustrator got it right with the van and Countryman in the foreground – both had correct ribbed roof with built-in ventilator and other details. I think I can still spot one little mistake, however – maybe you can find more.

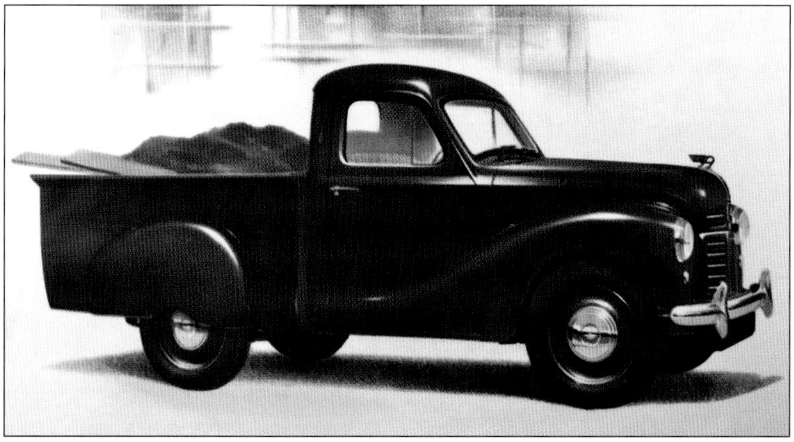

The pick-up, along with A40 van and Countryman, ran on 17in wheels.

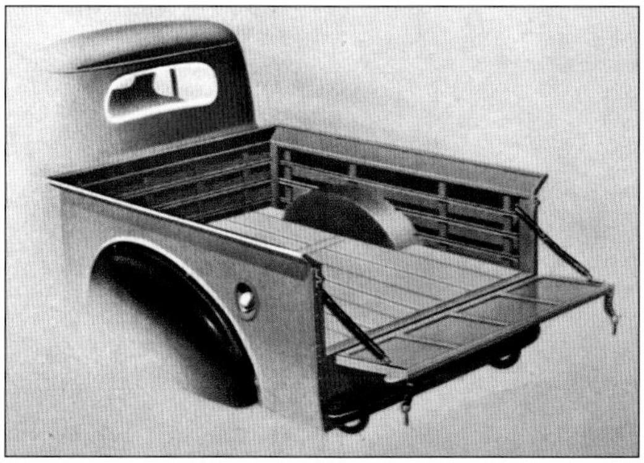

Front and side of pick-up body were composite steel and aluminium with wood framing. Tongued and grooved wood was used for the bed, which was just over 5ft 3in long and 3ft 3in between the wheelarches.

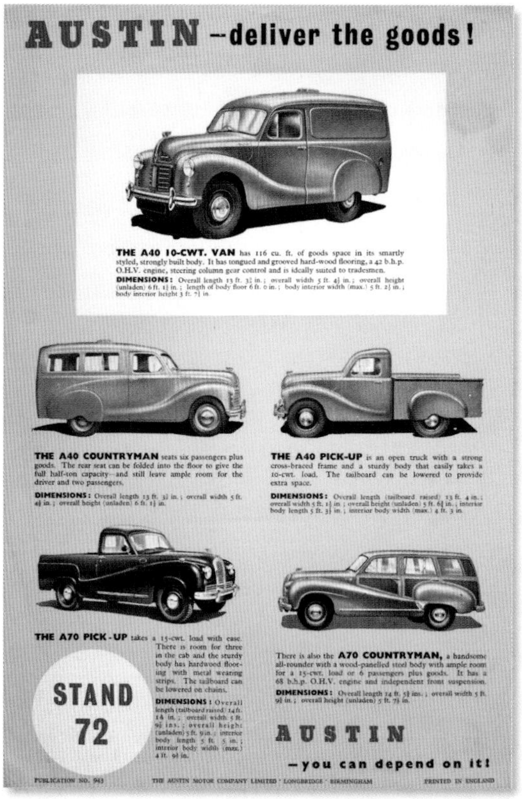

Austin's facelift light commercial range, when the A70 Hampshire had been replaced by the more bulbous Hereford. It did, however, convert into a particularly handsome "woodie" Countryman.

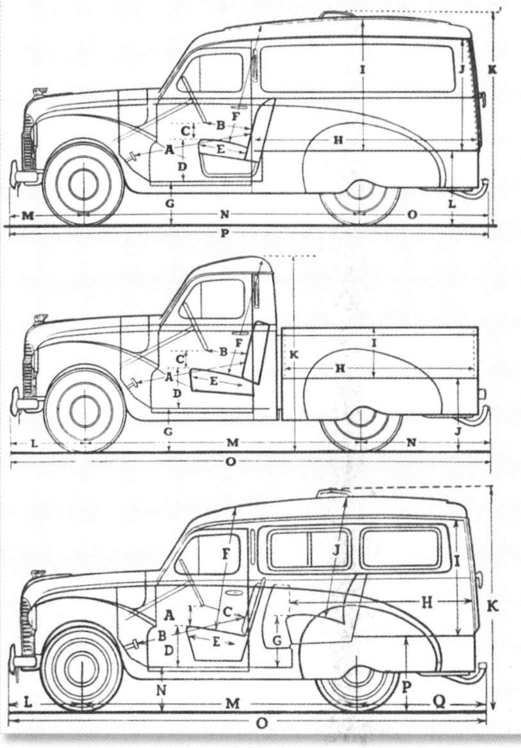

DIMENSIONS	VAN			PICK-UP			COUNTRY-MAN		
	ft.	in.	met.	ft.	in.	met.	ft.	in.	met.
A	3	3	0·99	3	0½	0·93		7	0·18
B	1	3	0·38	1	1	0·33	3	4	1·01
C		6¼	0·16		6¼	0·16	1	4½	0·42
D	1	1¼	0·34	1	1	0·33	1	0¼	0·31
E	1	5	0·43	1	5	0·43	1	7	0·48
F	3	3	0·99	3	2½	0·97	3	3	0·99
G	1	4	0·40	1	4	0·41	1	4½	0·42
H	6	0	1·83	5	3½	1·61	5	1¼	1·55
I	3	7¼	1·10	1	5	0·43	3	1	0·94
J	3	1	0·94	2	4½	0·72	3	2	0·96
K	6	1½	1·86	5	6¾	1·70	6	1½	1·86
L	2	5	0·74	2	0½	0·61	2	0½	0·62
M	2	0½	0·62	7	8½	2·35	7	8½	2·35
N	7	8½	2·35	3	7	1·09	1	2	0·35
O	3	6⅝	1·08	13	4	4·07	13	3⅜	4·05
P	13	3⅜	4·05		—	—	2	5	0·74
Q		—	—		—	—	3	6⅝	1·08
Overall width ...	5	4½	·64	5	1½	1·56	5	4½	1·64
Body interior width	5	2½	1·58	4	3	1·29	5	0	1·52
Width between wheelarches ...	3	3¼	1·00	3	3¼	1·00	3	3¼	1·00
Width of rear door opening	4	1¼	1·25		—	—	4	1¼	1·25
Back of rear seat to rear doors ...		—	—		—	—	2	10	0·86
Track, front at ground	4	0 13/16	1·24	4	0 13/16	1·24	4	0 13/16	1·24
Track, rear ...	4	2¾	1·29	4	2¾	1 29	4	2¾	1·29
Turning circle ...	38	0	11·58	38	0	11·58	38	0	11·58
Ground clearance...		7½	0·19		7½	0·19		7½	0·19
Body capacity ...	116 cu. ft.		3·29 cu. m.		—	—		—	—
Approx. weight (less spare wheel, tools and fuel, plus oil and water) ...	19½ cwt.		991 kg.	19½ cwt.		991 kg.	21 cwt.		1067 kg.

A completely redesigned dashboard layout for this version of the A70 – still with easy conversion to left-hand drive in mind. I think I rather prefer the earlier edition – see page 14

A70 pick-ups, whether the earlier Hampshire or the Hereford-based version shown here, had a four-cylinder, 2199cc motor that gave 68bhp at a leisurely 3800rpm. Like the A40 that acquired four-wheel hydraulic brakes, the later A70 followed suit, also featuring Girling hydraulics on all four corners.

A LIGHT OPEN TRUCK of 15-cwt. capacity, the Austin A70 Pick-Up has been specially developed to provide quick, economical and unfailing transport for those whose livelihood depends on the efficient delivery of goods and materials. Sturdily constructed, powerful and smooth in operation, the A70 Pick-Up can be relied on to give service first, service fast and dependable service always.

PRICES AT WORKS:
In Grey Priming **£581**
(Plus £100 3s. 11d. Purchase Tax)
In Standard Colour **£591**
(Plus £100 3s. 11d. Purchase Tax)

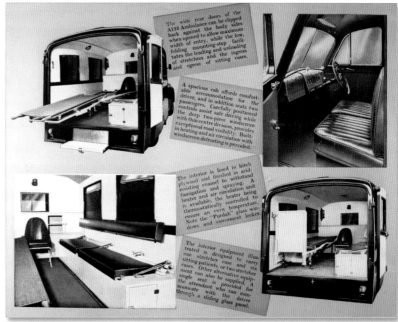

Whether or not you agree this is a light commercial, I could not bear to leave it out. I therefore give you the simply splendid Austin A125 Ambulance.

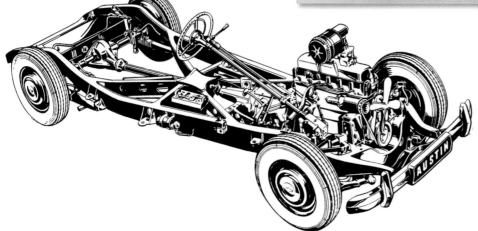

The A125 Ambulance's wheelbase was a whopping 11ft and its chassis was shared with Austin's rare top-of-the-range Sheerline limousine (the lesser regular Sheerline had a mere 9ft 11.3in wheelbase). The six-cylinder overhead-valve engine had a capacity of 3995cc and gave 130bhp at 3700rpm – every bit of which would doubtless be needed if an emergency dictated that the driver should attempt take its all-up weight of nearly 2½ tons to anywhere near its maximum of almost 80mph.

As a counter to the foregoing behemoth we have the complete reverse – the little A30 van. Austin had reintroduced its best-selling small car, or its name anyway, with the A30 Seven saloon in 1951 but it was not until mid-1954 that a van version was produced. Initially the pressed-steel bodies (both saloon and van) were made by Briggs of Dagenham but after the company's acquisition by Ford, Austin looked for an alternative supplier; from the summer of 1955, bodies were produced in-house by Fisher & Ludlow of Castle Bromwich, which had been owned by BMC since 1953.

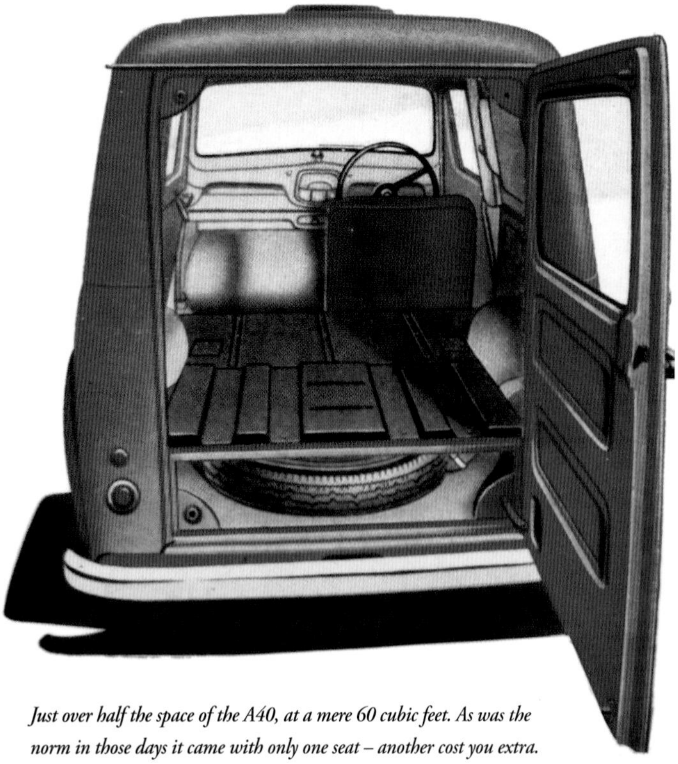

Just over half the space of the A40, at a mere 60 cubic feet. As was the norm in those days it came with only one seat – another cost you extra.

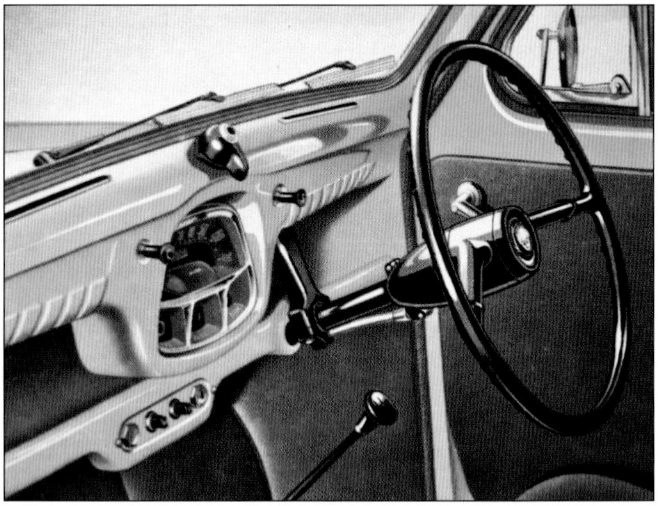

Building the A30 in right- or left-hand drive presented no problems as far as the modernistic central dash was concerned. The central switch just below the windscreen controlled the semaphore direction indicators.

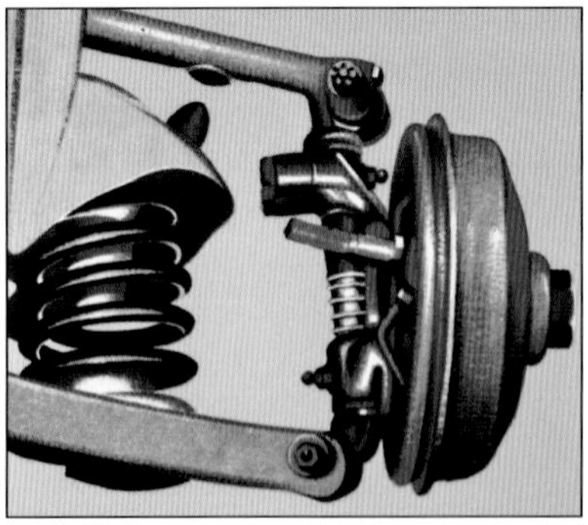

Front suspension was by coil and wishbone, while the rear was by underslung, reverse camber, semi-elliptic springs with double-acting hydraulic shock absorbers all round.

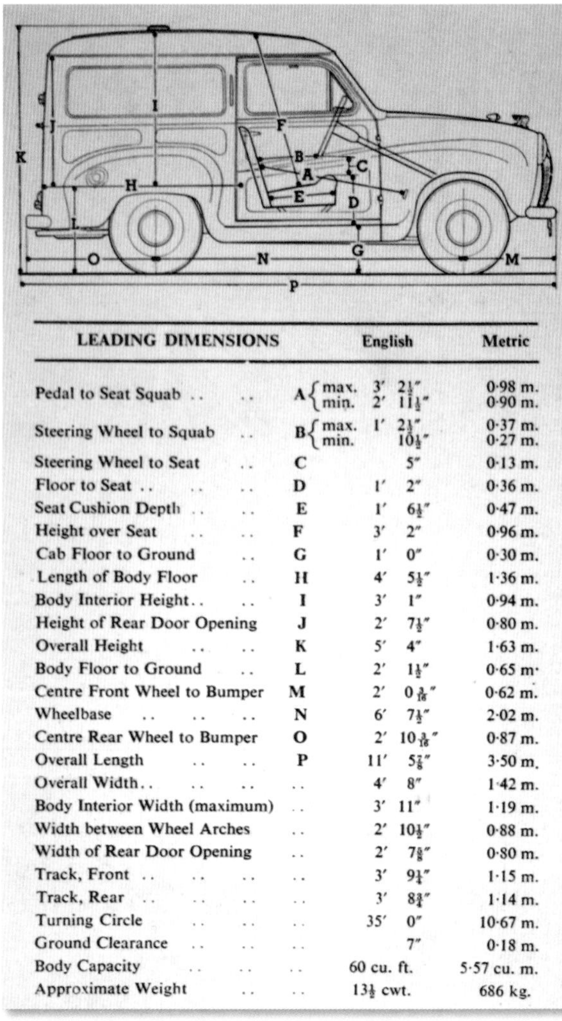

LEADING DIMENSIONS			English	Metric
Pedal to Seat Squab	A	max.	3′ 2½″	0·98 m.
		min.	2′ 11½″	0·90 m.
Steering Wheel to Squab	B	max.	1′ 2½″	0·37 m.
		min.	10½″	0·27 m.
Steering Wheel to Seat	C		5″	0·13 m.
Floor to Seat	D		1′ 2″	0·36 m.
Seat Cushion Depth	E		1′ 6½″	0·47 m.
Height over Seat	F		3′ 2″	0·96 m.
Cab Floor to Ground	G		1′ 0″	0·30 m.
Length of Body Floor	H		4′ 5½″	1·36 m.
Body Interior Height	I		3′ 1″	0·94 m.
Height of Rear Door Opening	J		2′ 7½″	0·80 m.
Overall Height	K		5′ 4″	1·63 m.
Body Floor to Ground	L		2′ 1½″	0·65 m.
Centre Front Wheel to Bumper	M		2′ 0 3/16″	0·62 m.
Wheelbase	N		6′ 7½″	2·02 m.
Centre Rear Wheel to Bumper	O		2′ 10 3/16″	0·87 m.
Overall Length	P		11′ 5⅞″	3·50 m.
Overall Width			4′ 8″	1·42 m.
Body Interior Width (maximum)			3′ 11″	1·19 m.
Width between Wheel Arches			2′ 10½″	0·88 m.
Width of Rear Door Opening			2′ 7⅝″	0·80 m.
Track, Front			3′ 9¼″	1·15 m.
Track, Rear			3′ 8¾″	1·14 m.
Turning Circle			35′ 0″	10·67 m.
Ground Clearance			7″	0·18 m.
Body Capacity			60 cu. ft.	5·57 cu. m.
Approximate Weight			13½ cwt.	686 kg.

The four-cylinder, 803cc engine, known as the A-series, produced 28bhp at 4800rpm. The upper ratio of the four-speed gearbox resulted in 12.67mph per 1000rpm. Fortunately these engines were happy at high-ish revs, as many of these little vans were persuaded (or perhaps I should say forced) to top 60mph – or more – on downhill straights.

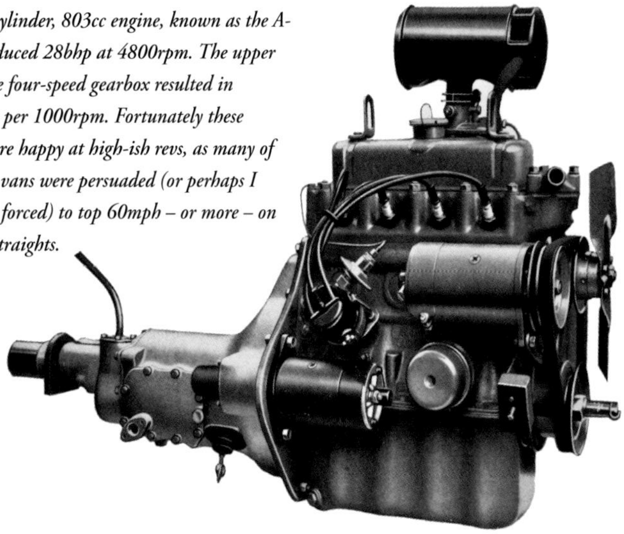

Austin's A35 had been launched as a replacement for the A30 at the 1956 motor show, and both van and pick-up versions were available from the outset. This brochure depicts the post-September 1962 6cwt model with larger engine and stronger road springs.

From every angle the bodywork was identical to its forebear, with just the lack of semaphore indicators and the addition of a pair of circular amber rear lights to tell them apart.

Until September 1962 the A35 had an A-series 998cc engine (34bhp at 4750rpm), from which point it was equipped with the 1098cc version. In later years, before its demise early in 1968, Austin's long-lived baby van was also available with another A-series variant of 848cc (34bhp at 5500rpm) to special order. Most customers went for the 1098cc engine, however, and well over 45,000 were sold against around 14,000 with the 848cc. The largest of the bunch gave out a thunderous 45bhp at 5100rpm and a genuine 75mph was easily achievable with its higher rear axle ratio. If this was not enough for the really adventurous there was always the opportunity to try for even more, if the BMC parts bin was raided for Spridget and other more sporting parts. All 35s regardless of engine capacity had a remote-change gearbox.

BMC's marketing department realised the A35 pick-up wouldn't be able to carry sheep or fencing posts, so Australia was a no-no but why try and foist it on the Dutch? It might be of of use to carry a couple of bunches of tulips, or even a small consignment of clogs but on a building site? I don't think so.

I can just picture queues forming at every street corner on the off chance a passing A35 pick-up might stop and offer them a ride.

The AUSTIN '152' Omnivan, Truck and Coach

Launched in the autumn of 1956 in conjunction with the Morris J2, the Austin 152 was BMC's first unitary construction van.

All the regular controls of the time, such as umbrella handbrake and steering column gear-change. Although there was provision for a heater and demister or a radio, such luxuries were optional extras. Newfangled flashing indicators were controlled by a switch in the centre of the steering wheel on the horn bar. Home-market vehicles had just a driver's seat as standard, whereas for export there was one for a passenger as well.

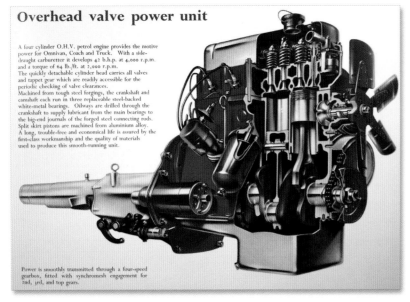

Overhead valve power unit

A four cylinder O.H.V. petrol engine provides the motive power for Omnivan, Coach and Truck. With a side-draught carburetter it develops 42 b.h.p. at 4,000 r.p.m. and a torque of 64 lb./ft. at 2,000 r.p.m.

The quickly detachable cylinder head carries all valves and tappet gear which are readily accessible for the periodic checking of valve clearances.

Machined from tough steel forgings, the crankshaft and camshaft each run in three replaceable steel-backed white-metal bearings. Oilways are drilled through the crankshaft to supply lubricant from the main bearings to the big-end journals of the forged steel connecting rods. Split skirt pistons are machined from aluminium alloy. A long, trouble-free and economical life is assured by the first-class workmanship and the quality of materials used to produce this smooth-running unit.

Power is smoothly transmitted through a four-speed gearbox, fitted with synchromesh engagement for 2nd, 3rd, and top gears.

A steel sub-frame welded to a one-piece pressed-steel floor formed the foundation for the main construction and carried mounting points for the engine and springs.

Mechanical components were pre-assembled like this as part of the production process. Brakes were 10in Lockheed hydraulics all round, but the driver needed strong right leg muscles with a full load.

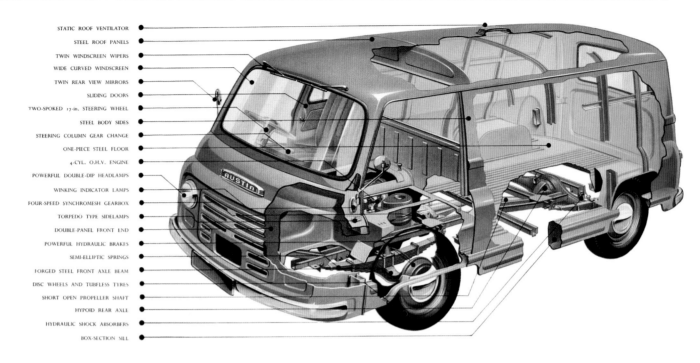

STATIC ROOF VENTILATOR
STEEL ROOF PANELS
TWIN WINDSCREEN WIPERS
WIDE CURVED WINDSCREEN
TWIN REAR VIEW MIRRORS
SLIDING DOORS
TWO-SPOKED 17-in. STEERING WHEEL
STEEL BODY SIDES
STEERING COLUMN GEAR CHANGE
ONE-PIECE STEEL FLOOR
4-CYL. O.H.V. ENGINE
POWERFUL DOUBLE-DIP HEADLAMPS
WINKING INDICATOR LAMPS
FOUR-SPEED SYNCHROMESH GEARBOX
TORPEDO TYPE SIDELAMPS
DOUBLE-PANEL FRONT END
POWERFUL HYDRAULIC BRAKES
SEMI-ELLIPTIC SPRINGS
FORGED STEEL FRONT AXLE BEAM
DISC WHEELS AND TUBELESS TYRES
SHORT OPEN PROPELLER SHAFT
HYPOID REAR AXLE
HYDRAULIC SHOCK ABSORBERS
BOX-SECTION SILL

The Omnivan normally came with sliding driver- and passenger-doors but hinged versions were an option. Cargo capacity was 200 cubic feet and the full-width pressed-steel bulkhead to the rear of the cab kept the cargo where it was supposed to be – a safety feature neglected by some other manufacturers.

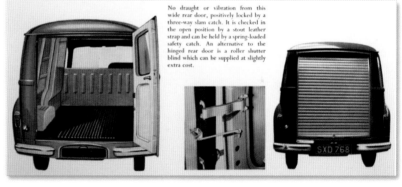

No draught or vibration from this wide rear door, positively locked by a three-way slam catch. It is checked in the open position by a stout leather strap and can be held by a spring-loaded safety catch. An alternative to the hinged rear door is a roller shutter blind which can be supplied at slightly extra cost.

"The nippy little Omnitruck is a boon to building contractors, plumbers, farmers and dairymen, to name a few," read the brochure.

Pressed-steel internal panels gave the pick-up body additional rigidity. Floor was 9ft long and, discounting wheelarches, over 5ft 6in wide.

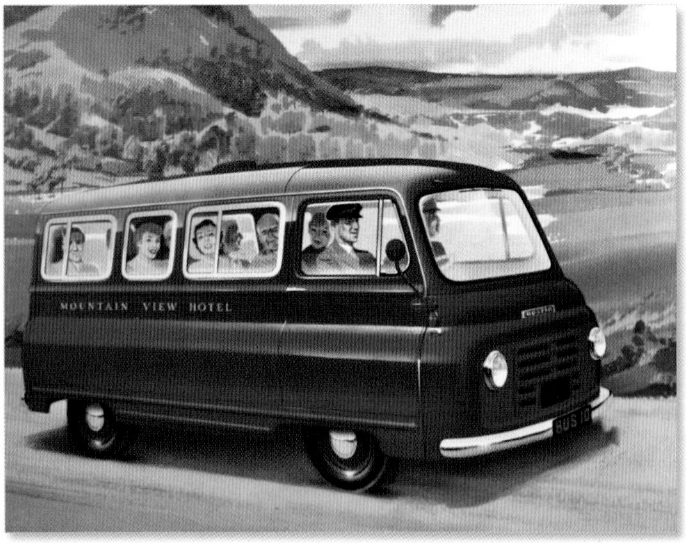

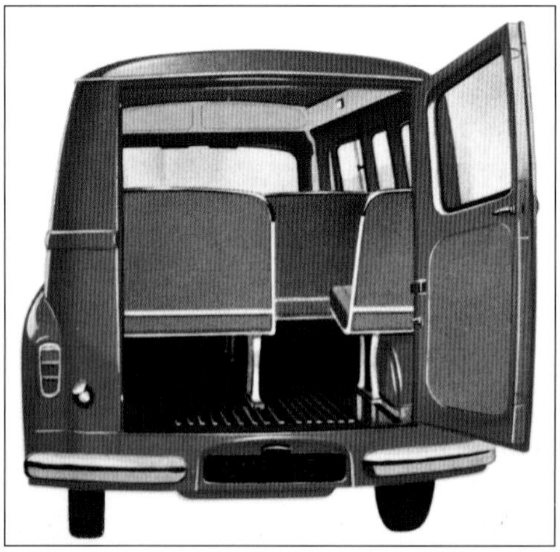

Normally the Omnicoach had seating for eight passengers at the rear plus one beside the driver (as shown here) but a utility version for 12 was available with 11 seats in the rear – six on one side and five on the other to allow for the door. The latter escaped purchase tax as it was classed as a public service vehicle, but to drive it you needed a PSV licence.

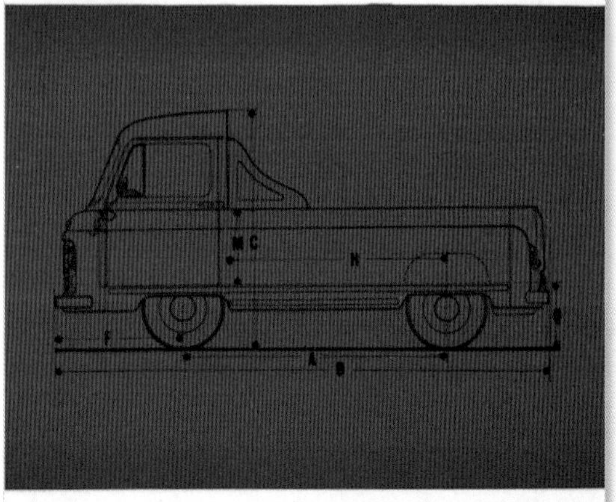

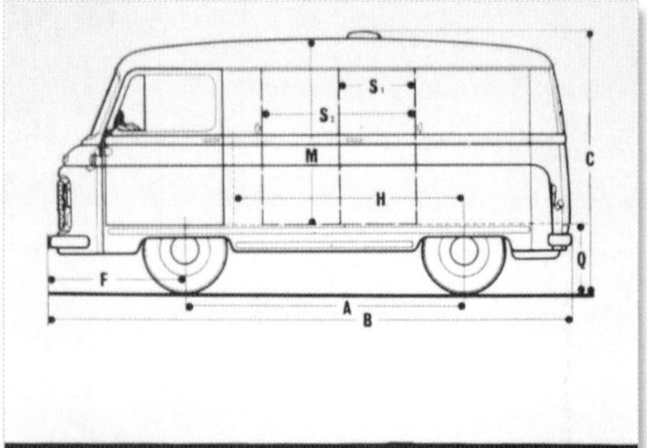

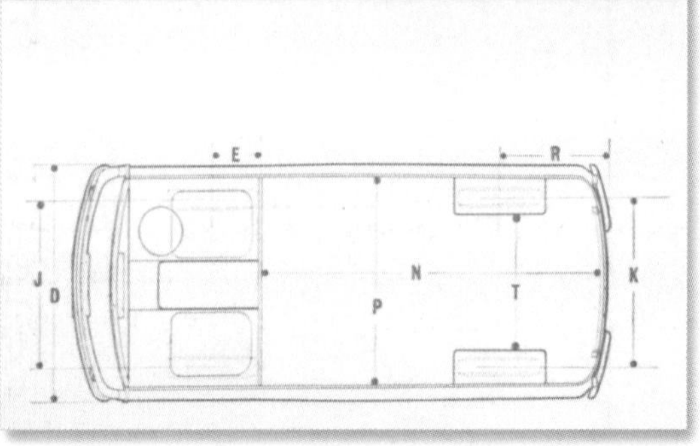

WEIGHTS & DIMENSIONS		OMNIVAN		OMNICOACH		OMNITRUCK	
Licensing Weight		2560 lb.	1161 kg.	2912 lb.	1320 kg.	2436 lb.	1105 kg.
Kerb Weights, Front		1691 lb.	767 kg.	1856 lb.	842 kg.	1729 lb.	784 kg.
Rear		1021 lb.	463 kg.	1171 lb.	431 kg.	826 lb.	375 kg.
Total		2712 lb.	1230 kg.	3027 lb.	1373 kg.	2555 lb.	1159 kg.
Wheelbase	A	7' 6"	2.28 m.	7' 6"	2.28 m	7' 6"	2.28 m.
Overall length	B	14' 2⅛"	4.32 m.	14' 2⅛"	4.32 m.	14' 2⅛"	4.32 m.
Overall height, laden ...	C	7' 1"	2.16 m.	7' 1"	2.16 m.	6' 7"	2.00 m.
Overall width	D	6' 1¾"	1.87 m.	6' 1¾"	1.87 m.	6' 1¾"	1.87 m.
Centre of front hub to back of bulkhead	E	1' 2 13/16"	0.38 m.	1' 2 13/16"	0.38 m.	1' 2 13/16"	0.38 m.
Centre of front hub to frontbumper	F	3' 8⅝"	1.13 m.	3' 8⅝"	1.13 m.	3' 8⅝"	1.13 m.
Centre of rear hub to back of bulkhead	H	6' 3 3/16"	1.90 m.	6' 3 3/16"	1.90 m.	6' 3 3/16"	1.90 m.
Track, front	J	4' 2 9/16"	1.28 m.	4' 2 9/16"	1.28 m.	4' 2 9/16"	1.28 m.
Track, rear	K	4' 5"	1.34 m.	4' 5"	1.34 m.	4' 5"	1.34 m.
Height of body interior ...	M	4' 9½"	1.46 m.	4' 9½"	1.46 m.	2' 1¼"	0.64 m.
Body interior length at floor	N	9' 0"	2.74 m.	9' 0"	2.74 m.	9' 0"	2.74 m.
Body interior width at floor	P	5' 7"	1.70 m.	5' 7"	1.70 m.	5' 7"	1.70 m.
Height of body floor, un- laden	Q	2' 0½"	0.62 m.	2' 0½"	0.62 m.	2' 0½"	0.62 m.
Centre of rear hub to rear bumper	R	2' 11½"	0.90 m.	2' 11½"	0.90 m.	2' 11½"	0.90 m.
Single side loading door entry width	S	2' 0¾"	0.63 m.	2' 0¾"	0.63 m.	—	—
Width between double side loading doors when open	S2	3' 0"	0.91 m.	—	—	—	—
Width between rear wheelarches	T	3' 6"	1.07 m.	3' 6"	1.07 m.	3' 6"	1.07 m.
Ground clearance		8"	0.20 m.	8"	0.20 m.	8"	0.20 m.
Turning circle		37' 0"	11.30 m.	37' 0"	11.30 m.	37' 0"	11.30 m.

MAX. GROSS VEHICLE WEIGHT 5152 lbs. 2337 kg.
MAX. ON FRONT AXLE 2604 lbs. 1181 kg.
MAX. ON REAR AXLE 2688 lbs. 1219 kg.

Add to kerb weights
Spare Wheel and Tyre 55 lbs. (24.9 kg.)
Heaters and Demisters 17½ lbs. (7.9 kg.)
Passenger Seat, Omnivan 25 lbs. (11.3 kg.)

BODY SPECIFICATIONS

GENERAL: All-steel integral construction, welded on to a robust sub-frame to form box-section throughout. A box section sill is also formed round the bottom of the entire vehicle, and the one-piece steel floor is corrugated for extra strength, and facilitates ease of loading and unloading. Sturdy rear corner panels prevent distortion of body ensuring a constant perfect fit for the single rear door. For increased safety, double panels are fitted on the front, the outer panel being an attractively styled grill carrying the headlamps. Body sides are carried outside the wheels, increasing load capacity and giving better distribution for the payload which is carried almost entirely between the front and rear axles.

The Austin A50 Cambridge saloon had first seen the light of day in 1954, and for 1957 had been upgraded to the A55; it was still equipped with the same 1.5-litre B-series engine, albeit with a slightly higher compression ratio that gave an extra horsepower or two. February 1957 saw a van version introduced, followed by a pick-up shortly after.

The A50 pick-up was introduced in May 1957. Like the van, it was given a chrome side flash, new grille and bumper plus other bits and pieces in late 1962; the larger 1622cc engine appeared a year later. Wheel size on both van and pick-up was reduced from 15in to 14in at the same time, with an increase in tyre section from 6.00 to 6.40. Both van and pick-up outlasted the scope of this book by several years, and their manufacture finally ceased in 1973.

A facelift model appeared in the autumn of 1962, which featured a redesigned and wider radiator grille, stronger fluted bumper, chrome mouldings on the body sides and one or two other details such as seat belt mounting points and a lid for the fascia compartment. The following year it was given the 1622cc version of the B-series engine.

The corrugated floor and flat-topped wheelarches were intended to facilitate loading of the van's 110 cubic feet capacity.

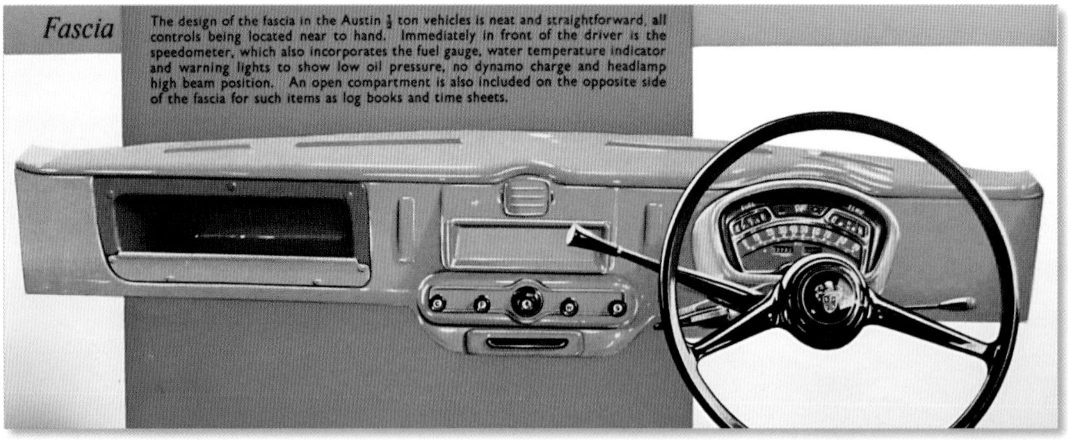
Fascia
The design of the fascia in the Austin ½ ton vehicles is neat and straightforward, all controls being located near to hand. Immediately in front of the driver is the speedometer, which also incorporates the fuel gauge, water temperature indicator and warning lights to show low oil pressure, no dynamo charge and headlamp high beam position. An open compartment is also included on the opposite side of the fascia for such items as log books and time sheets.

Brochure illustrations often showed two seats, although one for the passenger in this Austin, like many of the smaller commercials at this time, was an extra. Extra too would have been a heater.

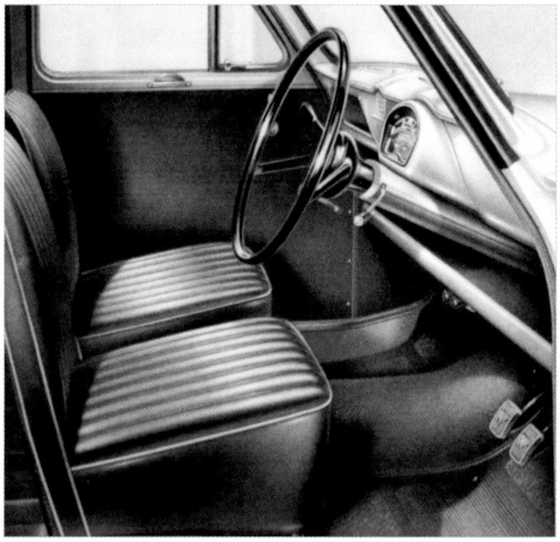

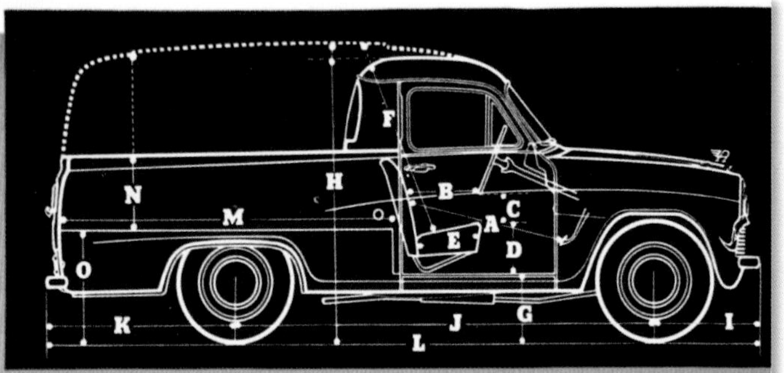
N
M
H
F
B
C
A
E
D
O
K
J
G
I
L

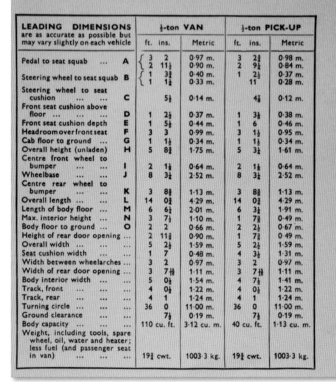

LEADING DIMENSIONS are as accurate as possible but may vary slightly on each vehicle		½-ton VAN ft.	ins.	Metric	½-ton PICK-UP ft.	ins.	Metric
Pedal to seat squab ...	A	3 2	2 11½	0·97 m. 0·90 m.	3 2	2¾ 9¼	0·98 m. 0·84 m.
Steering wheel to seat squab	B	1 1	3¾ 1¼	0·40 m. 0·33 m.	1	2½ 11	0·37 m. 0·28 m.
Steering wheel to seat cushion	C		5½	0·14 m.		4⅞	0·12 m.
Front seat cushion above floor	D	1	2½	0·37 m.	1	3⅛	0·38 m.
Front seat cushion depth	E	1	5½	0·44 m.	1	6	0·46 m.
Headroom over front seat	F	3	3	0·99 m.	3	1½	0·95 m.
Cab floor to ground ...	G	1	1½	0·34 m.	1	1½	0·34 m.
Overall height (unladen)	H	5	8¾	1·75 m.	5	3¼	1·61 m.
Centre front wheel to bumper	I	2	1⅛	0·64 m.	2	1⅛	0·64 m.
Wheelbase	J	8	3¼	2·52 m.	8	3¼	2·52 m.
Centre rear wheel to bumper	K	3	8⅝	1·13 m.	3	8⅝	1·13 m.
Overall length	L	14	0¾	4·29 m.	14	0¾	4·29 m.
Length of body floor ...	M	6	6¼	2·01 m.	6	3¼	1·91 m.
Max. interior height ...	N	3	7½	1·10 m.	1	7⅜	0·49 m.
Body floor to ground ...	O	2	2	0·66 m.	2	2½	0·67 m.
Height of rear door opening ...		2	11⅜	0·90 m.	1	7⅜	0·49 m.
Overall width		5	2½	1·59 m.	5	2½	1·59 m.
Seat cushion width		1	7	0·48 m.	4	3½	1·31 m.
Width between wheelarches ...		3	2	0·97 m.	3	2	0·97 m.
Width of rear door opening ...		3	7 13/16	1·11 m.	3	7 13/16	1·11 m.
Body interior width		5	0½	1·54 m.	4	7½	1·41 m.
Track, front		4	0½	1·22 m.	4	0½	1·22 m.
Track, rear		4	1	1·24 m.	4	1	1·24 m.
Turning circle		36	0	11·00 m.	36	0	11·00 m.
Ground clearance			7½	0·19 m.		7½	0·19 m.
Body capacity		110 cu. ft.		3·12 cu. m.	40 cu. ft.		1·13 cu. m.
Weight, including tools, spare wheel, oil, water and heater; less fuel (and passenger seat in van)		19¾ cwt.		1003·3 kg.	19¾ cwt.		1003·3 kg.

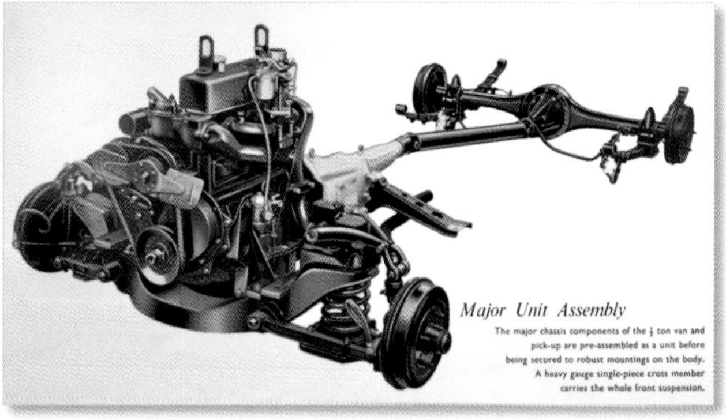
Major Unit Assembly
The major chassis components of the ½ ton van and pick-up are pre-assembled as a unit before being secured to robust mountings on the body. A heavy gauge single-piece cross member carries the whole front suspension.

With the operator's likely use of two-star petrol in mind the standard 1486cc engine had a compression ratio of 7.2:1, but by special request until 1962 a unit with 8.3:1 could be supplied for use with premium grade fuel. Girling 9in drum brakes all round, with twin leading shoes at the front, were quite adequate for the time but anyone who has driven only modern light commercials would likely be taken aback by their braking capabilities at anything above low speeds.

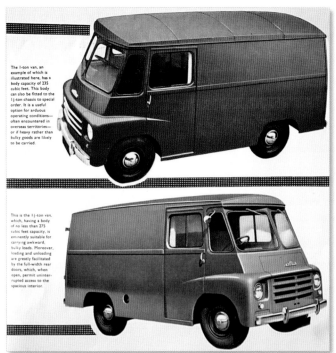

The 1-ton van, an example of which is illustrated here, has a body capacity of 235 cubic feet. This body can also be fitted to the 1½-ton chassis to special order. It is a useful option for arduous operating conditions—often encountered in overseas territories—or if heavy rather than bulky goods are likely to be carried.

This is the 1½-ton van, which, having a body of no less than 275 cubic feet capacity, is eminently suitable for carrying awkward, bulky loads. Moreover, loading and unloading are greatly facilitated by the full-width rear doors, which, when open, permit uninterrupted access to the spacious interior.

Austin's LD van was launched at the very end of 1954 as a replacement for its K8 Three-way. Being one of the recently-formed BMC's badge-engineering exercises – Austin out of Morris – the LD was manufactured in the old Morris factory at Adderley Park, Birmingham. Over the years the LD range was subjected to periodic updates but remained basically unchanged until it was replaced by the EA in 1967.

For the customer who wanted bodywork to their own specifications the LD was available either as a basic running chassis or with the front end of its body/cab fitted.

The metal-panelled body had a wooden frame and floor. Every time I look at a picture such as this it never ceases to amaze me that so many manufacturers felt it unnecessary to provide a bulkhead or division of some sort between driver and load area – especially in a vehicle of this capacity.

A diesel engine option was made available at an extra cost shortly after production commenced. This was BMC's own trusty four-cylinder 2.2-litre (actually 2178cc), which produced 55bhp at 3500rpm. Road speed per 1000rpm in top was 17mph for the 1-ton and 16mph for the 1½-ton, so in theory the diesel LDs should have had the legs of the lower-revving petrol LDs. All ran on 16in wheels, with 6.50 tyres for the 1-ton (7.00 was an option) and 7.50s for the 1½-ton.

Sliding doors gave access to a utilitarian and, even for the mid-'50s, somewhat dated driving compartment.

Tough, resilient, semi-elliptic leaf springs at front and rear insulate the vehicle from road shocks and vibration. Stability and a smooth ride are ensured by powerful, direct-acting hydraulic shock absorbers.

The standard petrol engine fitted to the LD was the good old 2199cc, four-cylinder A70 unit but emasculated down to a fairly feeble 46bhp at 3250rpm.

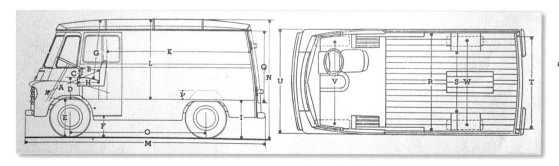

I-TON VAN (LD.I)

A	B	C	D	E	F	G	H	I	K	L	Turning circle 36' 0" (10·97 m.)
3' 7¼" (1·10 m.)	1' 2" (0·36 m.)	8" (0·20 m.)	1' 2¼" (0·37 m.)	2' 4¼" (0·72 m.)	1' 4" (0·41 m.)	3' 3" (0·99 m.)	1' 5" (0·43 m.)	2' 8¾" (0·83 m.)	9' 2" (2·79 m.)	4' 9" (1·45 m.)	
M	N	O	P	Q	R	S	T	U	V	W	Ground clearance 8¾" (0·22 m.)
14' 7½" (4·44 m.)	7' 5¼" (2·27 m.)	8' 4½" (2·55 m.)	6" (0·15 m.)	4' 2¼" (1·28 m.)	5' 10½" (1·79 m.)	3' 9" (1·14 m.)	5' 3½" (1·62 m.)	6' 4" (1·93 m.)	4' 10½" (1·49 m.)	4' 8¾" (1·43 m.)	Body capacity 235 cu. ft. (6·65 m.³)

I½-TON VAN (LD.2)

A	B	C	D	E	F	G	H	I	K	L	Turning circle 36' 0" (10·97 m.)
3' 6" (1·07 m.)	1' 2" (0·36 m.)	8" (0·20 m.)	1' 2¼" (0·37 m.)	2' 4¼" (0·72 m.)	1' 4" (0·41 m.)	3' 6" (1·07 m.)	1' 5" (0·43 m.)	2' 9¼" (0·85 m.)	9' 8¼" (2·95 m.)	5' 4" (1·62 m.)	
M	N	O	P	Q	R	S	T	U	V	W	Ground clearance 8¾" (0·22 m.)
15' 2¼" (4·63 m.)	8' 1¼" (2·47 m.)	8' 4½" (2·55 m.)	6" (0·15 m.)	4' 7" (1·40 m.)	5' 10½" (1·79 m.)	3' 9" (1·14 m.)	5' 5½" (1·66 m.)	6' 4" (1·93 m.)	4' 10½" (1·49 m.)	4' 10" (1·47 m.)	Body capacity 275 cu. ft. (7·78 m.³)

AUSTIN
se7en

¼-ton van and pick-up

A few months after the launch of BMC's revolutionary Mini, a van version was announced in January 1960. Its price would be £360 – just £3 cheaper than the current A35 van. A year later a pick-up was announced, and soon both were marketed with a full-colour brochure.

At last – two seats in a light commercial as standard equipment.

The Mini commercial's wheelbase was a little over 4in longer than the saloon's, so the extra was in the body structure, as the front and rear subframes were identical. Wheels on all Minis were 10in diameter that dictated small (7in) brake drums, with the result that stopping power was not the vehicle's strong point.

46 cu. ft. (1·30 m.²) of load space in an overall length of just under 11 ft. (3·35 m.)!
And there is a choice of a further 12 cu. ft. (·34 m.²) of usable space or an optional passenger seat beside the driver.
Such is the Austin Seven ¼-ton Van—delightfully easy to handle, extremely economical to operate, and specially engineered for manœuvring through the traffic-congested streets of today.
Similar to the world-beating, incredible Austin Seven Saloon, both of these new light commercials have all the identical features for ultra-safe, speedy, and dependable delivery service.

GENERAL STORE
HIGH ST. SMITHTOWN
PROP: S. JONES ● PHONE: 396

"Probably the most manoeuvrable and easily handled light commercial on the road today," read the blurb over 50 years ago, and I'm not entirely certain that it wouldn't hold true today if the original and "real" Mini was still in production. The pick-up had a useful 4½ft long load area too – or 6ft with the tailgate down.

Engine accessibility

Exceptional accessibility to the major mechanical components is permitted by the wide-opening bonnet. Engine sump, gearbox, and final drive differential have one oil filler and drain plug, and almost everything else of a mechanical nature needing periodical attention is handily situated beneath the bonnet. Servicing of these Austin ¼-ton commercials has been reduced to no more inconvenience than raising the bonnet top!

An oversight by the publicity department led to the use of the same illustration in both saloon and van brochures. This shows the former's removable anodised grille, whilst the commercial's is unitary and painted body colour.

"Saloon car comfort for the occupants," and, "a pleasant driving position." I'm not so sure! Having done many thousands of Mini miles in the '60s I have an idea that the combination of its driving position and seats were contributory to, if not the cause of, my own and others' lower back problems later on in life. Having said that, they were uproarious, mad, enjoyable miles as, providing you had some tread left on your front tyres, there wasn't much that could beat you on a twisty country road.

Engine

Based largely on the world-famous B.M.C. Series 'A' engine, the power pack of the Austin Seven ¼-ton light commercials is installed transversely, and included in its sump are the four-speed synchromesh gearbox and final drive differential. Revolutionary design producing a compact front-wheel-drive assembly with all the major mechanical components beneath the bonnet!

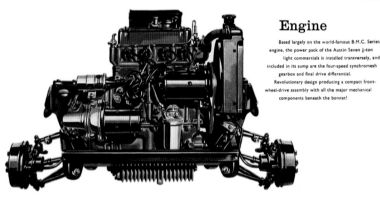

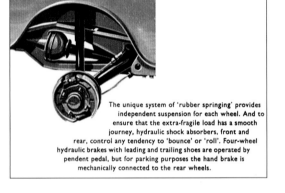

The unique system of 'rubber springing' provides independent suspension for each wheel. And to ensure that the extra-fragile load has a smooth journey, hydraulic shock absorbers, front and rear, control any tendency to 'bounce' or 'roll'. Four-wheel hydraulic brakes with leading and trailing shoes are operated by pendent pedal, but for parking purposes the hand brake is mechanically connected to the rear wheels.

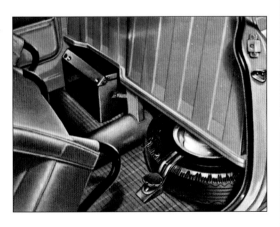

A Mini saloon's battery and spare wheel lived in the boot but in the commercials they were situated behind the seats. This is the pick-up version – note the pressed-steel bulkhead forming the rear of its cab.

LEADING DIMENSIONS

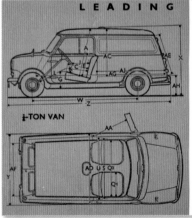

¼-TON VAN

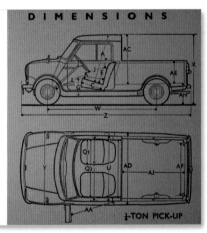

¼-TON PICK-UP

A	C	E	G	J (max.)	J (min.)	K	L (max.)
3 ft. 2 in. (·97 m.)	1 ft. 6 in. (·46 m.)	1 ft. 7 in. (·48 m.)	1 ft. 1½ in. (·34 m.)	1 ft. 4½ in. (·42 m.)	1 ft. 0½ in. (·32 m.)	6½ in. (·17 m.)	3 ft. 7½ in. (1·10 m.)
L (min.)	**Q1**	**Q2**	**S**	**U**	**W**	**X (Van)**	**X (Pick-up)**
3 ft. 5 in. (1·04 m.)	1 ft. 8 in. (·51 m.)	3 ft. 7½ in. (1·10 m.)	3 ft. 9½ in. (1·16 m.)	3 ft. 10 in. (1·17 m.)	7 ft. 0 4/32 in. (2·14 m.)	4 ft. 6½ in. (1·38 m.)	4 ft. 5½ in. (1·36 m.)
Y	**Z (Van)**	**Z (Pick-up)**	**AA**	**AC (Van)**	**AC(Pick-up)**	**AD**	**AE (Van)**
4 ft. 7½ in. (1·41 m.)	10 ft. 9⅞ in. (3·30 m.)	10 ft. 10½ in. (3·32 m.)	2 ft. 8 in. (·81 m.)	3 ft. 1½ in. (·95 m.)	3 ft. 1 in. (·94 m.)	4 ft. 5¾ in. (1·37 m.)	2 ft. 7½ in. (·81 m.)
AE(Pick-up)	**AF (Van)**	**AF (Pick-up)**	**AG (Van)**	**AH**	**AJ (Van)**	**AJ (Pick-up)**	**Approx. weight**
1 ft. 5½ in. (·44 m.)	3 ft. 4 in. (1·02 m.)	3 ft. 3 4/16 in. (1·00 m.)	8 ft. 6½ in. (2·61 m.)	1 ft. 5½ in. (·44 m.)	4 ft. 7 in. (1·40 m.)	4 ft. 6¾ in. (1·39 m.)	11½ cwt. (584 kg.)

There's a fine investment!

AUSTIN 10-12 cwt. van & pick-up

BMC felt it was missing a share of the small-to-medium commercial market, so the J4 was launched in 1960 as a more up-to-date and trimmer alternative to the 152 (J2) range for those who didn't need quite so much capacity. The J4 survived until 1974 when it was replaced by the Sherpa.

This left-hand-drive export model has the optional hinged side loading door but the artist made a mistake – a passenger seat came as standard on these models and was only an extra for the home market.

Can you remember laundry being collected or delivered wrapped in brown paper and tied with string? No? So who knows what's changing hands here… Wheels were 14in with 5.90 tyres, or 6.40s as an export option.

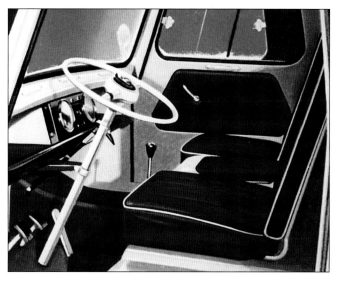

The sliding door option was probably the most popular but personally I preferred the hinged variety, even though they needed a good deal more space either side when parking.

An export model again and the artist has remembered to include a passenger seat. Apart from the steering, handbrake and foot controls, conversion from right- to left-drive was easy because all that was required, dashboard-wise, was to swap over the speedo and speaker grille for the optional radio.

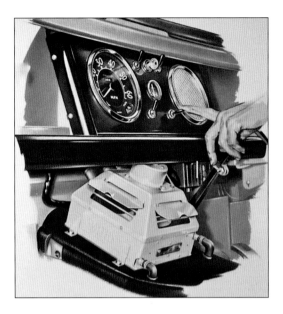

"Easy-to-read instruments, and 'quick flick' switches help concentration," read the brochure's caption. But not the poor artist's, as he got himself in a pickle with the juxtaposition of the speedo and speaker grille. To his credit, however, he made a wonderful job of depicting the optional heater.

Routine inspection of oil and water levels were by way of the central cover but it was necessary to remove the seats to get at them on either side. Interior noise was always an issue with this type of engine configuration, and manufacturers made attempts to quell it, but in those days it was an accepted characteristic of commercials whether light or heavy. As the gearbox was mounted conventionally behind the engine, a long linkage was necessary to connect it to the remote that was mounted on the forward base of the engine cowling.

The J4 body did not lend itself to the creation of a stylish pick-up but that was probably the last thing in the mind of those who had a need for such a vehicle.

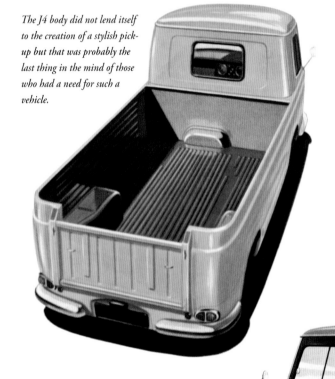

The optional tilt looked to be something of an afterthought and, unlike Austin's 152, there was no provision to secure it around the rear of the cab.

A chassis/cab version was available in drive-away form so that fleet or individual owners could equip it with bodywork to suit their special needs. For export it could be supplied in CKD (completely knocked down) form.

SUSPENSION

A distinct advantage, so far as road holding and general performance is concerned, is the inclusion of coil-spring independent front suspension. Semi-elliptic, leaf springs are fitted at the rear and to ensure perfect stability under laden conditions, the whole suspension system is controlled by hydraulic lever type shock absorbers.
Here again, numerous standardised components are already in use in other B.M.C. vehicles, and are therefore already available as spare parts through normal service channels.

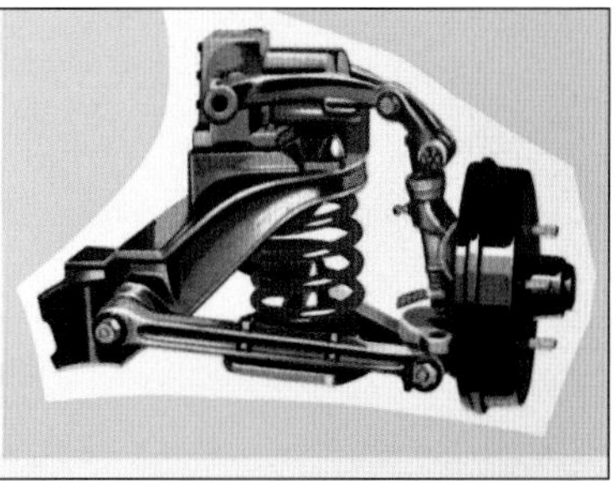

The brochure read well but when the shock absorbers got tired, and all too often they did, on certain road surfaces your J4 would assume a somewhat unnerving rhythmic bouncing gait at the front end – and an MoT failure to boot, if it was that time of the year.

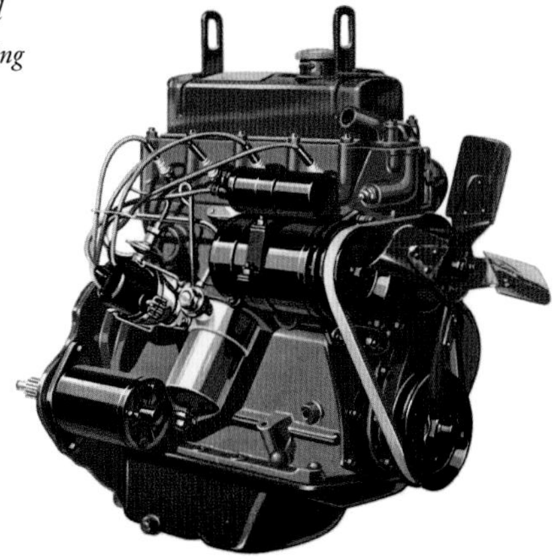

Yet another home for the B-series engine – this is the 1489cc version that gave out 42bhp at 4000rpm. From January 1964 J4s were fitted with a larger 1622cc B-series variant that was rated at 49bhp at 4000rpm.

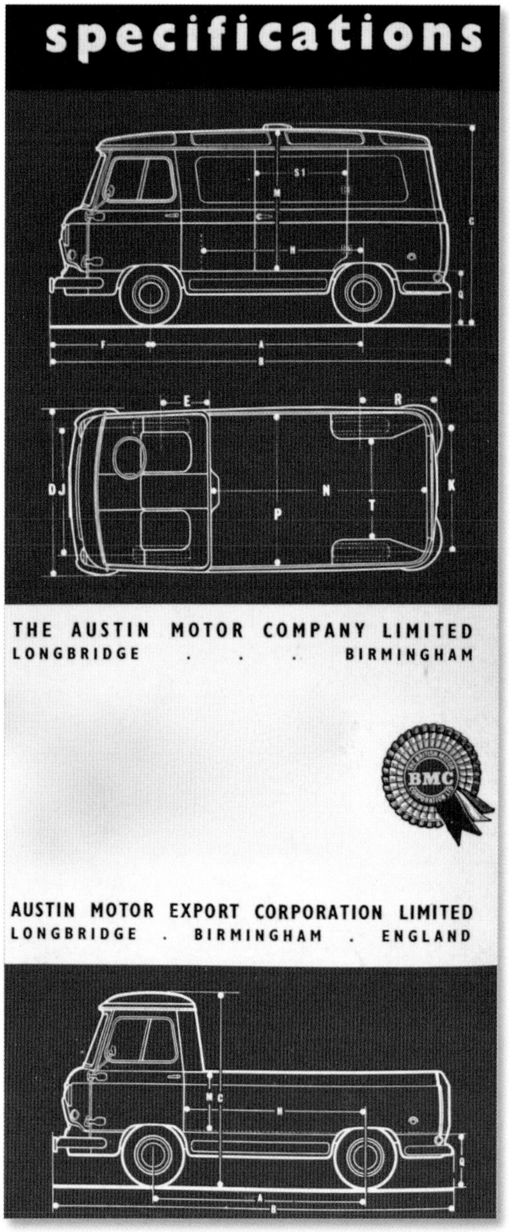
specifications
THE AUSTIN MOTOR COMPANY LIMITED
LONGBRIDGE . . . BIRMINGHAM
BMC
AUSTIN MOTOR EXPORT CORPORATION LIMITED
LONGBRIDGE . BIRMINGHAM . ENGLAND

SYNCHROMESH GEARBOX

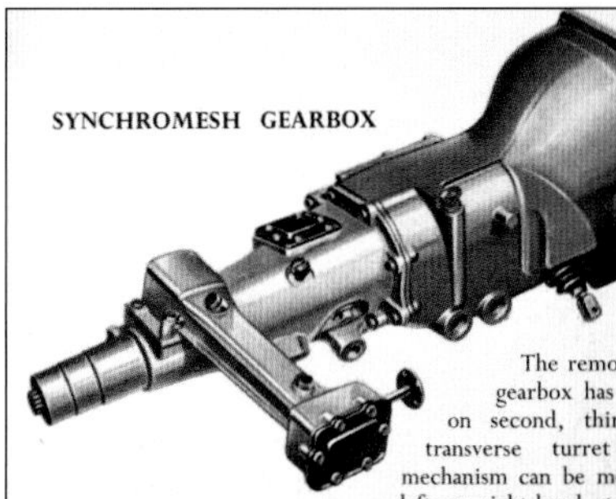

The remotely controlled four-speed gearbox has synchromesh engagement on second, third, and top gears. The transverse turret of the change-speed mechanism can be mounted either side to suit left- or right-hand steering, so that the floor-mounted gear lever can be kept as conveniently close to the driver as possible. The clutch has a single dry-plate, and is hydraulically operated.

The transverse turret of the gear-change mechanism could be mounted on either side depending on whether the vehicle was left- or right-hand drive – this is set up for the latter. The clutch was hydraulically operated and there was synchromesh on second, third and top, with just a touch over 24, 39 and 58mph on tap in each.

Weights and Dimensions	10/12 cwt. Van		10/12 cwt. Pick-up	
Max. gross vehicle weight	4,000 lbs.	1,814 kgs.	4,000 lbs.	1,814 kgs.
Max. on front axle ...	2,050 lbs.	930 kgs.	2,050 lbs.	930 kgs.
Max. on rear axle ...	2,200 lbs.	998 kgs.	2,200 lbs.	998 kgs.
*Licensing weight ...	2,282 lbs.	1,035 kgs.	†2,174 lbs.	986 kgs.
Kerb weights—front ...	1,435 lbs.	651 kgs.	†1,450 lbs.	658 kgs.
,, ,, rear ...	922 lbs.	418 kgs.	† 751 lbs.	341 kgs.
,, ,, Total ...	2,357 lbs.	1,069 kgs.	†2,201 lbs.	998 kgs.
*With side-loading door add	154 lbs.	70 kgs.	—	—
Wheelbase ... A	7′ 2″	2·19m.	7′ 2″	2·19m.
Overall length ... B	13′ 3″	4·04m.	13′ 3″	4·04m.
Overall height (laden) C	6′ 8″	2·03m.	6′ 3⅞″	1·93m.
Overall width ... D	5′ 9½″	1·77m.	5′ 9½″	1·77m.
Centre of front hub to back of bulkhead E	1′ 8½″	0·52m.	1′ 8½″	0·52m.
Centre of front hub to front bumper... F	3′ 3¼″	1·00m.	3′ 3¼″	1·00m.

Weights and Dimensions	10/12 cwt. Van		10/12 cwt. Pick-up	
Centre of rear hub to back of bulkhead H	5′ 5½″	1·66m.	5′ 5½″	1·66m.
Track (front) ... J	4′ 2⅜″	1·28m.	4 2⅜″	1·28m.
Track (rear) ... K	4′ 5″	1·35m.	4′ 5″	1·35m.
Height of body interior M	4′ 5½″	1·36m.	2′ 0″	0·61m.
Body interior length at floor ... ... N	7′ 11″	2·41m.	7′ 11″	2·41m.
Body interior width at floor ... ... P	5′ 0″	1·52m.	5′ 0″	1·52m.
Height of body floor (unladen) ... Q	1′ 11½″	0·60m.	1′ 11½″	0·60m.
Centre of rear hub to rear bumper ... R	2′ 9¾″	0·86m.	2′ 9¾″	0·86m.
Single side-loading door entry width ... S				
Width between rear wheelarches ... T	3′ 6½″	1·08m.	3′ 6½″	1·08m.
Ground clearance ...	7¼″	0·18m.	7¼″	0·18m.
Turning circle	33′ 0″	10·06m.	33′ 0″	10·06m.

† Estimated weights only

BEDFORD

Within a few years of acquiring Vauxhall Motors in 1925, General Motors had improved and extended the Vauxhall factory at Luton. Moreover, the firm had taken steps to encompass the manufacture of commercial vehicles, which were launched in 1931 under the name of Bedford.

Prior to this date, General Motors had assembled Canadian-sourced Chevrolet commercials at a plant in North London, marketing them as British Chevrolets.. More recently this operation had been transferred to Luton and the vehicles sold as Chevrolet Bedfords, named after the county in which the factory was situated.

Although the first Bedfords were very little different from their assembled forebears they gradually became more anglicised; even so, their six-cylinder engines owed much to the mother company, and when independent front suspension began to be featured it was GM's "knee action" design.

The first light commercial to carry the name was a 12cwt delivery van, and by the mid-'30s it had been supplemented by an 8cwt van based on the Vauxhall Light Six car. When the Vauxhall H-Type Ten-Four was announced in the autumn of 1937, a 5/6cwt van version soon followed. A year later, when the entire Bedford range was brought up to date with a fresh selection of heavier commercials, from 30cwt to 5 tons, the recently-introduced 5/6cwt was joined by a 10/12cwt derived from the new Vauxhall Twelve-Four.

Quite separately from the above, Bedford had been developing a 15cwt truck that had been submitted for British War Office trials in 1937, and as a result of its outstanding performance the MW was put on the list of suitably proven vehicles that could be called upon should the need arise. In September 1939 the long-expected eventuality arose, and over the next few years Bedford produced over 65,000 examples in many versions, ranging from the MWG anti-aircraft gun platform to the MWD general service truck.

The larger models of Bedford's civilian commercial range were also hastily reworked to make them suitable for a variety of military uses, and over 50,000 Q-types and 70,000 O-types saw service in all theatres of operations. In the aftermath of the Dunkirk debacle Vauxhall Motors was entrusted with the task of designing a heavy tank to replace the pitiful amount of (mainly outdated) heavy armour at the army's disposal, and less than a year later the Churchill went into production. By the end of the war over 5,500 had been manufactured at Luton and the large shadow factory at Dunstable, which had been built with government assistance to increase

The 5/6 cwt. Van
85 cubic feet loading space

truck production, becoming operational in 1942.

When peace returned, both the 5/6cwt HC and 10/12cwt JC were dusted off for a new lease of life. The former was discontinued in 1948, whilst the JC would have to do for a while longer – so it was given a weenie bit more power and a column gear-change to see it through until a replacement was ready.

During this period, too, the long-serving, ageing and soon-to-be-discontinued bullnose K-type was peddled to oilfield and outback markets in search of some export revenue – but did it really look the part? Even with the might of GM behind Bedford it was almost as though its smaller commercials were treading water until, early in 1952 and bearing not the slightest resemblance to its predecessor, the new 10/12cwt was announced. Gone were the rather rakish pre-war, long-bonnet, Vauxhall saloon looks and in their place was a dumpy, boxy load carrier with the frontal appearance reminiscent of a contented pug dog. But would the public take to it?

The answer was quick in coming, and by the time the 10/12cwt was replaced by the Bedford CF 17 years later around 370,000 had been sold.

Without realising it at the time, Bedford and its CA were in the vanguard of what would become the norm for 10-to-20cwt commercials. Forward and semi-forward-control was nothing new – for example the Morris PV and J-type vans – but despite its homely looks the new Bedford had reasonable performance and was quite pleasant to drive. Vauxhall's new Wyvern engine provided the power and in common with the latter a three-speed gearbox was considered quite sufficient. This remained the sole formula until 1961, when a Perkins diesel became an option, with a four-speed gearbox, if required, the following year. It was not until 1965 that the 1.6-litre Victor engine found its way into the CA. In

Above: The Bedford Utilecon is an all-purpose car. It can be used as a comfortable 4-seater saloon or, with the rear seat folded flat into the floor, as a roomy van. This is the 5-6 cwt. 4-seater Utilecon, there is a larger 10-12 cwt. 7-seater model. There are dozens of uses for the Utilecon on the modern farm.

other respects, too, so "right" was the original concept that little more than a few changes were asked for or deemed necessary, other than versions with a longer wheelbase or greater capacity.

There was, however, an almost immediate call for specialised bodywork, and the although the CA's original purpose was that of a goods vehicle it is perhaps remembered more fondly in one of its camper van configurations – the generic term Dormobile conjuring up an image of a CA in that guise amongst many of the older generation.

Bedford's forward-control TK series of 1960 would prove to be as popular amongst heavier goods vehicle operators as the CA, and its success gave it an even longer life that would span nearly 20 years – although the last of Bedford's lightweights within our timeframe reverted back to the private car-based van.

If the 5/6 cwt wasn't quite large enough there was the JC, which had been introduced in 1939 with the Vauxhall Twelve-Four's 1442cc overhead-valve engine. It too had a three-speed gearbox, independent front suspension and Lockheed hydraulic brakes, but its 17in wheels had larger 5.25 tyres. The bodywork of both models was panelled in steel on a wooden frame, and 10 cubic feet should be subtracted from the advertised loading space of each if the optional passenger seat was fitted.

The 10/12 cwt. Van
120 cubic feet loading space

The late summer of 1948 saw the discontinuation of the 5/6cwt and the announcement of a mildly revamped version of the 10/12cwt, when it became the PC – receiving a slightly improved version of the 1442cc motor from the Vauxhall Wyvern that gave 35bhp at 3600rpm. The gearbox was still a three-speed but was largely redesigned and had a column gear-change that, coupled with a handbrake under the dash, was supposed to enable the driver to use either door. When tested by The Commercial Motor *the new 10/12 returned the remarkably good consumption of 39mpg fully loaded. I'd like to see someone repeat that today!*

NEW BEDFORD VANS

10/12 cwt Light Delivery Van
(AS ILLUSTRATED)

30 cwt 3-Way Loader Van

Since the late 1940s, if someone wanted a little quarter-ton commercial there had been no Bedford to fit their needs, because Vauxhall manufactured no suitable car. Nevertheless, it must have been obvious that BMC, Ford and others were profiting from this situation, so the introduction of Vauxhall's Viva in 1963 provided the opportunity to remedy the problem. The Viva was also manufactured as the Bedford HA, with a load capability of either 6cwt or 8cwt. Although late to the market it proved very popular, and many utility companies ran fleets of HAs. Less well remembered than the Bedford CA or TK it nevertheless outlived both with a lifespan of 20 years, during which its body remained unchanged whereas the Viva's styling was redesigned on more than one occasion.

Much was hoped for the CF when it replaced the CA in 1969, but by that time Ford's Transit was holding sway and, because the standard combination of the rough overhead-cam Victor engine and a three-speed gearbox delivered an inferior driving experience, the CF was forever destined to be second best. From 1980 there was a better petrol engine or Opel's bulletproof diesel, and two years later an electric version received government funding for a while; sadly, battery technology and price, amongst other factors, proved to be insuperable.

The revered (or reviled) Margaret Thatcher may have allocated a few of the taxpayer's pounds to the electric project but there are those who would maintain that the favouritism she showed to Leyland in granting of military vehicle contracts, as well as the denial of the firm's overtures to acquire Land Rover, prompted GM to call it a day in the UK. Whatever the reasons, Bedford production was brought to a halt in 1986.

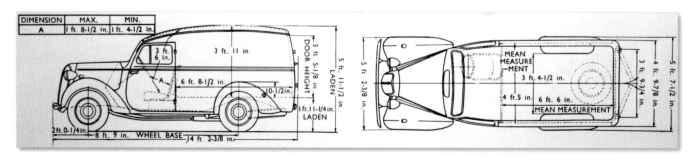

Bedford vans of this period were supplied in primer and there was no advertised range of colours. Wings, wheels and hubcaps were normally finished in black, but I suppose a customer could have chosen green.

Wide rear doors hung on self-aligning hinges make it easy to load and unload the 10/12 cwt. van. The spare tyre is carried at the rear and is reached through a hinged flap below the doors.

7-SEATER UTILECON

The 10/12cwt Utilecon was built upon the same 8ft 9in wheelbase chassis as the van and could also be supplied as an ambulance equipped to carry one stretcher patient, attendant and driver, or six sitting cases and driver. In this form it could be fitted with an extra door on the nearside, and the estate car could be fitted with one or two additional side doors – all at extra cost.

BEDFORD PICK-UP TRUCKS

Bedford's rugged, no-nonsense pick-ups on the 120in K chassis were specifically intended for export. They were fitted with a six-cylinder, overhead-valve, 3521cc motor that served all the firm's larger commercials. This brochure gave its output as 72bhp at 3000rpm but by going to 3200rpm it would give about 76bhp. A four-speed gearbox was coupled to the lower axle option for the K chassis of 5.28:1, and there were hydraulic brakes all round with a tandem master cylinder.

BEDFORD CREW UTILITY PICK-UP

DEVELOPED specially to meet the requirements of surveyors, engineers, farmers, and all who need a general utility vehicle with accommodation for passengers in addition to a useful load space, the Crew Utility Pick-up provides passenger car comfort for driver and crew. The Bedford K chassis, modified to include ambulance type springs and shock absorbers to improve the riding qualities, has a maximum gross laden weight of 6,500 lb. (2948 kg.), giving an allowance of 1,860 lb. (844 kg.) for passengers and luggage in addition to the driver. These figures are for first and second class roads and should be de-rated for bad surfaces. Body sides and tailboards are of double skin steel construction. The cab roof is of aluminium, extended to form a canopy over the fore part of the body space, with the cavity between inner and outer panels filled with Isoflex insulation material.

The cab of this left-hand-drive crew utility looked as though it might have been destined for a country with a hot climate, but was the seating really in buff leather as the brochure stated? Driver's side windscreen panel opened outwards on quadrants and the door windows were full-drop direct-lift railway carriage type.

BEDFORD HEAVY DUTY PICK-UP

FOR general utility work this handy vehicle on the Bedford K chassis has ambulance type springs and shock absorbers to give smooth riding on bad roads. The maximum gross laden weight of 6,500 lb. (2948 kg.) gives a payload of 1,900 lb. (862 kg.) in addition to driver and mate for main roads and good secondary roads, but for lower grade roads these figures should be de-rated to suit local conditions. Of all-steel welded construction, the body has a low loading line and detachable hinged tailboard with rubber-covered supporting chains.

The cab is designed to accommodate driver and one passenger on individual bucket type seats which give body support just where it is needed for a comfortable driving position. The driver's windscreen panel hinges outwards on quadrants and full-drop windows in the doors can be raised or lowered at the touch of a finger. Windows and doors can be locked. A fixed window at the rear of the cab facilitates reversing.

Bedford Pick-up Chassis Features

Robust chassis frame cold squeeze riveted for hard service.

Long life engine—28 h.p., 6 cylinders, smooth and economical.

Engine over axle for ideal weight distribution.

Six phase carburation to give top performance with maximum economy.

Automatic Ignition Control by centrifugal governor and vacuum unit.

Heavy duty gearbox—sturdy, compact and efficient.

Hydraulic brakes — self-sealing with double safety factor.

External brake cylinders, away from the heat of the drums.

NEW *front-end styling*
NEW *interior comfort and luxury*
NEW *improved vision*

NEW *steering and handling ease*
NEW *flashing direction indicators (front and rear)*
NEW *longer-life piston rings (top rings chromium plated)*

The brilliant new

VAUXHALL 10 CWT. COUPE UTILITY

23.44 h.p. 6 CYLINDER O.H.V.

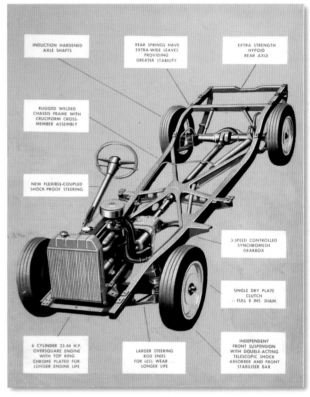

INDUCTION HARDENED AXLE SHAFTS

REAR SPRINGS HAVE EXTRA-WIDE LEAVES PROVIDING GREATER STABILITY

EXTRA STRENGTH HYPOID REAR AXLE

RUGGED WELDED CHASSIS FRAME WITH CRUCIFORM CROSS-MEMBER ASSEMBLY

NEW FLEXIBLE-COUPLED SHOCK-PROOF STEERING

3-SPEED CONTROLLED SYNCHROMESH GEARBOX

SINGLE DRY PLATE CLUTCH – FULL 8 INS. DIAM.

6 CYLINDER 23.44 H.P. OVERSQUARE ENGINE WITH TOP RING CHROME PLATED FOR LONGER ENGINE LIFE

LARGER STEERING ROD ENDS FOR LESS WEAR LONGER LIFE

INDEPENDENT FRONT SUSPENSION WITH DOUBLE-ACTING TELESCOPIC SHOCK ABSORBER AND FRONT STABILISER BAR

Not strictly a Bedford, but I had to include this delicious vehicle – especially because a friend of mine owns one, and the model was part of the Vauxhall/Bedford export drive. The Vauxhall Velox Coupe Utility was peculiar to the antipodes, as far as I know, and was made from 1955 to 1957.

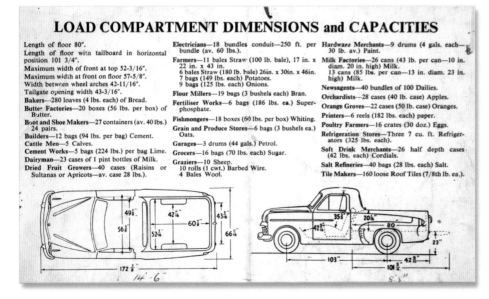

LOAD COMPARTMENT DIMENSIONS and CAPACITIES

Length of floor 80".
Length of floor with tailboard in horizontal position 101 3/4".
Maximum width of front at top 52-3/16".
Maximum width at front on floor 57-5/8".
Width between wheel arches 42-11/16".
Tailgate opening width 43-3/16".
Bakers—280 loaves (4 lbs. each) of Bread.
Butter Factories—20 boxes (56 lbs. per box) of Butter.
Boot and Shoe Makers—27 containers (av. 40 lbs.) 24 pairs.
Builders—12 bags (94 lbs. per bag) Cement.
Cattle Men—5 Calves.
Cement Works—5 bags (224 lbs.) per bag Lime.
Dairyman—23 cases of 1 pint bottles of Milk.
Dried Fruit Growers—40 cases (Raisins or Sultanas or Apricots—av. case 28 lbs.).

Electricians—18 bundles conduit—250 ft. per bundle (av. 60 lbs.).
Farmers—11 bales Straw (100 lb. bale), 17 in. x 22 in. x 43 in.
6 bales Straw (180 lb. bale) 26in. x 30in. x 46in.
7 bags (149 lbs. each) Potatoes.
9 bags (125 lbs. each) Onions.
Flour Millers—19 bags (3 bushels each) Bran.
Fertiliser Works—6 bags (186 lbs. ea.) Super-phosphate.
Fishmongers—18 boxes (60 lbs. per box) Whiting.
Grain and Produce Stores—6 bags (3 bushels ea.) Oats.
Garages—3 drums (44 gals.) Petrol.
Grocers—16 bags (70 lbs. each) Sugar.
Graziers—10 Sheep.
10 rolls (1 cwt.) Barbed Wire.
4 Bales Wool.

Hardware Merchants—9 drums (4 gals. each— 30 lb. av.) Paint.
Milk Factories—26 cans (43 lb. per can—10 in. diam. 20 in. high) Milk.
13 cans (85 lbs. per can—13 in. diam. 23 in. high) Milk.
Newsagents—40 bundles of 100 Dailies.
Orchardists—28 cases (40 lb. case) Apples.
Orange Groves—22 cases (50 lb. case) Oranges.
Printers—6 reels (182 lbs. each) paper.
Poultry Farmers—16 crates (30 doz.) Eggs.
Refrigeration Stores—Three 7 cu. ft. Refrigerators (325 lbs. each).
Soft Drink Merchants—26 half depth cases (42 lbs. each) Cordials.
Salt Refineries—40 bags (28 lbs. each) Salt.
Tile Makers—160 loose Roof Tiles (7/8th lb. ea.).

What a REALLY sensible and informative specification sheet.

It may look old fashioned now but the semi-forward-control Bedford CA was almost revolutionary when it was launched at the beginning of 1952, pre-empting the basic form that medium-sized vans were to adopt that lasts, with modern interpretation, to this day.

Larger Loads....
Longer Life....
Lower Costs....

The New

BEDFORD 10/12 cwt. Van

DESIGNED TO DO A VAN'S JOB BETTER

Super Efficient Square Engine gives more power for less petrol

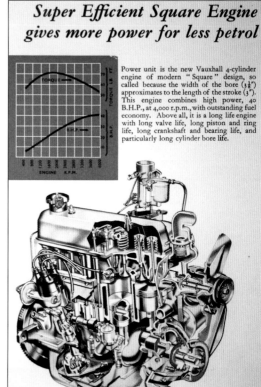

Power unit is the new Vauxhall 4-cylinder engine of modern "Square" design, so called because the width of the bore (3⅛") approximates to the length of the stroke (3"). This engine combines high power, 40 B.H.P., at 4,000 r.p.m., with outstanding fuel economy. Above all, it is a long life engine with long valve life, long piston and ring life, long crankshaft and bearing life, and particularly long cylinder bore life.

COIL SPRING INDEPENDENT FRONT SUSPENSION

The ends of the deep cruciform bracing structure extend to the ends of the side members. Cruciform and side members are welded together to form a strong box section. The cross member of the front suspension unit is bolted to the frame side members. There is an additional cross member at the front, and two more at the rear.

The Grosvenor

CANOPY PICK-UP

The Grosvenor Canopy Pick-Up, like the Estate Wagon, is based on the new Bedford 10/12 cwt. Light Van. It has an all-steel body, wide front sliding doors, semi-forward control, a 40 b.h.p. 4-cylinder "Square" engine, exceptionally comfortable independent front-wheel springing, and its turning circle is only 33 ft.

THIS model is designed to meet the requirements of builders, decorators, surveyors, engineers, farmers, etc. It has accommodation for three passengers, or crew under the canopy, and a useful load space. Behind the driver there is a polished wood partition with a sliding communication window. Sliding windows are fitted in the sliding cab doors. A full width bench seat and a back-rest with Dunlopillo cushion and squab are provided beneath the canopy. Pick-up body has fixed sides and a hinged tailboard fitted with retaining chains and locking pins.

WEIGHTS & DIMENSIONS

Taxation weight: 1 ton 0 cwt.	Interior length:
Gross laden weight: 1 ton 13 cwt.	(behind partition) 6 ft. 5½ in.
	Height of sides : 1 ft. 10 in.
Interior width:	Overall length: 12 ft. 10 in.
(panel to panel) 5 ft. 1 in.	„ width: 5 ft. 10 in.
(inside wheel arches) 3 ft. 7½ in.	„ height : (unladen) 6 ft. 3 in.

The right is reserved to alter any details of price, specification or equipment without notice.   VAUXHALL MOTORS LTD., LUTON, BEDS.

The Grosvenor Carriage Company of Kilburn, North West London, was the first to offer specialised coachwork on the new CA by the summer of 1952, within months of its launch. The Grosvenor nine-seater Estate Wagon could also be used as a two- or five-seater with plenty of luggage room, a two-seater with full 12cwt load, an emergency ambulance to carry a recumbent patient with two seated attendants and driver, or turned into a single- or double-sleeper.

The canopy pick-up had seating for three additional rearward-facing passengers beneath its canopy, with a sliding communication window in the polished wood partition at the rear of the cab.

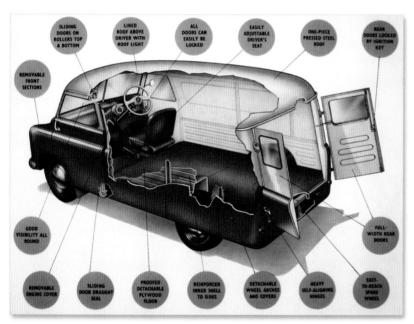

Full-width rear doors on self-aligning hinges make it easy to load and unload this new Bedford van from the rear. Load space is 135 cu. ft.—plus 10 cu. ft. more beside the driver. Spare wheel is neatly stowed behind a hinged flap under the doors.

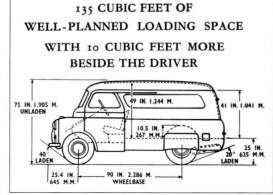

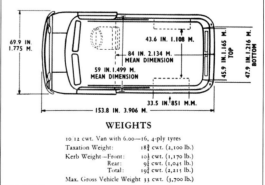

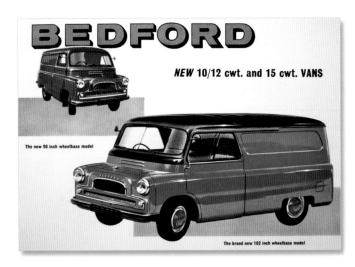

BEDFORD

NEW 10/12 cwt. and 15 cwt. VANS

The new 90 inch wheelbase model

The brand new 102 inch wheelbase model!

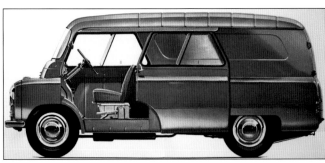

For 1959 the CA acquired a one-piece curved windscreen and a restyled radiator grille, but more significantly there was now a choice between the existing 90in wheelbase (from now on known as the CAS or 90) and one of 102in, which was titled the CAL or 102. There was also the option of a 15cwt payload for either CAS or CAL, which was equipped with heavy-duty rear springs along with 6.40x15in six-ply tubeless tyres, whilst the 10/12cwt version had 6.00x15in six-ply tubeless.

Doors on the 102-inch wheelbase CAL were 12in wider than those on the CAS, and the safety catch held the door open in three positions on the former and two on the latter. I did once hear the most dreadful tale about someone who was badly, if not mortally, injured when one of these failed and the door slammed on them while they were leaning out and braking, but maybe it was an old wives' tale. After all, the brochure did categorically state, "The door cannot over-ride catch unless handle is turned."

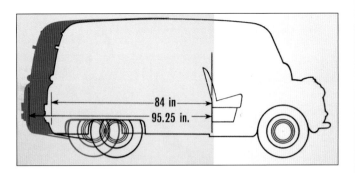

The difference between the 90 and 102in wheelbase translated into an extra 27 cubic feet of load space – so the short-wheelbase had 134 cubic feet (one less than in the 1952 brochure!), whilst the long-wheelbase had 161.

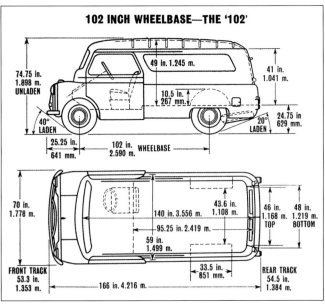

102 INCH WHEELBASE—THE '102'

FRONT-END SHEET METAL AND FRONT DOORS DETACHABLE FOR SERVICE OR REPLACEMENT

HINGED ENGINE COVER WITH QUICK-RELEASE HANDLE AND EFFICIENT DRAUGHT AND FUME SEAL

NEW, EXTRA COMFORTABLE BOX-SPRING SEAT WITH THICK LATEX FOAM OVERLAY. TOOL COMPARTMENT IN BASE

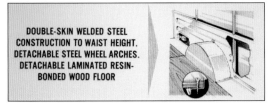

DOUBLE-SKIN WELDED STEEL CONSTRUCTION TO WAIST HEIGHT. DETACHABLE STEEL WHEEL ARCHES. DETACHABLE LAMINATED RESIN-BONDED WOOD FLOOR

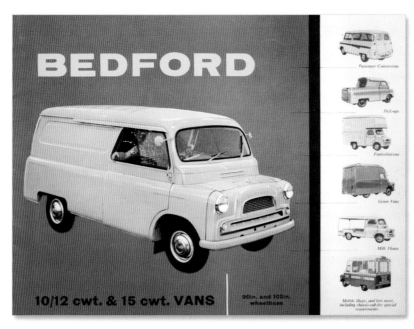

This spring 1961 brochure was filled with all manner of CAs with both standard and specialised bodies.

This is the '102' van, with a total loading space of 171 cu. ft. The passenger seat shown is an optional extra. Cherry Red is a factory-finished colour option.

The 102 in Cherry Red, which was one of three current factory colour options – the others being Ash Grey and Strata Blue. A reduction in wheel diameter to 13in with 6.40-section tyres gave all kinds of advantages, according to the manufacturer. But by consulting the various dimensional drawings you find the new floor level was a mere ½in lower. Did any operator really notice?

Here's a 90 in the popular Strata Blue finish.

The ultimate option for Dormobile, Utilabrake or Workobus was the de luxe special-equipment body with glazed rear quarters, chrome bumpers and other exterior embellishments.

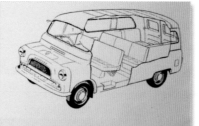

THE DORMOBILE COMPACT

This is a brand new model, available as a 4-seater on the '90' or a 6-seater on the '102'. Ample loading space is provided in this dual-purpose luxury vehicle, and the seats will fold to form two beds. Alternatively, the rear seats can be folded against the body sides, giving additional baggage space. Model '102' shown.

	'90'	'102'
Taxation weight	21¼ cwt.	22¾ cwt.
Maximum G.V.W.	34¼ cwt.	35¾ cwt.

THE UTILABRAKE 12-SEATER

Driver's and front passenger seat fold forward for easy access to three forward-facing intermediate seats. Centre intermediate seat folds aside for access to rear upholstered seats, which seat three a side, or two with folding armrests in use. Also available as a 'Farmer's Model', with wood-slatted rear seats.

	'90'	'102'
Taxation weight	22¼ cwt.	22¼ cwt.
Maximum G.V.W.	38¼ cwt.	39¾ cwt.

Normally the standard version was in a single colour but this one had been given the optional two-tone treatment.

The mobile shop was built only on the 15cwt chassis. It came completely fitted out with all necessary equipment – whether for butchers, fishmongers, bakers or greengrocers – by the maker, Smiths Delivery Vehicles Ltd. A door on the passenger side was not normally fitted, and the shop could be directly accessed from the cab. There was standing room for three or four customers, who entered by a sliding door at the rear. This is the Viandette, which cost either £919 10s or £966 10s depending on whether you ordered a 90 or a 102. I wonder how many picked up on the significance of its rather charming name..

This is the Kenebrake 12-seater conversion of the 15cwt van by Kenex of Dover. For the brochure it's been dressed up with optional extras such as roof lights, two-tone colour scheme and chromium bumpers. Seating was three abreast in the front, another row of three behind and six facing each other at the rear with three on each side.

The Busette, by Marshall Motor Bodies Ltd, was another 12-seater conversion of the 15cwt and, like all others, it could be based on either the 90 or 102. A little less luxurious for the rear six passengers, however, as their seats were slatted wood.

"Small enough to be an economical runabout, big enough to carry a useful load," Walker's dropside truck was available on both long- and short-wheelbase, as well as 10/12cwt and 15cwt chassis. The dropside body was constructed of tongued and grooved wood, and a ladder rack was an optional extra. A tipper or platform truck could be supplied with the same range of chassis cabs as a basis. Doors on these cabs were hinged at the front.

Even with a crew of five there was still plenty of room for equipment at the rear of the Canopy pick-up made by B Walker & Son of Watford. There was a sliding window between cab and rear, whilst the rear-facing hinged seat under the canopy was fully upholstered.

Marketed with the rather uninspiring name of the All Metal Van and built by Hawson, the 90 version had a 200 cubic feet capacity, whilst the 102 boasted 235 cubic feet. It was constructed on a welded steel frame with steel sides and an aluminium roof; the floor, however, was of tongued and grooved wood.

"A well appointed vehicle that meets the needs of the dress trade for a really large-capacity van that will be easy to handle in crowded city streets." Made by Spurlings Motor Bodies of North London, the Gown Van's interior had framed skirt panels and three hanging rails, with a pair of ceiling lamps to illuminate your haute couture clothing. All doors were hinged and had step wells plus slam locks with recessed outside handles.

Built by RW Osborne Ltd Of Saffron Walden, the Milk Float was another special that could be had on the 15cwt version of either 90 or 102 chassis. Despite its name the brochure pointed out that it was also very suitable for other distributive trades such as greengrocery, mineral waters or any other dealing with goods handled in crates or drums.

Also only built on a 15cwt chassis was the Baby Pantechnicon by Gregory's of Uxbridge, with 320 cubic feet of space in the 90 version and 363 in the 102. Its body was panelled in aluminium with the exception of the roof, which was translucent fibreglass; doors on the steel cab unit were forward-hinged.

This rugged Bedford chassis is the foundation of every Bedford van, conversion or special body

The Bedford chassis is available in either the 90 in. or the 102 in. wheelbase, and in two payload ratings. Rigid, cruciform crossbracing plus three crossbearers strengthens the channel section sidemembers. Additional strengthening webs are fitted for increased durability. The '102' has frame side members of heavier gauge, and a propeller shaft of increased diameter.

A chassis-and-cab version is also available.

ICE-CREAM CANTEENS
on the 15 cwt. chassis
THE "CORNETTE" Mk. 2 and Mk. 3

TWO ENTIRELY DIFFERENT MODELS are available. The Mark 2, illustrated in colour, and the new Mark 3 version. Body frames are of hardwood, with aluminium and Fibreglass exterior panels. Interiors are fully equipped and finished in plastics, stainless-steel and glass for cleanliness and ease of maintenance. Service windows on both sides. Cold-storage equipment extra to choice.

WEIGHTS AND DIMENSIONS

	Mark 2	'90'	Mark 3	'90'
Overall length		13 ft. 3 in.		13 ft. 3 in.
width		6 ft. 0 in.		5 ft. 11 in.
height		8 ft. 1¼ in.		8 ft. 3 in.
Interior headroom		6 ft. 0 in.		6 ft. 0 in.
Taxation weight		24 cwt.		24 cwt.
Maximum G.V.W.		38¼ cwt.		38¼ cwt.

Smith's Delivery Vehicles of Gateshead-on-Tyne made both these ice cream vans. I much prefer the look of the Mk 2 – how about you?

New diesel-engined Bedford 10/12 cwt. and 15 cwt. vans

90 in. or 102 in. wheelbases

The diesel option became available in 1961 for all models. Perkins' 4.99 was, the brochure said, "Specially modified to suit the Bedford van."

BEDFORD'S UNIQUE PROTECTION AGAINST CORROSION MEANS LONGER VEHICLE LIFE

Every Bedford van goes through a special process which gives triple protection against rust and corrosion for the life of the vehicle. This consists of cleansing and de-oxidosing, followed by Bedford's special primer dip. All the vulnerable underbody parts, including double skin and wheelarch interiors, receive this anti-corrosion protection. Red oxide primer follows, inside and outside, followed by baking and wet sanding before two coats of special dark grey primer are applied.

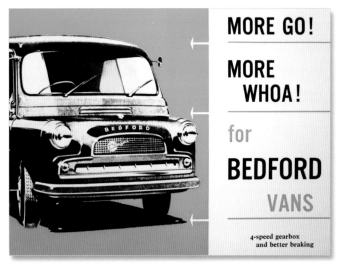

MORE GO!
MORE WHOA!
for
BEDFORD
VANS

4-speed gearbox and better braking

At last, for 1962, some overdue improvements and a larger range of colours. The optional four-speed gearbox added £12 to the price.

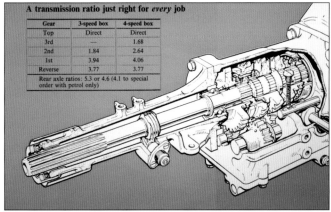

A transmission ratio just right for *every* job

Gear	3-speed box	4-speed box
Top	Direct	Direct
3rd	—	1.68
2nd	1.84	2.64
1st	3.94	4.06
Reverse	3.77	3.77

Rear axle ratios: 5.3 or 4.6 (4.1 to special order with petrol only)

CHERRY RED

STRATA BLUE

FIR GREEN

NAVY BLUE

ASH GREY

Choice of five smart factory-finished colours for only £15.10 extra

and remember that when you buy a Bedford van in factory-finished colour you get a *complete* painting job—*inside* as well as outside.

For the basic price a Bedford came in primer, so unless you wanted to paint it yourself there was always a little bit extra to pay for one of the standard range of colours, which for 1962 was extended.

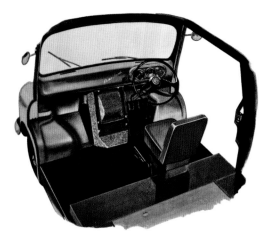

New for 1963 came several minor improvements that gave the excuse for a fresh brochure. The engine cowl had been redesigned to give easier cross-cab access and better sound deadening. Underneath was the same motor, however, and it would be a couple of years before the larger 1594cc Victor unit powered the CA range.

Spurling also did a security conversion of the CAL van with built-in cash box, steel trellis rear gate and armoured glass.

"It's a car…It's a truck…It's boss transport. This is the truck for the owner of the business, the manager of men – a vehicle he will be pleased and proud to drive," read one of the 1960 brochures for Bedford's new commercial. It was no slouch either, as The Commercial Motor found when it managed to extract over 80mph out of one on test in 1961.

"There's plenty of room for husky drivers in the spacious Bedford cab," – looking very stateside with a large bench seat, but they dressed it up with extras such as a fire extinguisher, radio and heater for the brochure.

The transatlantic styling of Bedford's half-tonner shouldn't come as too much of a surprise to those who know that Bedford had been owned by General Motors since its inception. I always thought the flashing indicators perched on the front wings rather detracted from their lines and I see that the artist left them out in this view, so perhaps he thought so too. Tilt frame sockets were provided in case you wanted such a thing, although it wasn't on the list of options. If you needed a dropside truck Walker & Son did an all-steel version with reinforced floor and sides, or if you had a special body in mind you could buy a chassis with front cowl or chassis complete with cab. All came with 15in wheels shod with 6.70-section tyres.

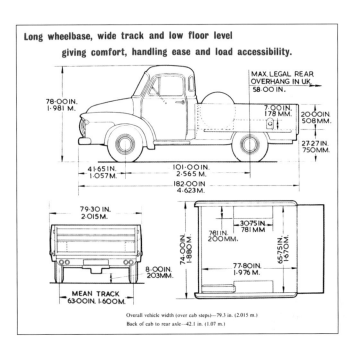

Vauxhall's newest edition of the six-cylinder overhead-valve Cresta engine was exactly square, with a bore and stroke of 82.55mm and displacement of 2651cc. The firm didn't let us know what revs were needed to attain its 104bhp, but maximum torque of 140lb/ft came in at 2400rpm. It was mated to a three-speed gearbox with column change, and alternative back axle ratios gave either 4.11:1 or 4.62:1.

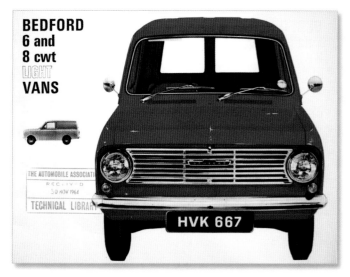

HVK 667

With the launch of its Viva in September 1963 Vauxhall took the opportunity to manufacture a van version, which could claim a share of a market that the firm had neglected since the demise of its 5/6cwt at the end of the 1940s.

Like other Bedfords, HAs were priced in primer but, "For a small additional charge," they could be painted, "inside and out," in one of the following factory colours: Matador Red, Navy Blue, Strata Blue, Ash Green or Fir Green. As this had to take place prior to assembly, it beats me why the firm didn't include the paintwork in a slightly increased price – but then I've never been in marketing. It is also something of a mystery why manufacturers so often used colour schemes they didn't offer in their colour brochures – like this 6cwt HA.

HAE 65

"High (39in), wide (57in) and lengthsome (67in), in sensible proportions these new Bedford vans meet your needs in easy-to-get-at, easy-to-handle loadspace." But was the, "70 cubic feet total load capacity," calculated with or without the optional passenger seat?

The 8cwt version was given the following de luxe features – bright metal moulding to body sides, bright anodised radiator grille, chrome insert to windscreen surround, chrome rear-view mirrors and, on the inside, chrome instrument bezels, parcel shelf below dash, additional floor mat and an interior roof lamp with door courtesy switches.

The parcel shelf tells us that this is the 8cwt model but otherwise the view is identical to the 6cwt. Rocker switches are very '60s and, although it is barely visible, there's a stalk to the right side of the steering column that controls flashing indicators, horn, main or dipped beam and headlamp flashers.

Front suspension was independent by transverse leaf spring and double wishbones mounted on a detachable crossmember, while the rear was by semi-elliptic and a rear axle with short torque tube. The 8cwt model had a heavy-duty axle, rear springs and wheels – with 4Jx12in wheels as opposed to 3.50x12s on the 6cwt. Tyres were 5.50 six-ply tubeless.

The 1057cc four-cylinder overhead-valve engine had an over-square bore and stroke ratio of 74.3mm to 60.96mm that resulted in its 40hp (net) being developed at a high-ish 5200rpm. This was mated to a four-speed all-synchromesh gearbox with short remote floor change. Final drive ratio was 4.12:1. High-speed road tests utilising a section of motorway were possible by this time and The Commercial Motor *returned over 41mpg with an average speed of 55mph.*

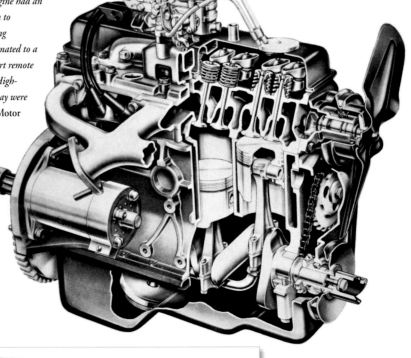

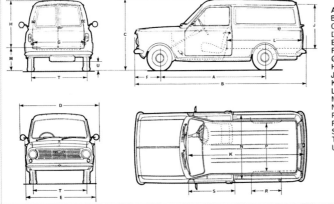

A	wheelbase	91.5 in.
B	overall length	150.2 in.
C	overall height, unladen	59.5 in.
D	overall width	08.0 in.
E	body width	59.4 in.
F	front overhang	22.2 in.
G	door opening width, floor level	40.5 in.
H	body interior height	39.2 in.
J	door opening height	35.2 in.
K	dash to rear doors	114.0 in.
L	body floor length	67.2 in.
M	floor height from ground, unladen	20.0 in.
N	body interior width	57.0 in.
P	width between wheel arches	38.2 in.
R	wheel arch length	25.0 in.
S	cab door width	40.5 in.
T	track, mean	18.0 in.
U	ground clearance	5.0 in.
	maximum leg room	44.0 in.
	maximum head room	41.3 in.
	seat adjustment, fore and aft	5.0 in

BOND

Strictly speaking, this manufacturer should be referred to as Sharp's Commercials, but as the majority of its products are known as Bonds (after Laurie Bond, whose concepts the firm put into production at its Preston, Lancashire factory) this is how I have titled them.

Bond's little two/three-seater open three-wheeler car first saw the light of day at the very beginning of 1949 – a basic device powered by a Villiers 122cc two-stroke motorcycle engine and three-speed gearbox, its kick-start operated via cable by a handle under the dash. Equally Heath Robinson was the steering by wire and bobbin – a system that had been employed by some of the less desirable cycle cars of the 1920s. Surprisingly, in retrospect, it sold well, and by the end of the year boasted the larger 197cc Villiers with the steering upgraded to rack and pinion by mid-1950.

Spring 1951 saw an improved Mk B version on the market, and at this time the company built a prototype that was intended to go into production as the Sharp's Commercial 3cwt. With a 250cc Brockhouse sidevalve motor with three-speed and reverse gearbox it benefitted from a little more pulling power, as it was envisaged as a tug to tow luggage trains at stations and airports, as well as a light commercial. Providing it could satisfy the criteria set out by the Ministry of Pensions, Sharp's also intended to break into the lucrative invalid carriage market with a suitable version, and to this end the chassis had, from the outset, been given central steering and single central seat.

Events, however, overtook the project, and although it was exhibited at the Motor Cycle Show, only the one was built. Instead a (very) light commercial version of the open car, the Sharp's Minitruck, came to the market in the spring of 1951, followed shortly by the Sharp's Minivan.

A definite downside of Minicar, Minitruck or Minivan ownership was the lack of reverse gear, which, fairly obviously, made some manoeuvres a hardship if not a virtual impossibility – so with the advent of the Mk C Minicar (announced in the Autumn of 1952) came a partial salvation. Worm-and-sector steering was incorporated, giving the single front wheel an operational radius of 180 degrees, which allowed the little vehicle to turn in its own length. Apart from a single prototype van no more commercials were made with the introduction of this improved model, and it was not until the Mk F had been in production for two years that a commercial variant named the Ranger was offered early in 1960.

By now Bonds boasted a 250cc Villiers engine

The 90mpg claim related to the Minicar, but even when loaded the little 122cc commercials could have approached this figure.

THE WORLD'S MOST ECONOMICAL CAR

Petrol 90 m.p.g. Tax £5.

THE SHARPS MINITRUCK

£265

INCLUDING PURCHASE TAX

SHARP'S COMMERCIALS LTD
(EST. 1922)

PRESTON

Sole Manufacturers

● BOND MINICAR ●
● SHARPS MINITRUCK ●
● SHARPS MINIVAN ●

Agents apply for terms

All models to be seen on Stand 45 at Earls Court

Just where and to whom might this young lady have been setting out for once she had loaded her packages?

switch to enable the driver to stop and restart the two-stroke engine in the opposite direction of rotation.

As you are probably wondering, yes some adventurous individuals (very often "rockers" taking an involuntary sabbatical from two wheels due to injury) did progress through the gears while the engine was running in reverse mode, and yes, this all-too-often led to a little accident.

The first Ranger was nothing more than a normal saloon with its rear side windows deleted and a small tailgate added, but shortly after its introduction a Ranger van was offered. In order to increase its carrying capacity the van had just one front seat, but it was not popular for the simple reason that the kind of economy-minded small businessman who would buy such a thing would also want to use it to double as the family car; less than 40 examples were made before it was discontinued.

During 1961 the final, Mk G, incarnation of the quirky little Bond three-wheeler appeared, and the following year a Ranger version with large tailgate and a carrying capacity of 4cwt became available.

along with four-speed gearbox and a Siba Dynastart – a device that made up for the lack of reverse in the motorcycle gearbox by using a three-way ignition

It looks like it's doing 70mph or more but the manufacturer's claimed top speed was 55mph, with a cruising speed of 35-to-45mph. No mention of the type of terrain used to calculate these figures, however – they didn't cope with hilly country too well.

In 1963 the company brought out its first four-wheeler, the Equipe GT, and shortly afterwards it became officially known as Bond Cars. The Equipe was marketed as several different models during its life but was initially based on the Triumph Herald chassis; cars subsequent to 1967 used either the Triumph Spitfire or Vitesse as a basis.

In 1966 Bond came up with a far more sophisticated three-wheeled saloon that utilised a Hillman Imp van motor and transaxle. It was named the 875 and, in line with previous practice, a Ranger version came along a few months later.

The final vehicle to bear the Bond name was the totally extraordinary three-wheeler Bug of the early 1970s, but by this time the company was owned by Reliant and was a Bond in name only – a name that died with the Bug in 1974.

MIN EXPENSE & MAX PERFORMANCE

tell you it's a great vehicle!

MAX — What impresses me so much about the Bond Ranger is its low running costs . . . absolutely at a minimum!

MIN — Yes, and there's no Purchase Tax either, so it's amazingly cheap to buy.

MAX — And notice how roomy the interior is—plenty of space available to meet all needs.

MIN — It really is spacious!

MAX — The construction details make interesting reading. Just take a look.

MIN — You mean all that technical stuff? Like fully independent suspension and hydraulic brakes?

MAX — That's it. See for yourself, it's all printed there . . .

❋ **The BOND RANGER can do over 70 miles per gallon**

❋ **Generous capacity of 42 cubic feet**

❋ **The hand-built aluminium — and — glass fibre body gives sure freedom from corrosion**

❋ **There is a choice of attractive colours**

BRUSH

This brochure shows the range of Brush electric commercials available under Hawker Siddeley's ownership in the early 1960s.

During the last quarter of the nineteenth century the use of electricity was becoming increasingly widespread – no doubt spurred on by Edison's success in producing a commercially viable light bulb. Equally important was the development of the dynamo, and it was to exploit the patents of the American Charles Frances Brush in this sphere that the Anglo-American Brush Electric Light Corporation set up in business at Lambeth in London.

Within ten years it had outgrown its initial premises, and in 1889 commenced relocating to the Falcon Engineering and Car Works at Loughborough, Leicestershire – a large site that had formally been Hughes' locomotive workshops.

By the early years of the twentieth century the Brush Electrical Engineering Company (as it was now called) had a workforce that numbered over 2000, predominantly engaged in the manufacture of steam locomotives, railway and tramway rolling stock, as well as all manner of heavy electrical equipment.

Throughout the First World War, besides continuing with many of its staple products, the company was also called upon to manufacture munitions that included some 650 of various types of aircraft for the RNAS. Post-armistice, there was strong demand for Brush's large turbines and related equipment, which was created by a boom in the construction of factories and small municipal electricity plants, along with an increase in the electric traction and trolleybus side of its business; it put the firm in a good position to weather the lean years ahead, and the '30s proved to be times of expansion and acquisition.

Come the Second World War the Yeovil, Somerset-based engine manufacturer Petter and the Associated British Oil Engine Company had become part of the group. As a result, and to a greater extent than during the 1914-to-1918 conflict, the company was able to contribute greatly to the war effort, making a profit in the process. As an example, Brush's coachworks alone built more than 300 de Havilland aircraft, as well as producing wings for heavy bombers during the period.

With the war over, the coachworks returned to making bus and coach bodies, before ceasing operations in the early 1950s. But elsewhere on the extensive Loughborough factory complex a small range of goods vehicles was being made: launched in 1946 and badged Brush, all were battery-electric three-wheelers. Smallest was the Pony, with either a dairy or van body, then a 10-to-14cwt van for milk or general deliveries, with an 18-to-22cwt version to complete the initial range. London Jaguar dealer Henlys was quick to see the possibilities and secured

the distributorship for the capital and Home Counties – staging an electric vehicle show at its Great West Road headquarters in January 1947.

The ensuing years saw the little battery-electric vehicle range expanded, despite remaining a tiny part of an organisation that in 1950, by way of various takeovers, mergers, amalgamations and arrangements, was acknowledged, amongst other things, to be the largest manufacturer of heavy diesels outside the USA.

By 1953 what was known as the Brush ABOE Group consisted of Brush Electrical Engineering Co and Associated British Oil Engines, which contained J&H McLaren, Mirrlees, Bickerton & Day, Petters, National Gas and Oil Engine Co, and Henry Meadows.

In 1956 the conglomerate became known simply as the Brush Group. A year later, and short of capital, it accepted an offer from Hawker Siddeley that resulted in Brush becoming part of its group of companies but retaining its individual trading names and products.

At the time, some 100-or-so employees were engaged in the manufacture of the diminutive electric commercials by Brush Electrical Engineering – a drop in the ocean compared with the number working on railway locomotives being built by Brush Traction (which, incidentally, was involved in the construction of Eurotunnel locomotives more than 40 years on).

Fifteen years later Hawker Siddeley Aviation and Dynamics was nationalised, and 20 after that – in 1992 – the remainder, now known as the Hawker Siddeley Group, was taken over by BTR. In 1996

The "PONY" FOOD CARRIER for hospital, canteen use, etc. Open type body with drop canvas side and end curtains; alternatively with back filled in and either sliding doors or roller shutters to sides. One intermediate platform tier as standard. The trays are sliding and detachable. Variations on this design available to suit particular size food containers and urns. General dimensions as Pony Open Dairy Model.

the FKI Group acquired Hawker Siddeley Electric Power (which included the various remaining Brush industries) from BTR, and as of now is part of FKI Energy Technologies, which has been owned by Melrose plc since 2008.

The "PONY" ENCLOSED VAN designed for the efficient delivery of foodstuffs and general merchandise. Overall length 10' 7¾" by 4' 10½" wide. Floor space 4' 8½" by 4' 5½" wide. Overall height 6' 5¾" laden. 4' 4" door clearance. Floor height 1' 7¾" laden. Payload 18 cwt. Turning radius 7' 8". With or without doors to cab.

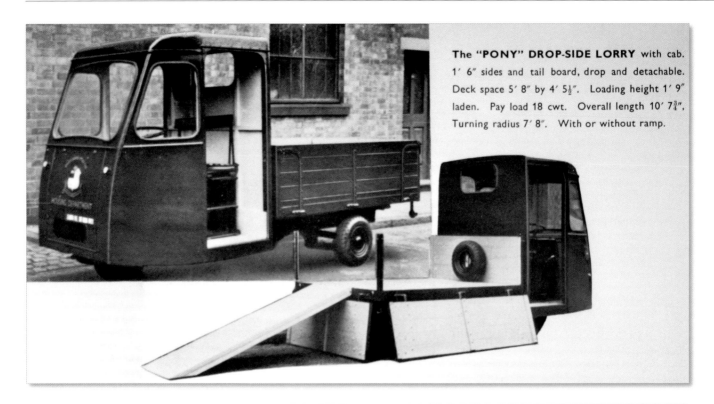

The "PONY" DROP-SIDE LORRY with cab. 1' 6" sides and tail board, drop and detachable. Deck space 5' 8" by 4' 5½". Loading height 1' 9" laden. Pay load 18 cwt. Overall length 10' 7¾", Turning radius 7' 8". With or without ramp.

"PONY" BATTERY ELECTRIC VEHICLE

CHASSIS SPECIFICATION

FRAME
Robust channel section welded frame, adequately braced to give maximum strength and rigidity.

REAR AXLE
Solid type, comprising forged steel stub axles, welded into strong angle section giving a wide track for stability. Hubs are fitted with adjustable taper bearings.

MOTOR
Totally enclosed highly efficient 2.3 hp series-wound traction type, designed for heavy duty. Built to B.S. 173:1941, Class "B" insulation. Large conducting surfaces on commutator and brushes. Dirt and moisture-proof ball bearings. Large hand holes are provided, allowing adequate access to the commutator and brushes.

POWER UNIT
This is a self-contained unit driving from the totally enclosed motor through a duplex roller chain and sprocket, and a spur reduction gear to the front axle and wheel. The whole power unit is fully enclosed, forming part of the steering column, and is mounted on radial ball bearings. The complete unit, which is interchangeable, can be removed from the chassis by releasing eight bolts and disconnecting the motor leads.

CONTROLLER
This is mounted above the motor on a steel sub-frame which also carries the contactor and forward and reverse switches and resistance. The con-troller is of the series battery type, having five speeds forward and reverse, giving a progressive acceleration throughout its range. It is foot-operated. On the forward and reverse control lever there is a removable key for isolating the vehicle when left unattended. The whole assembly is extremely accessible for routine inspection.

BRAKES
Are Girling type rod-operated with 8in. diameter cast steel brake drums fitted to rear wheels, both foot and hand-operated. A pistol grip hand brake is provided for parking purposes.

STEERING
This is of the direct type, operating through the motor and power unit, giving an amazingly small turning circle of 6ft. 3in. radius with perfect control at all speeds.

WHEELS AND TYRES
Heavy duty 18×7 tyres are mounted on pressed steel wheels and are interchangeable.

ROAD SPRINGS
Long, wide, semi-elliptic springs are fitted to the rear axle mounted near to the hubs, giving greater purchase and stability. Rubber bushes are fitted at the spring ends, rendering lubrication unnecessary.

BATTERY
Traction type 15-cell. Choice of three standard makes and various capacities to suit range required. Housed in a robust steel container which is easily removable and forms part of the seat. A charging point is provided to the front of the chassis. To insert charging plug a cover must be slid clear which operates an interlock with the controller pedal. This device ensures that whilst battery is being charged, the vehicle cannot be driven.

CHARGER
Fully automatic metal rectifier type, incorporating an M.J.V. time relay, available in standard form of 200/250 V., 50-cycle, single-phase, a.c. supply, d.c. charger to special requirements.

EQUIPMENT—Full kit of tools.

EQUIPMENT WITH COMPLETE VEHICLE
Electric side lamps, Electric horn. Driving mirrors. Regulation rear lighting and reflectors. Licence-holder. Windscreen wiper when supplied with enclosed cab.

PAINTING
(a) In priming grey as standard.
(b) Vehicle finish in best enamel, colour to purchaser's choice and lettering as required. (Extra).

The design and manufacture of BRUSH Battery Electric Vehicles are subject to constant improvement, and the illustrations and specification may, therefore, vary in some detail from the equipment supplied.

PERFORMANCE DATA—

Approximate mileage rate under normal conditions of use with average payload and taking into consideration 8 stop/starts per mile, vehicle fitted with any of the following batteries:

Battery 15 Cell	160	ampere hour capacity	– 13	Miles Range on one charge
,,	207	,, ,, ,,	– 16	,, ,, ,, ,,
,,	220	,, ,, ,,	– 17	,, ,, ,, ,,
,,	231	,, ,, ,,	– 19	,, ,, ,, ,,
,,	264	,, ,, ,,	– 22	,, ,, ,, ,,
,,	282	,, ,, ,,	– 24	,, ,, ,, ,,

Speed — up to 8 miles per Hour

The BRUSH "PONY" AMBULANCE for operating within hospital confines. Body length behind driver 7' 6"—8' 0". Inside width 5' 0". Inside height 6' 0" at body centre. Various inside fitments available include box type seat for 4 and folding stretcher carrier—2 box type seats for 8—box type seat for 4 and space for trolley stretcher. Extras: sliding ramp—folding step—cabinet, shelves, etc.

COMMER

Commercial Cars was founded in London during 1905 but within a short while relocated to Luton and began to manufacture lorries for UK and foreign consumption. By World War I its products were sufficiently well regarded for the firm to be awarded government contracts that resulted in an output of around 3000 military lorries between 1914 and 1918.

However, after the war the firm lost its way, and insolvency threatened until it was bought by Humber in 1926. Under new ownership the name was abbreviated to Commer and a fresh range of commercials of up to 4½-ton payload was announced; but within two years Commer, along with its erstwhile benefactor Humber, became part of the burgeoning Rootes empire.

William Rootes' acquisition of Commer provided a base to go into large-scale manufacture of reasonably-priced commercials, the first of which was the Humber Snipe-engined 2-ton Invader of 1929. In 1931 another evocatively named Commer joined the ranks in the form of the 1½-ton Raider; within a year or two it was available with a Perkins diesel, thus starting a long-term relationship between the two companies. The following year a forward-control 1-tonner was introduced, and although I'd love to able to tell you it was called the Attacker I have to report that it was simply known as the N1.

The long-established firm of Karrier in Huddersfield appeared to have weathered the depression in good shape, with an increasing range of passenger and goods vehicles. But that was a delusion, and Karrier fell prey to Rootes after the official receiver was called in. Lorry production was moved down to Luton, and from then Karrier would concentrate on lighter vehicles than Commer, although there was some similarity between the two makes.

There was an already current exception, however, in the shape of the Commer Supervan, which had been introduced in 1933 – in reality a reworked Hillman Minx, but a Commer all the same.

On the eve of the Second World War, Commer had recently replaced its medium-to-heavyweight trucks with the Q or Superpoise range of between 1½- to 6-ton capacity, available with normal or forward control and Rootes petrol or Perkins diesel engines. They came along at just the right time, and the Ministry of Supply kept the Luton factory busy throughout the war, to the extent that over 25,000 militarised Superpoise vehicles were produced.

But this was only a small part of the story, and other vehicles produced by Rootes during the time included some 20,000 Hillman Light Utility Trucks, as well as thousands of Humber armoured cars, heavy utilities and the staff cars immortalised by General Montgomery's open version, Old Faithful. Rootes also operated huge shadow factories that produced aircraft, notably the Bristol Blenheim and Handley Page Halifax – one at Speke near Liverpool and another at Ryton-under-Dunsmore near Coventry.

After the war Commer found itself in a better position than many competitors insomuch as its Superpoise

The first Hillman Minx-based Commer Supervans had taken to the road in 1933, and this was the, "New," post-war model, "restyled in the modern manner," even though it was rather a case of old wine in a new bottle.

The NEW COMMER 8 cwt. Supervan

WITH 'SYNCHROMATIC' FINGER-TIP GEAR CONTROL

SUPER CAPACITY
SUPER APPEARANCE
SUPER PERFORMANCE

P. H. WAKEFIELD LTD.
MOTOR AGENTS.
35, FOREGATE ST. WORCESTER.
Phone WORCESTER 4348

COMMER

STURDIEST LIGHT VAN ON THE ROAD

"Britain's smartest, handiest and most economical light delivery van," was without a doubt the roomiest 8cwt van on the road, having a cleared loading space of 100 cubic feet behind the driver. No mention of extra space beside the driver, as the Commer came with two seats as standard.

commercials had been new to the market in 1939, so had a relatively modern appearance. Also, because any faults or weaknesses had been exposed and dealt with as a result of several years' arduous testing at the government's expense, the model was put straight back into civilian production.

The Hillman Minx-based Supervan, whose close relative the Tilly had also performed sterling wartime service, was also put back onto the civilian market as soon as conditions permitted. It had an early update when the MkII Minx was announced towards the end of 1947 – a steering column gear-change being virtually the only mechanical alteration. A year later the wide-bodied MkIII Minx arrived and the Commer's 8cwt

Supervan followed suit. Then, when the MkIV Minx came on the scene in autumn '49 with an extra 80cc added to its old sidevalve engine, Commer was encouraged to re-title its 8cwt the Express Delivery Van.

Hillman's Minx got a 1390cc overhead-valve engine in 1954 but the poor old Express Delivery and its 8cwt pick-up sibling had to make do with the ancient sidevalve through the '50s until the last version of the ageing Express was given the new 1592cc overhead-valve Minx engine for 1962.

In 1954 Hillman brought out a small estate car named the Husky, based on the MkVIII Minx; two years later Rootes introduced a van version named the Cob – early models had the old sidevalve engine but from 1957 they were given 1390cc overhead-valve units.

During this period the long-running Superpoise range had been updated but was now beginning to show its age, and even the smallest left a gap that was finally filled in 1960 when Commer introduced its 15cwt FC. The gap, in fact, only existed among Commer's own products, as it had been well catered for by competitors for several seasons – namely Bedford's CA, BMC's J2 or more recently Ford's Thames 10/12cwt or 15cwt.

Nevertheless, on a "better late than never" principle Commer went ahead, and an array of in-house conversions and bodywork was catalogued. A caravan version emanated from the Len Engineering Works at Maidstone, which was based at a grandiose modernist garage complex that William (Lord William since 1942) Rootes built in the late 1930s on the site of the aero engine repair facility he had established during the First War. The site had formed one of the foundations of what would become his vast Rootes Group empire – an empire that, like all others, would have a limited lifespan. And the clock was ticking.

In the meantime, the new Commer sold better than it perhaps deserved, and although late to the market it would go on to enjoy several updates and a longer production run than its contemporaries. Its final incarnation was the Spacevan from 1974 until 1983 – but by that time it was called a Dodge, and would have been killed off earlier had not the Post Office insisted on placing repeat orders for the things.

Back to 1963, and Rootes at last launched its answer to the Mini – the Hillman Imp, a basically excellent little vehicle that bears much of the blame

Alligator bonnets had already been in use on small Rootes vehicles but this Supervan's type, as well as its frontal styling and many other features, were pure MkII Hillman Minx – both were announced in the autumn of 1947. Easiclean wheels had also been replaced by plain 16in discs shod with 5.25-section tyres.

Power unit was the long-running, four-cylinder, 1185cc, sidevalve Hillman Minx engine that had been around since the early '30s. Its 35bhp at 4100rpm was perfectly acceptable for the time.

THE NEW 'SYNCHROMATIC' FINGER-TIP GEAR CONTROL

Avoids complicated mechanism and thus achieves maximum efficiency of operation.

for what was soon to transpire.

The Imp, which would be followed by a Commer van version two years later, had taken a deal of time and lots of money to bring to fruition; but that had been expected. What had not been, however, was the attitude of the British government, which forced Rootes to build a vast new factory to the east of Glasgow – admittedly with a regional assistance grant – in order to provide employment for ex-Clydebank shipyard workers. That was all very well, but the staff had no experience of motorcar production and the plant was out on a limb from the traditional epicentre of the British car industry – leading to an immense amount of toing and froing between Lynwood and Ryton. What's more, industrial relations nosedived, and in 1964 there were around 30 stoppages at Lynwood alone, which conspired with the already inefficient workforce and unfeasible logistics to return an output amounting to less than 50 per cent of the plant's capability.

Rootes' financial woes were by no means confined to the Imp saga, however, and by 1964 its eventual takeover by Chrysler (which had aspirations in that direction for some while) had became a certainty. The year ended with Lord Rootes' unexpected death in December.

In 1967 the company finally became Chrysler's but brand names and models were continued for as long as it suited; the troubled Imp lasted until 1976. By that time the whole of Chrysler was in enough trouble for the British government to bail out its UK operation, but in the future Commers became Dodges, and there

would be no more Hillmans or Sunbeams. Two years later the remains of Chrysler UK were sold to Peugeot SA, which disposed of the commercial vehicles operations to Renault Vehicules Industriels (RVI) in 1983. In 2001 RVI was sold to Volvo.

Rootes' newfangled, transatlantic-inspired column gearchange was fitted to both Supervan and MkII Minx, as well its Humbers.

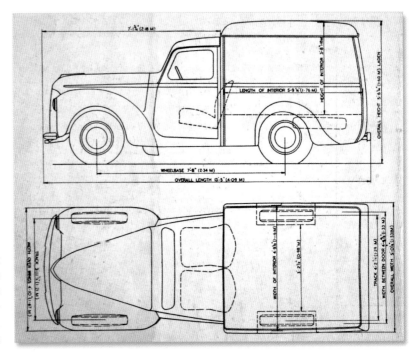

THE COMMER 8 CWT SUPERVAN
with independent front suspension and finger-tip gear control

The motor show of 1948 launched the wide-bodied Hillman Minx MkIII, and with it came a commercial version in the form of Commer's complementary Supervan. Wheelbase was 1in up on the previous model's at 7ft 9in.

Engine was still the same little four-cylinder sidevalve with steering column-controlled four-speed 'box, but the beam front axle had been replaced with this independent suspension setup. The wheels were now 15in with 5.50 tyres but the Lockheed hydraulic brakes with twin leading shoes at the front were carried over from the earlier model.

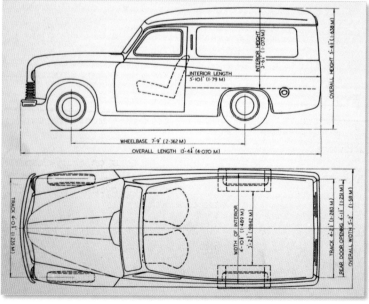

Completely different bodywork from the previous model but the manufacturer still claimed the same 100 cubic feet load area and the passenger seat was still included in the basic price, as were chromium-plated bumpers and hubcaps. Listed options were simply a radio, electric clock or heater.

SMARTEST AND STURDIEST LIGHT VAN ON THE ROAD

For the 1950 season came the Express Delivery Van but under the skin, except for the motor, all was as before; styling changes amounted to little more than a mildly redone radiator grille, as well as a side flash on each flank.

To warrant the new title the old engine had been given an extension to its useful career by increasing the bore by 2mm, which resulted in a capacity of 1265cc. Power was now 37.5bhp at 4200rpm – some Express!

It's 1962 and the Express Delivery is still a current model due to the numerous minor facelifts during its long career – this is its last incarnation.

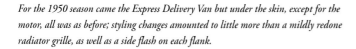

It had always been one of the most spacious light vans on the road, with its 100 cubic feet of load space.

"Power-packed for performance," the publicity department proudly announced. Quite right, too – the Express Delivery now had was the latest 1592cc Hillman Minx engine, which boasted 54bhp at 4400rpm.

Pick-up versions of Express Delivery vans were almost exclusively aimed at overseas markets, and here's an export brochure circa 1957. Both were still fitted with the 1265cc sidevalve Minx engine.

Very much in the style of the Australian coupé utility, Commer's pick-up was a good-looking vehicle. This one was right-hand drive, too, so the advertising was surely slanted towards the antipodean market. A tilt or tonneau cover was available as an extra but chromium bumpers and hubcaps, tool kit, jack and wheel brace were included in the standard specification.

COMMER LIGHT *Pick-up*

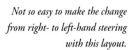

Not so easy to make the change from right- to left-hand steering with this layout.

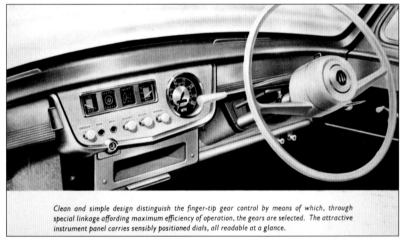

Clean and simple design distinguish the finger-tip gear control by means of which, through special linkage affording maximum efficiency of operation, the gears are selected. The attractive instrument panel carries sensibly positioned dials, all readable at a glance.

The bench seat had a split backrest that gave access to a small luggage area. As the manufacturer pointed out, "Sporting equipment such as guns, golf clubs or light miscellaneous purchases made when shopping in town can be safely kept under lock and key."

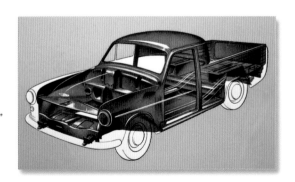

Cab, bodyshell and under-frame were of unitary construction.

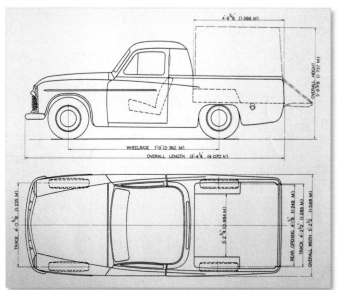

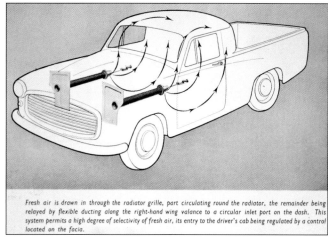

Fresh air is drawn in through the radiator grille, part circulating round the radiator, the remainder being relayed by flexible ducting along the right-hand wing valance to a circular inlet port on the dash. This system permits a high degree of selectivity of fresh air, its entry to the driver's cab being regulated by a control located on the facia.

If the optional heater was added to this system a blower unit was not needed.

Commer's Q or Superpoise range had been introduced on the eve of World War II; as a result the bulk of production was soon taken up by the government, with some 25,000 produced for the military by 1945. Early post-war vehicles were virtually indistinguishable from the 1939 models but someone had taken a good look at transatlantic styling before Rootes came up with this good looking pick-up for 1950. Under the bonnet, or perhaps I should say hood, was a different story, though. Rootes could have slotted in one of its six-cylinder Snipe motors that ranged from 2.7 to over 4-litres, but instead used the latest Humber Hawk four-cylinder sidevalve motor of 2267cc, with all of 50bhp to move an all-up laden weight of almost for 2½ tons. That aside, I'd still like to own one.

The 16in wheels were shod with chunky 7.00-section tyres. To save you checking the dimensional chart, the pick-up bed was a very generous 7ft 6in long and nearly 4ft wide. Despite the brochure cover's illustration, this model was intended for export to countries that drove on the right side of the road and was only right-hand drive to order.

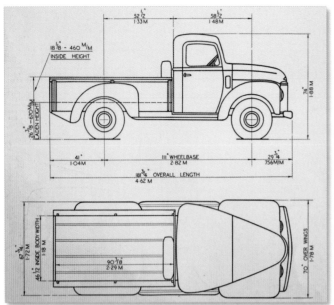

The Superpoise van also had something of an American look and it was spacious too, with nearly 200 cubic feet of load space. This was a 1953 edition and had opening quarterlights by the side windows.

With its 10ft 3in wheelbase and rugged construction the 25cwt Superpoise chassis cab provided plenty of scope for the customer with special requirements. On all commercials of this size, Commer's patented Diaflex four-point rubber mountings attached the superstructure, carrying radiator, wings, bonnet, scuttle and cab.

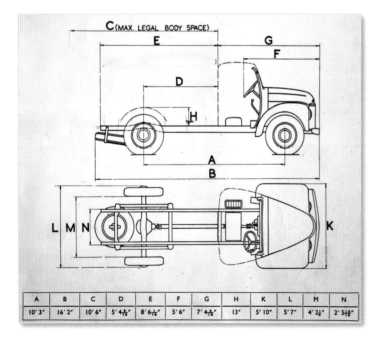

A	B	C	D	E	F	G	H	K	L	M	N
10'3"	16'2"	10'6"	5'4½"	8'6½"	5'6"	7'4½"	13"	5'10"	5'7"	4'2½"	2'5½"

The 2267cc sidevalve engine and its hefty four-speed gearbox were carried on three rubber mountings. Advertised speeds through the gears at 3200rpm were 8, 15, 28 and 48mph.

Restyled and fitted with a more powerful engine for 1956 it became the Superpoise B – but the artist left out the blue van's swivelling quarterlights. All models had a 9ft 4in wheelbase unless you wanted a longer chassis for your 1½-tonner, in which case its wheelbase was 10ft 4in. On test with a full 25cwt on board the petrol-engined model would exceed 60mph and return 23mpg.

"Providing superb accommodation for three persons," said the brochure of the pick-up's cab, which had now been given two rear windows; but who on earth are these three? The driver looks to be a nice clean-cut young man, whilst the fellow on the right has the appearance of a real hard-bitten thug. So where are they off to with the chap in the middle looking for all the world like a shop dummy? Surely they're up to no good!

ADVANCED DESIGN O.H.V. PETROL ENGINE

POWERFUL! ECONOMICAL! SMOOTH! RELIABLE!

Perfected after long research, the Commer four-cylinder o.h.v. engine has been fully proved in rigorous tests under extreme road and climatic conditions. Robust and lively, it is rated at 16 h.p. and yields more power than its famous side-valve forbear, developing a gross b.h.p. of 56 at 3,400 r.p.m. and a torque of 104 lb. ft. at 1,600 r.p.m. Excellent pulling power, brisk acceleration and a great reserve of power even when dealing with maximum loads expedite deliveries, while outstanding reliability and fuel economy cut operating costs to a minimum. Extra power and smooth operation originate from a highly efficient cylinder head of clean, compact design, while easy engine accessibility stemming from the overhead valve arrangement greatly facilitates maintenance. Salient features include separate inlet and exhaust ports for each cylinder, a compression ratio of 6.25:1, large diameter inlet valves, unobstructed inlet and exhaust porting, whilst a thermostatically-controlled manifold system in conjunction with a highly efficient carburettor ensures quick starting from cold, greater operational efficiency, together with maximum power and low fuel consumption. Fundamentally simple in design, this brilliant engine provides ample power and smooth, trouble-free performance whatever the demands made upon it. Finally, for operators who demand even greater longevity than that provided by the standard power unit, porous chrome cylinder bores which, four times harder than cast iron, extend engine life to a phenomenal degree are available as an optional extra.

Chrome Bores available as optional extra

This overhead-valve version of the 2267cc Humber Hawk motor was introduced towards the end of 1954.

FOR LONG-LASTING ECONOMY AND LONG-LIVED RELIABILITY

NEW COMMER LIGHT DIESEL ENGINE

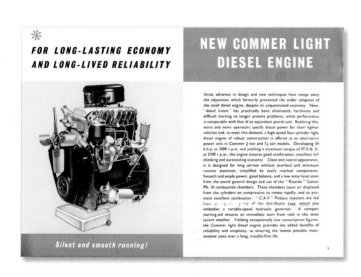

Great advances in design and new techniques have swept away the objections which formerly prevented the wider adoption of the small diesel engine, despite its unquestioned economy. Now, 'diesel knock' has practically been eliminated, harshness and difficult starting no longer present problems, while performance is comparable with that of an equivalent petrol unit. Realising this, more and more operators specify diesel power for their lighter vehicles and, to meet this demand, a high-speed four-cylinder light diesel engine of robust construction is offered as an alternative power unit in Commer ¾ ton and 1¼ ton models. Developing 54 b.h.p. at 3000 r.p.m. and yielding a maximum torque of 97.5 lb. ft. at 2100 r.p.m., the engine ensures good acceleration, excellent hill climbing and outstanding economy. Clean and neat in appearance, it is designed for long service without overhaul and minimum routine attention, simplified by easily reached components. Smooth and ample power, good balance, and a low noise level stem from the sound general design and use of the "Ricardo" Comet Mk. III combustion chambers. These chambers cause air displaced from the cylinders on compression to rotate rapidly, and so promote excellent combustion. "C.A.V." Pintaux injectors are fed from an advanced type of distributor type, which also embodies a variable-speed hydraulic governor. A compact starting-aid ensures an immediate start from cold in the most severe weather. Yielding exceptionally low consumption figures, the Commer light diesel engine provides the added benefits of reliability and simplicity, so ensuring the lowest possible maintenance costs over a long, trouble-free life.

Silent and smooth running!

No reference to its source but this was Standard's 2260cc motor that saw service in Vanguards, as well as the Ferguson tractor.

SECTIONED VIEW
SHOWING CONSTRUCTIONAL FEATURES

1. Hardwood framing, rigidly constructed.
2. Adjustable roof strainers eliminate panel drumming.
3. Interior, hardboard-panelled to waist level.
4. Steel floor runners prevent wear and facilitate easy handling of goods.
5. Full width partition behind driver.
6. One-piece roof pressing prevents leaks.
7. All-steel doors sponge-rubber sealed, and fitted with anti-rattle buffers.
8. Check arms allow doors to be held securely in any position throughout a 90° travel.
9. Detachable rear wings.
10. Van completely dust sealed throughout.

Here's the autumn 1960 brochure for the forward-control and Superpoise range of light commercials.

View of exceptionally capacious interior showing the full-length rear doors clipped to the bodysides in the open position. Note also, roof light and easily-accessible spare wheel. A passenger seat and support can be supplied at extra cost.

From this angle just an extra foot or so of floor length distinguished the 1-ton from the 1½-ton van.

There was also a 1½-ton version with a capacity of over 300 cubic feet, which had a 12in longer wheelbase. Here's the autumn 1960 brochure for the forward-control and Superpoise range of light commercials.

The ¾-ton pick up.

When required the hinged tailboard can be lowered to provide extra capacity when the length of goods carried exceeds the normal length of body.

A tilt cover to protect the load from effects of adverse weather can be supplied as an optional extra.

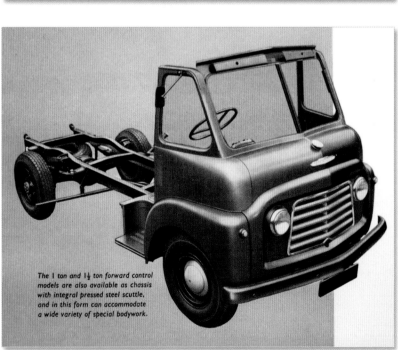

Interior of new and spacious cab fitted to 'Superpoise' models. With ample room for three, a 6" seat adjustment, together with a repositioning of change speed and hand brake levers, gives maximum comfort and more leg-room. Sealing has been given special consideration, and is effected by generous sponge rubber strips round the doors and rubber gaiters around the control levers and pedals. The floor is covered by a rubber mat with felt underlay.

The 1 ton and 1½ ton forward control models are also available as chassis with integral pressed steel scuttle, and in this form can accommodate a wide variety of special bodywork.

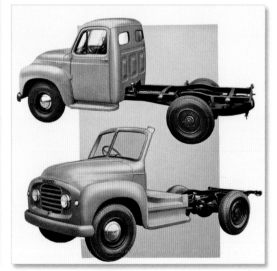

Superpoise ¾-ton and 1½-ton chassis with integral pressed-steel scuttle or a complete cab were available to operators who needed to fit specialised bodywork.

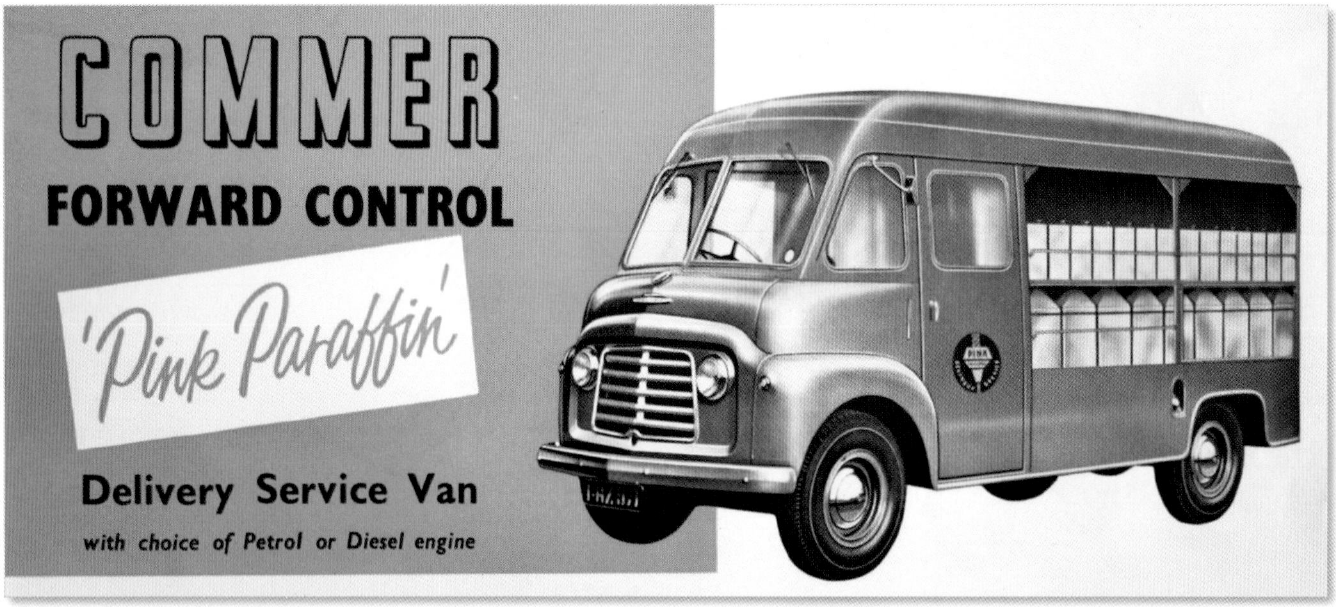

Designed in conjunction with Shell-Mex BP the body, which could carry 54 five-gallon drums and 224 one-gallon cans, had a moulded fibreglass roof.

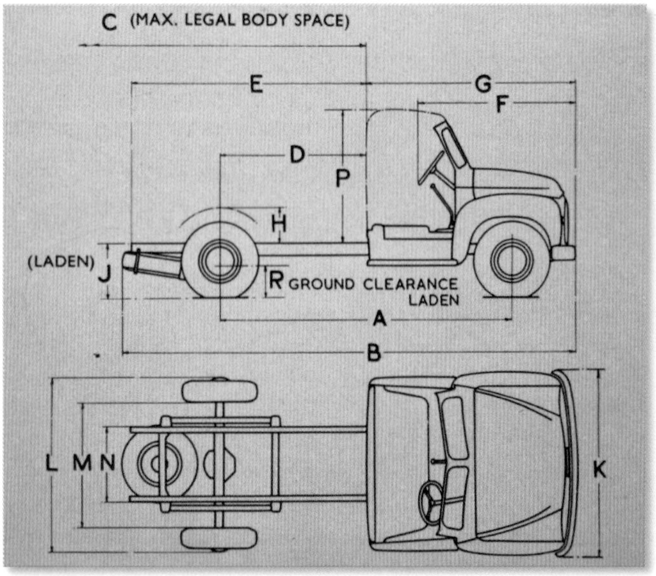

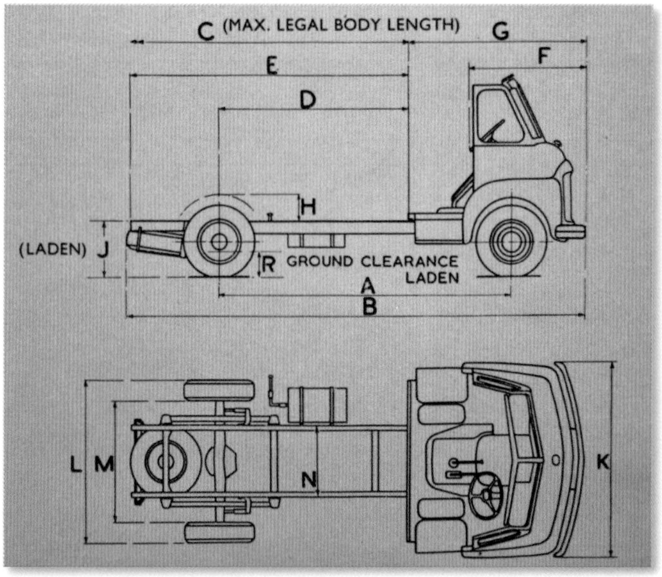

	Model	A	B	C	D	E	F	G	H	J	K	L	M	N	P	R
'SUPERPOISE' NORMAL CONTROL	¾ Ton	112″	178″	93″	46¼″	83¾″	66⅝″	86⅝″	12 1/16″	22⅝″	74⅝″	66⅛″	50⅞″	29 13/16″	53¾″	6⅞″
	'Pick-Up'	112″	169 13/16″	93″	46 9/16″	77⅜″	66⅝″	86⅝″	12 1/16″	22″	74⅝″	66⅛″	50⅞″	29 13/16″	53¾″	6⅞″
	1½ Ton	112″	178″	93″	46¼″	83¾″	66⅝″	86⅝″	13 1/16″	23⅞″	74⅝″	66½″	50⅛″	29 13/16″	53¾″	7⅜″
		124″	191″	111″	58¼″	95¾″	66⅝″	86⅝″	13 1/16″	23⅞″	74⅝″	66½″	50⅛″	29 13/16″	53¾″	7⅜″
FORWARD CONTROL	1 Ton	111″	184¾″	111″	68¼″	105¾″	49 9/16″	74 13/16″	12⅝″	22¾″	80⅞″	66 7/16″	50 9/16″	29 13/16″	—	7⅛″
	1½ Ton	123″	196¾″	132″	80¼″	117¾″	49 9/16″	74 13/16″	12⅞″	23¼″	80⅞″	66⅞″	50⅛″	29 13/16″	—	7⅝″

In 1954 Hillman had introduced a small station wagon named the Husky that was based upon the Minx MkVIII, and for 1956 a van version known as the Cob was marketed. By this time the Minx had been given a larger overhead valve engine but both Husky and Cob retained the old 1265cc sidevalve unit. More costly than its direct rivals from BMC and Ford – so it never sold in huge numbers – the Cob was nevertheless a thoroughly workmanlike little vehicle. This brochure is for its replacement, the Series I, which was announced in the autumn of 1957 and was the first Cob to be badged as such – the previous Husky derivative simply wearing Commer badges.

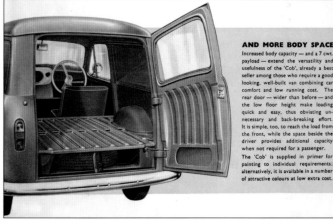

AND MORE BODY SPACE

Increased body capacity — and a 7 cwt. payload — extend the versatility and usefulness of the 'Cob', already a best looking, well-built van combining car comfort and low running cost. The rear door — wider than before — and the low floor height make loading quick and easy, thus obviating unnecessary and back-breaking effort. It is simple, too, to reach the load from the front, while the space beside the driver provides additional capacity when not required for a passenger. The 'Cob' is supplied in primer for painting to individual requirements; alternatively, it is available in a number of attractive colours at low extra cost.

Wheels were 15in with 5.50-section tyres, and brakes were Lockheed hydraulic with twin leading shoes at the front and 8in drums. Chromium-plated bumpers and hubcaps were standard, but the passenger seat was no longer complementary and had joined a list of extras that included a radio, roof rack, exterior sun visor, mascot, windscreen washer kit, clock or thermometer, cigar lighter and overriders as depicted here. The basic-price paint job for a Cob was grey primer but for an extra tenner Commer would do you a nice gloss finish in one of the model's standard colours of Antelope, Fiesta Blue, Thistle Grey or Seacrest Green – all with red trim.

A SMOOTH, SURE RIDE

The new Commer front suspension, working in conjunction with hydraulic dampers, employs ball joints and embodies coil springs with double wishbone links. Exceptional handling and road holding qualities with protection for fragile loads are thus ensured, while extra low pressure tyres further promote driver comfort. Other advantages include longer life, reduced wear, and simplified servicing. Fully proved in service, this new suspension is robustly constructed to withstand many years of full load operation.

NEW, ROBUST O.H.V. ENGINE

... a lively, powerful and fully proved unit

The "new" engine was the 1390cc Minx unit that had been around for a couple of years or so. It produced 43bhp at 4000rpm. It was mated to a four-speed gearbox with floor change.

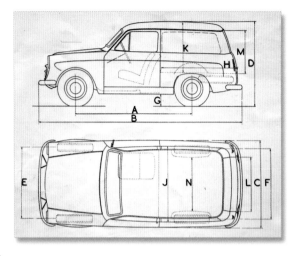

DIMENSIONS		
A.	Wheelbase	86 in.
B.	Overall length	149½ in.
C.	Overall width	60¼ in.
D.	Overall height (unladen)	61¾ in.
E.	Front track (at ground)	49 in.
F.	Rear track	48½ in.
G.	Minimum ground clearance (laden)	7 in.
H.	Interior length	57½ in.
J.	Interior width (maximum)	54¼ in.
K.	Interior height (maximum)	35¾ in.
L.	Width of rear door aperture	37 in.
M.	Height of rear door aperture	30¼ in.
N.	Width between wheel-arches	37½ in.
Loading height unladen		25½ in.
Turning circle (approx.)		31 ft. 6 in.
Body capacity		47 cu. ft.
Petrol tank capacity		6½ gallons
Vehicle weight without passenger seat (less fuel, water and spare wheel)		17½ cwt.
Vehicle weight without passenger seat (with fuel, water and spare wheel)		18½ cwt.
Maximum Gross Vehicle Weight		26½ cwt.

The square (bore 76.2mm/stroke 76.2mm) 1390cc engine was up to 47.5bhp at 4400rpm courtesy of revised manifolding and carburettor, along with other minor improvements for the Series II Cob. There was a sportier gearbox too, with closer ratios and a remote change.

ROBUST FOUR-CYLINDER O.H.V. ENGINE OF 1390 c.c. CAPACITY

. . . a lively, economical and fully-proved power unit

COMMER

'COB' LIGHT VAN

A ROOTES PRODUCT

REAL CAR COMFORT

A deeper and wider windscreen provides even greater visibility, and together with a bucket seat of improved design, increased legroom, and smooth responsive controls, make the 'Cob' comfortable, safe, and a pleasure to drive. Fully-proved steering and suspension units assure a splendid ride, and lift handling qualities and safety into the highest class. There's a full-length parcel shelf, provision for heater and radio, and everything else you'd expect in a driving compartment built to car specification.

Passenger seat is an accessory.

The Series II Cob of 1960 had a new grille (still with combined sidelights and flashing indicators at its extremities) and headlamp bezels that assisted the lower, ribbed, roofline and deeper screen to give the illusion of an entirely redesigned model. In some respects I suppose it was, as it had lost a few cubic feet of space behind the driver. Rootes still stuck to the policy of sending out vehicles in primer unless you were prepared to pay a bit extra, but now the choice of colours had been extended to Caramel, Powder Blue, Wickham Blue, Lake Green, Glen Green or Pippin Red – all with red trim.

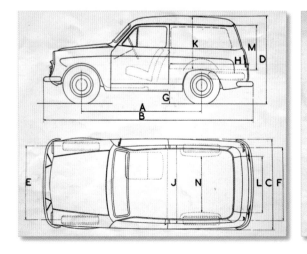

DIMENSIONS		
A.	Wheelbase	86 in.
B.	Overall length	149½ in.
C.	Overall width	60¼ in.
D.	Overall height (unladen)	60½ in.
E.	Front track (at ground)	49 in.
F.	Rear track	48½ in.
G.	Minimum ground clearance (laden)	7 in.
H.	Interior length	56½ in.
J.	Interior width (maximum)	54¼ in.
K.	Interior height (maximum)	34½ in.
L.	Width of rear door aperture	37 in.
M.	Height of rear door aperture	30½ in.
N.	Width between wheel-arches	37½ in.
Loading height unladen		25½ in.
Turning circle (approx.)		31 ft. 6 in.
Body capacity		44½ cu. ft.
Petrol tank capacity		6½ gallons
Vehicle weight without passenger seat (less fuel, water and spare wheel)		17½ cwt.
Vehicle weight without passenger seat (with fuel, water and spare wheel)		18½ cwt.
Maximum Gross Vehicle Weight		26½ cwt.

ROOTES special accessories

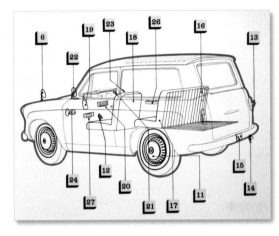

		£	s.	d.
1.	Overriders (set of 4) ...	4	10	0
2.	Badge bar (fitted in conjunction with lamp carriers) ...	1	17	6
	Lamp carriers (R.H. or L.H.) ...		19	6
3.	Fog lamp ...	2	18	6
4.	Driving lamp ...	2	18	6
5.	Mascot ...		17	6
6.	Rebound wing mirror (straight stem) ...	1	5	0
	Rebound wing mirror (curved stem) ...	1	5	0
7.	Exterior sun visor (in primer) ...	4	2	6
8.	Roof rack ...	3	15	0
9.	Rimfinishers (set of 5) ...	5	5	0
10.	White wall tyre trims (set of 4) ...no longer available			
11.	Wheel discs (set of 4) ...		8	5	0
12.	Pedal rubber ... (set of 3)		3	6
13.	Petrol locking cap ...	1	1	0
14.	Reverse lamp kit ...	3	17	6
15.	Tow bar attachment ...	6	17	6
16.	Rear compartment mat ...	2	9	6
17.	Rear folding seat kit ...	20	0	0
18.	Passenger seat kit ...	10	5	0
19.	Windscreen washer ...	1	15	0
20.	Radio—Ekco ... CR/915/RB	22	1	0*
	Radiomobile ... 50/Td	25	0	8*
	Pye ... TCR/1000	19	17	11*

		£	s.	d.
21.	Either electric clock ...	4	16	6*
	or thermometer ...	2	12	6
22.	Door mirror ...		19	6
23.	Cigar lighter ...	1	7	5*
24.	Second windtone horn kit ...	2	6	6
26.	Door arm rests (kit of 2) ...	1	15	0
27.	Heater kit ...	12	10	0
	Blower unit ...	4	15	0
ALSO AVAILABLE :				
Vanity mirror ...			9	7*
Bonnet lock ...			14	6
Fire extinguisher ...		2	15	0
Safety belt (front seats only) ... each		3	5	0
Multi-purpose cushion ...		1	15	0
Tool kit ...		1	16	6
Radiator blind ...		3	6	0
Badge clips ...			3/6 & 5/3	
Perspex interior sun visor ...		1	12	6*
Paint touch-in brush ...			4	3
Liquid polish ...			3	6
Interior cleaner ...			4	6
Floor ashtray ...		1	2	2*
Roof headlining kit ...		12	0	0
Paint spray (limited range) ...			10	6
Paint touch-in matching kit (limited range)			8	6

The Commer FC was launched in 1960 and from the outset the main colour brochure outlined a wide variety of models. Standard finishes other than primer were Toledo Red, Wickham Blue, April Yellow, Seacrest Green or Foam White, all with red trim.

Durability of the highest degree is offered by the bodyshell and underframe of unitary construction — an all-steel, all-welded structure of minimum weight and maximum strength which is protected on the underside by a stoved bitumen compound. This proved and practical form of construction has many advantages. Being of exceptional strength it will not distort even under extreme loading and this in turn ensures complete absence of drumming and enables the structure to resist the most rigorous use over long periods of regular service.

NOTE THESE FEATURES

1 Battery easy of access.
2 Extremely comfortable seating.
3 Twin screen wipers.
4 Roof projects over windscreen.
5 Grab handles on screen pillars.
6 Twin mirrors.
7 Deep panoramic windscreen.
8 Large diameter steering wheel.
9 Instruments in neat cluster.
10 Controlled fresh-air ventilation.
11 Engine accessibly positioned beneath centre seat.
12 Full-width parcel shelf.
13 Flashing indicators.
14 Independent front suspension.
15 Powerful hydraulic brakes.
16 Two jacking points on each side.
17 Hypoid rear axle unit.
18 Extra long rear leaf springs.
19 Wide rear doors with metal checks.

The lively o.h.v. PETROL
unit of 1494 c.c. capacity

At first the FC was fitted with the current 52bhp Minx engine (79mm x 76.2mm stroke) but before long it was uprated with a bored-out 1592cc (81.5mm x 76.2mm stroke) version that, in the FC, was rated at 54bhp at 4400rpm.

The fully-proved DIESEL
unit of 1621 c.c. capacity

If diesels were your kettle of fish the 1621cc Perkins 4.99 was an option but 42-odd horsepower at 3600rpm was its mark, and its wet-liner engine was prone to internal water leaks and other maladies including cracked cylinder heads. Around 1970 I ran one of these for a while and, although I never experienced engine trouble, its pitiful performance combined with the motor's harsh diesel clatter (admittedly when loaded to the gunwales) has always stuck in my memory.

The ¾-ton FC was also available as a chassis and cab unit that was suitable for a variety of bodywork. If an open-topped body was envisaged, the manufacturer stipulated the use of cab reinforcing members.

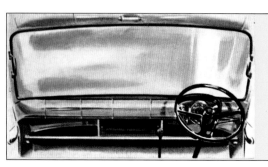

Unique front three-seat capacity

Design allows for the fitting of three comfortable seats in the driver's compartment — those for passengers are optional extras — and their positioning gives ample legroom. The driver's seat is fully adjustable. Furthermore, due to the toeboard mounted gear lever, a clear floor area allows entry or exit from either side of vehicle. Seat frames are made from tubular steel, the cushions from interwoven springs and plastic foam, whilst the entire seats are trimmed with strong, hard-wearing P.V.C. fabric.

Extra-wide vision wrap-round screen

Panoramic vision is provided by the extra-wide, wrap-round screen of toughened plate safety-glass which is fitted with dual central drive wipers for full visibility in inclement weather. Thus the driver has an uninterrupted view of the road, and all controls both major and minor, are within his easy reach.

What Rootes referred to as the Drive-Away unit was suitable as a basis for more highly specialised bodywork; cab reinforcing members were still needed if it was to be an open version.

The Walker had the standard unitary construction body with the addition of either a full-width, half-height bulkhead with blind behind the driver or, as an optional extra, a full-height bulkhead with glass sliding hatch.

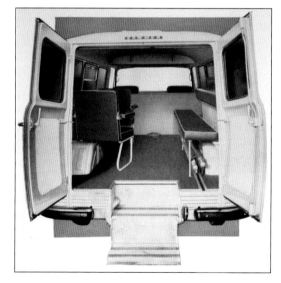

This was the B6 model that would accommodate up to six inward-facing and two forward-facing patients, or two forward-facing sitting patients and one stretcher case.

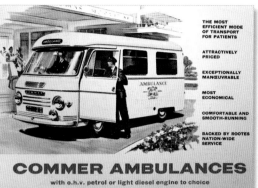

Almost from its inception the FC was available as a fully-equipped and ready-to-go ambulance. There were two models, and this was the Lomas Junior. The entire body was of aluminium with an ash frame.

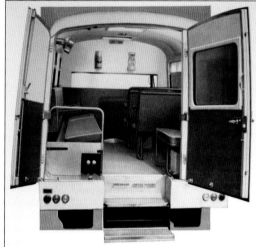

To access the rear for loading patients there was this configuration or conventional double doors. This is the type F interior that would accommodate nine or ten sitting patients, or five sitting and one stretcher case once the combined seat and stretcher platform had been erected on the nearside.

Anxious to cover all possible markets, Commer published individual brochures for some of the specialised bodywork that was available on its ¾-ton FC. This February 1961 example still listed the 1494cc petrol engine.

To create the High Top with nearly 325 cubic feet of load area, the standard roof was cut away above gutter level and replaced with a fibreglass moulding that incorporated an opening rear hatch; when opened, it increased the loading height to 5ft 6in. The original cab canopy was retained and built up to provide a large shelf above the driver.

"Housewives welcome the chance of shopping from their own front doors and this small mobile shop, eye catching in appearance and a first class economic proposition, will make sales soar." Side windows were for display and the sales counter was accessed through sliding doors at the rear.

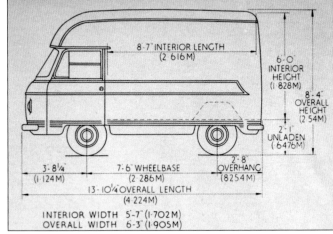

"Pick-ups for every purpose", this brochure could have been titled.

Standard pick-up

The standard pick-up model — based on the Commer ½-ton forward control chassis/cab — is a popular and truly versatile vehicle which provides the means of transporting relatively small but necessary tools and materials; a model designed to withstand arduous operating conditions which will prove its worth in a wide variety of trades and occupations.

Body is of welded steel construction throughout, and incorporates a swaged-steel floor with steel wheelboxes. Body sides are double-skinned with 18 s.w.g. inner and 20 s.w.g. outer mild steel panels pressed to conform to the cab contours. Triangulated gusset pressings reinforce the front end of the body and cab, and tilt sockets are provided in the top of each body side.

Easy loading is effected by a full width tailboard aperture and the tailboard, a single mild steel hinged panel with rolled top and bottom edges, is retained by quick-release fasteners and fitted with robust drop chains.

For protection against inclement weather, three tilt tubes and a canvas tilt cover, which stow behind the cab when not in use, are included in the range of optional equipment available.

Standard vehicle is finished in either grey primer, or it can be paint finished to customer's requirements.

DIMENSIONS. Overall length 14 ft. 0 in.; Overall width 6 ft. 3 in.; Overall height 6 ft. 9 in.; Body interior length 8 ft. 10 in.; Body interior width 5 ft. 4¼ in.; Height of sides 2 ft. 0 in.; Loading height (unladen) 2 ft. 1¼ in.

The canopy pick-up was aimed at the building and allied trades, with seating for three in the cab and three at the rear, as well as a good carrying capacity.

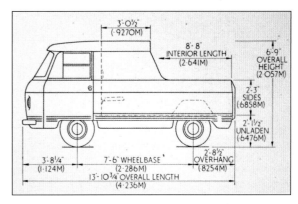

A Dropsider pick-up was another alternative that was particularly easy to load and unload – especially in the case of bricks, building blocks, sand, gravel or, as illustrated here, heavy packing cases. All other bodies in this range incorporated reinforcement at the rear of the cab to prevent structural flexing but with the dropsider this was not possible, so a framework that served the same purpose was braced to the floor on each side.

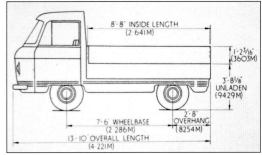

Other vehicles in Commer's pick-up range had hinged doors but the Bottle Float, as it was called (being sure not to restrict sales only to milkmen, I suppose), was equipped with sliding doors for ease of ingress and egress in confined conditions.

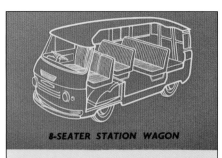

8-SEATER STATION WAGON

The Station Wagon provides first-class travelling conditions for eight persons, all facing forward, with ample space for luggage at the rear.

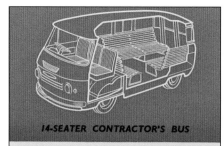

14-SEATER CONTRACTOR'S BUS

Sturdily constructed seats accommodate eleven passengers in the main compartment together with three in the driver's compartment.

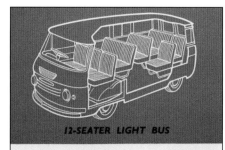

12-SEATER LIGHT BUS

With seating accommodation for twelve persons, the Light Bus provides maximum comfort for its passengers, all of whom face forward.

The FC passenger range also attempted to fill all niches in the market.

Due to popular demand Commer introduced a 1-ton version (soon to be known as the 2500) of the FC in autumn 1962. Besides the 200 cubic feet (210 if you left out the passenger seat) van depicted on the brochure's cover, a comprehensive range was available. Engine options remained either 1592cc petrol or 1621cc diesel, but interestingly this brochure gave theoretical maximum speeds. With the standard 5.125:1 axle ratio and 6.70x15in tyres the petrol FC would be doing 70.5mph at the 44000rpm that delivered its peak of 54bhp. The diesel, on the other hand, with its lower ratio of 5.625:1 and 6.70x15in tyres, would be doing 52.5mph at its governed maximum of 3600rpm.

The ¾-ton and 1-ton Commers had been marketed as the 1500 and 2500 for some while but in September 1965 they were updated and re-engined. As an example of the former, the separate sidelights and flashers were now a legal requirement; meanwhile, big changes took place in the drivetrain. Petrol Commers were now equipped with Rootes' new five-bearing 1724cc motor, which also went into Minxes and Sunbeam Alpines in varying states of tune, and was not unduly stressed pushing out 62bhp at 4000rpm. The more expensive diesel versions were now fitted with the 1752cc Perkins 4.108 that gave 52bhp at 4000rpm – an improved design that utilised dry (as opposed to the 4.99's wet) cylinder liners.

There was a new manual gearbox too, with synchromesh on all gears.

Seating was now in black with up-to the-minute pleated panels.

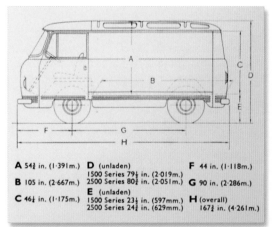

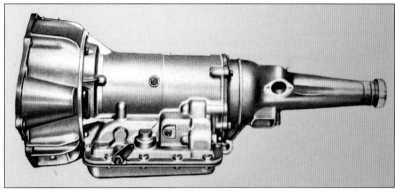

A 54¾ in. (1·391m.)
B 105 in. (2·667m.)
C 46¼ in. (1·175m.)

D (unladen)
1500 Series 79½ in. (2·019m.)
2500 Series 80¾ in. (2·051m.)
E (unladen)
1500 Series 23½ in. (597mm.)
2500 Series 24¾ in. (629mm.)

F 44 in. (1·118m.)
G 90 in. (2·286m.)
H (overall)
167¾ in. (4·261m.)

A most unusual option was introduced in the form of the Borg-Warner model 35 automatic gearbox. Specifically intended for use in the lighter-capacity 1500 Commer it could, however, be specified in the 2500 providing the sales engineer department okayed the intended operating conditions. Normally the 1500 had 10in brakes at the front and 9in at the rear whilst the 2500 had 10in all round, but the automatic 1500 also featured 10s.

As a postscript to the FC here's a mildly customised FC from a Rootes accessory brochure to demonstrate what went on back then with encouragement from this manufacturer.

NEW COMMER IMP VAN ACCELERATES DELIVERY TIME LIKE NO OTHER VAN HAS EVER DONE BEFORE

The Imp never attained the iconic status of the Mini and is all but forgotten. Yet the Imp was enormous fun to drive, with a responsive rear engine coupled to a delightful all-synchro gearbox, rack-and-pinion steering, and all-independent suspension. Its 12in wheels were shod with 5.50 Dunlop tyres and the brakes were 8in drums all round with twin leading shoes at the front. Standard colours for the van were Tartan Red, Polar White, Orchid Green, Capri Blue or Bermuda Blue.

Hillman's rear-engined challenge to the Mini had come onto the market in 1963 but it was not until the autumn of 1965 that a van version was introduced. It was manufactured at a new purpose-built factory at Linwood in Scotland.

The Coventry Climax FWM-inspired 875cc engine had a single overhead cam and die-cast aluminium cylinder block fitted with dry liners and an aluminium cylinder head. Rootes' brochure credited it with 36bhp at 4500rpm but the little engine would happily go on to five, six or even more without any ill effects. But whatever you do, don't *do what I once did! In the early '70s, a friend and I were hammering up the E40 from Ostend to Brussels late one night in his canary yellow van when it began to seriously overheat. We pulled over and I tipped about a gallon of water into the filler that is exposed when the tailgate is opened (you can see it at the bottom of this picture). Despite looking like a radiator filler cap, I couldn't have been more wrong! The radiator filler lived under a panel on the left (you will see this too), but I had mistakenly gone for the engine oil filler. What fun it was, lying on my back trying to crack open the sump plug sufficiently to let out water but not too much oil – all done by feel whilst truck after truck roared past only inches away.*

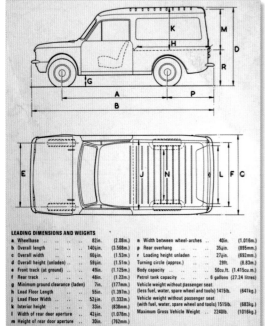

LEADING DIMENSIONS AND WEIGHTS

a	Wheelbase	82in.	(2.08m.)	n Width between wheel-arches	40in.	(1.016m.)
b	Overall length	140½in.	(3.568m.)	p Rear overhang	35½in.	(895mm.)
c	Overall width	60½in.	(1.53m.)	r Loading height unladen	27½in.	(692mm.)
d	Overall height (unladen)	59½in.	(1.51m.)	s Body capacity	50cu.ft.	(1.415cu.m.)
e	Front track (at ground)	49in.	(1.125m.)	Petrol tank capacity	6 gallons	(27.24 litres)
f	Rear track	48in.	(1.22m.)	Vehicle weight without passenger seat		
g	Minimum ground clearance (laden)	7in.	(177mm.)	(less fuel, water, spare wheel and tools)	1415lb.	(641kg.)
h	Load Floor Length	55in.	(1.397m.)	Vehicle weight without passenger seat		
j	Load Floor Width	52½in.	(1.332m.)	(with fuel, water, spare wheel and tools)	1515lb.	(683kg.)
k	Interior height	33in.	(838mm.)	Maximum Gross Vehicle Weight	2240lb.	(1016kg.)
l	Width of rear door aperture	42in.	(1.078m.)			
m	Height of rear door aperture	30in.	(762mm.)			

You'd never think it from this view but there's 50 cubic feet of space in the back of one of these – plus another 3½ cubic feet behind the seats and under the floor if you had small packages or something to hide.

DOUGLAS

The strictly utilitarian plywood/aluminium laminate bodywork had some novel features. The Douglas could be had as a van, pick-up or open-sided for milk delivery.

When Douglas Engineering made its first motorcycle in 1907, the motor built to power it was a horizontally-opposed flat twin, and five years later a brace of twins placed first and second in the Isle of Man Lightweight TT – these becoming the firm's hallmark for the next 50-or-so years.

Come the Great War, a lucrative contract with the government saw thousands of Douglas machines in France and elsewhere; their legendary reputation for reli-

ability standing them in good stead when peace returned and ensuring a ready queue of customers throughout the post-war boom.

One more TT win came along when hard-man Freddie Dixon hitched his own design of sidecar to one of the company's bikes, and its dirt-track model ruled the sport for a while. But by the early '30s the glory days were over.

Douglas lurched through the next few years with unsuccessful models and was beset with financial diffi- culties that led to changes of ownership – the last of which resulted in the company being bought by the British Pacific Trust with the idea of using its extensive engineering facilities to expand the manufacture of aero engines, which had hitherto been a sideline.

World War II could have allowed the expansion but instead the company, now known as Aero Engines Ltd, found a renewed and enlarged demand for the Douglas Industrial Truck that it had made since the '20s. These robust little tug-come-pick-ups, powered by the firm's air-cooled twins, had even been supplied to other motor manufacturers such as Austin for use around their facto- ries, but now they really came into their own, shifting materials within many of the establishments engaged in war work.

The company's motorcycle-based twins also found their way into thousands of generator sets, as well as radar equipment, and the factory also produced wings for various aircraft. But, as motorcycle manufacture had been discontinued a few years earlier, it was not called upon to supply military machines.

Peace saw fresh investors in the company and a change of name to Douglas (Kingswood) Ltd in 1946. Within a short space of time a brand-new motorcycle with torsion bar rear suspension and an updated over- head-valve flat-twin was announced, as was a range of battery-powered commercials called Douglas ACM Electric. Designed with the assistance of Morrison – which was already established as a manufacturer of similar vehicles – the Douglas differed from the latter in many respects: it had twin motors, each driving a rear wheel, while the Morrison had but one, and Girling hydraulic brakes as opposed to its competitor's Bendix. Intended to operate in relatively flat urban areas it was

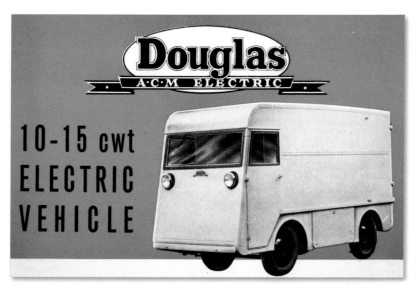

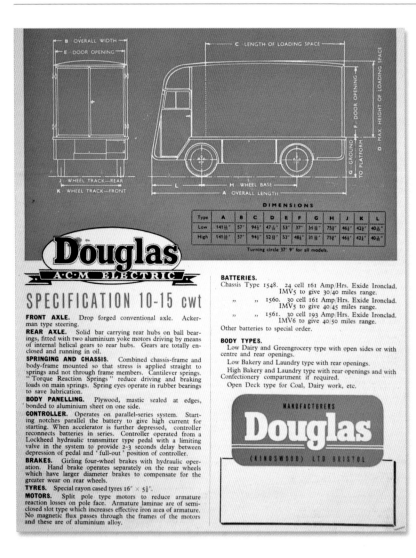

Douglas
A·C·M ELECTRIC

SPECIFICATION 10-15 cwt

FRONT AXLE. Drop forged conventional axle. Ackerman type steering.

REAR AXLE. Solid bar carrying rear hubs on ball bearings, fitted with two aluminium yoke motors driving by means of internal helical gears to rear hubs. Gears are totally enclosed and running in oil.

SPRINGING AND CHASSIS. Combined chassis-frame and body-frame mounted so that stress is applied straight to springs and not through frame members. Cantilever springs. "Torque Reaction Springs" reduce driving and braking loads on main springs. Spring eyes operate in rubber bearings to save lubrication.

BODY PANELLING. Plywood, mastic sealed at edges, bonded to aluminium sheet on one side.

CONTROLLER. Operates on parallel-series system. Starting notches parallel the battery to give high current for starting. When accelerator is further depressed, controller reconnects batteries in series. Controller operated from a Lockheed hydraulic transmitter type pedal with a limiting valve in the system to provide 2-3 seconds delay between depression of pedal and 'full-out' position of controller.

BRAKES. Girling four-wheel brakes with hydraulic operation. Hand brake operates separately on the rear wheels which have larger diameter brakes to compensate for the greater wear on rear wheels.

TYRES. Special rayon cased tyres 16" × 5¼".

MOTORS. Split pole type motors to reduce armature reaction losses on pole face. Armature laminae are of semi-closed slot type which increases effective iron area of armature. No magnetic flux passes through the frames of the motors and these are of aluminium alloy.

BATTERIES.

Chassis Type 1548. 24 cell 161 Amp/Hrs. Exide Ironclad. IMV5 to give 30/40 miles range.
,, ,, 1560. 30 cell 161 Amp/Hrs. Exide Ironclad. IMV5 to give 40/45 miles range.
,, ,, 1561. 30 cell 193 Amp/Hrs. Exide Ironclad. IMV6 to give 40/50 miles range.

Other batteries to special order.

BODY TYPES.

Low Dairy and Greengrocery type with open sides or with centre and rear openings.
Low Bakery and Laundry type with rear openings.
High Bakery and Laundry type with rear openings and with Confectionery compartment if required.
Open Deck type for Coal, Dairy work, etc.

MANUFACTURERS

Douglas
(KINGSWOOD) LTD. BRISTOL

available in van, open-side or pick-up form and, depending on load and battery capacity, offered up to nearly 50 miles on full charge.

Due to the restrictions imposed by their motive power, electric vehicles have always had limited sales, and the Douglas went out of production in 1952 – by which time the company had once again all but gone broke and was running under receivership.

Why the well-equipped and well-placed Kingswood factory should be continually up against it financially is hard to understand, especially when the firm had so many other irons in the fire. In addition to manufacturing electric commercials and motorcycles, it was undertaking a large amount of subcontract work for the Bristol Aeroplane Company, as well as building Vespa scooters under licence, having negotiated very favourable rights with the Italian parent firm of Piaggio, granting not only the UK market but also that of the entire Commonwealth.

Fresh hopes for a change of fortune were pinned on a new motorcycle, the distinctively styled Dragonfly twin, which was unveiled late in 1954. But sales failed to meet expectations and the company was still in the hands of the receiver when it was taken over by Chippenham-based Westinghouse Brake and Signal two years later. A good part of the extensive premises was thereafter given over to the new owner's products – such as railway braking equipment – and although the Dragonfly was fairly soon killed off, Douglas Vespa scooters lasted until well into the '60s.

By that time Westinghouse itself had been acquired by Hawker Siddeley, but the old Douglas Kingswood factory continued to manufacture braking equipment whilst the Douglas name lived on as an importer of small Italian motorcycles.

In 1971 Westinghouse merged with Bendix, and brake manufacture continued on the old Douglas site. Nationalisation of Hawker Siddeley Aviation and Dynamics occurred in 1977, while the remainder became the Hawker Siddeley Group; in 1992 it was acquired for £1.5bn by BTR. Seven years later BTR merged with Siebe, and what remained that hadn't been shut down or sold off was renamed Invensys.

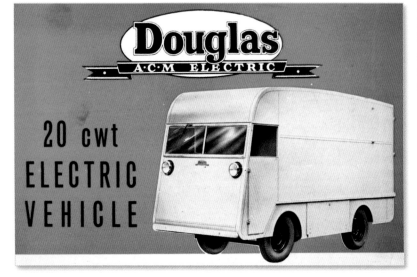

Externally the 20cwt Douglas van was easily distinguishable by its split windscreen but its chassis had been given a 7in longer wheelbase and 2in wider track, while the entire vehicle was stretched by 2ft.

FORD

Henry Ford's Detroit-based Ford Motor Company was a mere eight years old when he established a factory at Trafford Park, Manchester in 1911 to assemble Model Ts from imported parts. It was his first factory outside North America and the first of many that would literally encircle the globe in years to come.

By 1914 the Manchester factory was sourcing an increasing amount of components in the Midlands, and production had been speeded up considerably with the introduction of moving assembly lines. Some 6000 cars had been sold in 1913, with output during the year that war broke out set to be even higher; this gave Ford a large percentage of the British market, even though a strict one-model policy was adhered to. The T, however, was available with various styles of open and closed bodywork, as well as a light van or even a chassis if you wanted to have your own body built.

Initially, the First World War was far removed from the United States and its people, despite the fact that so many had roots in Europe. But Henry Ford was a pacifist, and even travelled to Europe with a delegation aboard the infamous Peace Ship that he financed at the end of 1915. Ford's mission achieved nothing but public awareness, and opinions grew until Germany's extraordinary efforts to enlist Mexico as an ally against the US – coupled with U-boats sinking several of its ships – forced the president's hand. By April 1917 America too was at war.

A year earlier, Ford's advertising was claiming its Trafford Park operation was capable of turning out 25,000 cars annually; although I believe that figure was somewhat optimistic, large numbers of ambulances, service wagons and water carriers based on the T chassis were supplied to our forces in Europe and the Middle East. Open tourers, too, were supplied for general duties, but as far as I am aware no actual weapons were manufactured.

With the war won it was a simple matter to return Trafford Park's T production lines to the output of civilian vehicles, and in 1919 the TT 1-ton truck with a heavier chassis and rear axle was introduced to the British range. Ford's keen pricing ensured an enormous demand, and soon the Manchester factory would be outgrown, so the search began for new premises.

Trafford Park had originally been chosen due to its proximity to the Manchester Ship Canal but there was no room for expansion, so in the mid '20s a large tract of marshland beside the River Thames at Dagenham, ten miles East of London, was purchased. Construction began just as the economic slump hit Britain, and the country was still in a very bad way when the largest car factory in Europe was completed and operational late in 1931.

Production of the T had ended in 1927, with Henry Ford watching the landmark 15-millionth off

This little brochure (K.8317/594) is something of an oddball and almost certainly dates from September 1945. However, the artist depicted a pre-war 7Y Eight 5cwt on the cover with what are acknowledged to be post-war hubcaps – several months after the introduction of the EO4C. Furthermore, the photo within was of a pure pre-war van with Ford script on the hubcaps, along with clam shell ventilators on the side of the scuttle and wings without peripheral ribbing – but scuttle mounted wipers, which I am assured are post-war. The spare wheel mounting gave something of a military look, but was an interior space saver.

Fordson 5 cwt.

A FEW OF MANY GOOD FEATURES

Large load space. Interior dimensions are: length 4 ft. 3 in.; width 4 ft.; height 3 ft. 4 in. Total capacity 65 cu. ft.

Full-width rear doors facilitate loading and off-loading, simplify the handling of wide trays and bulky articles.

It is easily adapted to meet the special needs of such trades as bakers, butchers, fishmongers, grocers, etc.

Designed and built to withstand the heavy wear and tear of delivery work. Rear doors are stoutly made and strongly hinged. All doors can be locked. Rear doors have windows for improved visibility and ventilating louvres. Hand-brake lever is accessibly mounted under the scuttle and is of pistol-grip type. Three-forward-speed gearbox has exceptionally easy synchronised change and silent helical-type intermediate gear. Modern equipment includes indirectly-lighted instruments of attractive design; powerful headlights controlled by convenient foot dimmer switch; ignition lock, etc.

On the pre-war 7Y Eight and the first of the post-war EO4C vans (until late 1946) the petrol tank was at the rear – the filler cap seen here on the valance to the nearside of the number plate.

the Highland Park, Detroit production line. The T had been replaced by the A, so the new cars, along with AA trucks, were initially manufactured in Manchester before production got under way at Dagenham.

In common with several other European countries Britain imposed a horsepower tax on a car's engine size; so, because US-made As were rated at 24hp, a 2033cc version rated at 14.9hp was produced by Dagenham. Even this attracted a road tax that in today's values would equate to well over £1000 a year on what was supposed to be a cheap car for the masses, who in the prevailing economic climate, would find it nigh on impossible to afford the vehicle alone. To make matters worse, the 14.9hp drank just as much petrol as the larger motor but its performance, especially on hills, was severely compromised. Sales fell far short of expectations.

With amazing equanimity and speed, Ford's designers back in the US formulated a smaller car that would be acceptable in Great Britain, as well as Europe. In 1932, and looking for all the world like a downsized version of its new US-made V8, Ford launched its Dagenham-built 8hp Model Y onto the British market.

At the same time the almost-identical Koln was unveiled in Germany, where it would be built at Ford's Cologne factory. Originally designed as a two- or four-door saloon, its overall size and four-cylinder, sidevalve, 993cc engine gave it reasonable performance and economy that compared well with the opposition, and soon van and pick-up versions were introduced. By the time it was replaced by the completely restyled 7Y Eight in 1937 its manufacturer had achieved the distinction of selling the most basic Popular model for just £100 – the cheapest-ever four-seat saloon.

The 7Y Eight was also made as a light commercial, and in 1938 it was joined by the larger E83W, which had an 1172cc sidevalve engine and a full ½-ton carrying capacity.

By this time war was once again in the offing and the old Trafford Park factory was being entirely redeveloped under the shadow factory plan – during the ensuing hostilities, around 35,000 Rolls-Royce Merlin engines would be made there.

Ford Dagenham, on the other hand, concentrated on vehicles of all kinds, with something in the neighbourhood of 350,000 turned out in total. At random, but from an HMSO listing, these included 9059 WOA-2 utility cars, 59,498 WOT-2 15cwt trucks, 17,966 WOT-3 30cwt trucks, 134,478 Fordson tractors and 15,516 10cwt vans (the last of which were, of course, E83Ws).

Briggs Motor Bodies (which supplied Ford with bodies and within ten years would be owned by the firm) was also located at Dagenham, and produced in the region of 275,000 armoured and other bodies – almost exclusively for Ford – as well as a vast array of equipment such as 11 million steel helmets and 20 million jerry cans.

Over in the United States, the old and ailing Henry Ford began by reiterating his pacifist sentiments but when it came to his own country's direct participation, the company he had started was thrown wholeheartedly into the war effort. Perhaps its most impressive contribution was the production of some 9000 B-24 aircraft at the giant Willow Run facility that Ford ordered to be purpose-built.

Peace was probably greeted with a mixture of relief and a sense of an anticlimax when the Dagenham workforce returned to normal production – which as far as light commercials were concerned meant continuance of the E83W and the 5cwt 7Y Eight, soon to be renamed the EO4C; both had proved themselves, so why make changes?

With the exception of a name change from Fordson to Thames and slight alterations that turned the EO4C into the E494C in the late '40s, Ford's light vans and pick-ups continued as they were until the autumn of 1954 when the smallest was replaced by an entirely new 5cwt model – on the face of it, at any rate. Anyone opening the bonnet would immediately recognise the trusty little sidevalve engine nestling in the spacious engine bay, but in virtually every other respect the 300E was utterly different from its predecessor – from its unit-construction body made "just across the road" by Briggs (which had become a subsidiary of Ford a year earlier) to its MacPherson strut front suspension in place of the E494C's front end that had been around since before the First World War.

This wasn't quite the end of the end of the beam axle and transverse spring hangover from the T, however, as it would soldier on as the old 10cwt's underpinnings for another three years – finally being replaced by the 400E. This time the sidevalve engine had been discarded as well, in favour of the short-stroke Consul overhead-valve unit; but the new 10cwt did retain a separate, albeit completely redesigned, chassis – a feature that the sales material pointed out was, "Ideal for a hundred and one uses not possible with vehicles of integral body-and-chassis construc-

5cwt. chassis

tion." The chassis was certainly no bad thing, but in common with the majority of medium-capacity forward-controls of that era the 400E was a bit short in the wheelbase and narrow of track. Still, it did the job and was stable enough at the speeds it was capable of.

The 1172cc flat-head motor had a stay of execution until it was finally made redundant when the last of Ford's 100E series saloons was discontinued in the summer of 1962 – a year after its light commercial equivalent, the 300E, had been superseded by a van version of the latest Anglia 105E.

With its American styling influences and ultra-short-stroke, pushrod overhead-valve motor the new Anglia saloon was launched in 1959. It marked the next step in the gradual change of persona for Ford's (British-built) passenger cars that had been taking place throughout the '50s with the Consul/Zephyr series. Now the utilitarian image and almost agricultural engineering had been swept away and replaced by products that appealed to the modern – and especially younger – generation.

The winds of change had blown across the Atlantic, as Ford in America had awoken to the market that

Transverse-leaf and radius-rod front and rear suspension, along with torque-tube rear axles, were a Ford tradition that had been around since pre-First World War Model Ts, and there was no reason to break with it just yet. The van's four-cylinder, 933cc, sidevalve engine was advertised to give 23bhp at 4000rpm and was mated to a three-speed gearbox with synchromesh on second and top. Wheelbase was 7ft 6in and its 17in wheels carried 4.50-section tyres. From this viewpoint you can clearly see the pre-1948 radiator grille that lacked a central division.

Ford's long-running small sidevalve engine is best remembered in its 1172cc form that was achieved by increasing the bore of the 933cc version from 56.6mm to 63.5mm – stroke remained constant at 92.5mm. Back in the days of slow-revving and under-stressed Model Ts and As, Ford had seen no need for pressure-fed crankshafts – relying on dip and splash for lubrication – but this motor had a submerged oil pump that fed both crank and camshaft; filtering was by nothing other than gauze. This was the 1172cc unit as fitted to the 10cwt, although visually there was little (if any) difference.

Fordson 10 cwt.

No filler cap in the rear valance of the 10cwt, as the tank was mounted on the nearside of the chassis midway between the axles.

Wheelbase of the 10cwt was identical to its smaller 5cwt brother but, as you can see, the chassis frame was entirely different and the engine was offset, which necessitated an offset torque tube and a rear axle with unequal-length radius rods. Like the 5cwt, however, suspension was by transverse leaf and the four-wheel drum brakes were mechanical; wheels and tyres were larger, at 18x5.00. Its 1172cc motor produced 30bhp at 4000rpm and was coupled to a three-speed gearbox.

The E83W Fordson 10cwt van had a capacity of 110 cubic feet and, although the brochure didn't tell us, I suspect this was inclusive of the space beside the driver. No mention of optional passenger seat for either 5 or 10cwt vans, but as there was only one for the driver in interior photos it's safe to assume that's what was fitted. Besides, the combination of semi-forward-control and the engine being offset to the nearside on the 10cwt meant there was precious little room for a passenger's feet. Unladen weight was 17cwt. This illustration is from the February 1946 brochure (L.4023/624), so whether it depicted an immediately pre- or post-war vehicle is questionable.

than for simply getting from A to B, and the under-40s wanted the looks and promise of just that – Dearborn's Total Performance image of the '60s bringing this to fruition for many. It was preached and practised here too, and in the future there'd be many a driver at the wheel of a Cortina or an Escort van who was only too aware of competition successes enjoyed by its close relatives.

In 1961 Britain much of this had still to unfold, but even so Ford entered the decade with a pair of acceptably modernistic light commercials; the larger model could be ordered with pretty much whatever type of body you needed, while the Anglia-based 5cwt van was that pure and simple.

But behind the scenes something was afoot, and in the autumn of 1965 the 400E's replacement was launched – the Transit is still with us, and its name long ago became generic. Ford's Cologne plant had been making a 1000kg Taunus van of the same name for several years but the design of the new Transit had begun with a clean sheet of paper. What emerged was an up-to-the-minute range of commercials that would happily cope with loads from 12 to 35cwt, with a choice of two wheelbases and a multiplicity of configurations – a little like the 400E had offered but potentially far more comprehensive.

Even the shorter wheelbase was bigger – at 106in – compared with similar vehicles that had gone before, whilst the longer version had an additional 12in, plus twin rear wheels. The track was wider than the norm for the class of vehicle, and at the front its maker had reverted to a beam axle albeit with conventional, but

existed amongst those who had been born between the wars and the far larger one that was about to arrive when the baby-boomer generation came of age.

Motoring was increasingly seen as something other

Rear-view of the Fordson 10 cwt. Van. The sturdy steel-panelled doors are equipped with large windows to provide exceptionally good rearward visibility, and the doors are also provided with ventilating louvres. Spare wheel enclosed in separate locker under floor at the rear.

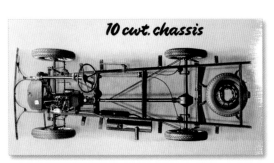

10 cwt. chassis

GENERAL DIMENSIONS—

	5-cwt. Van	10-cwt. Van	10-cwt. Truck
Wheelbase	90 in.	90 in.	90 in.
Overall length	11 ft. 5 in.	13 ft. 1½ in.	13 ft. 6 in.
Overall width	4 ft. 11 in.	5 ft. 4 in.	5 ft. 5 in.
Overall height	5 ft. 6½ in.	6 ft. 1½ in.	6 ft. 2 in.
Load space length	4 ft. 3 in.	6 ft. 7 in.	6 ft. 8 in.
Load space width	4 ft. 0 in.	4 ft. 6 in.	5 ft. 2 in.
Load space height	3 ft. 4 in.	3 ft. 9½ in.	1 ft. 6 in.
Approx. unladen weight	11¾ cwt.	17 cwt.	17½ cwt.
Gross laden weight	20 cwt.	31 cwt.	31 cwt.
Rear door opening width	3 ft. 9 in.	4 ft. 4 in.	—
Rear door opening height	3 ft. 1 in.	3 ft. 4½ in.	—
Approx. loading height	1 ft. 9 in.	2 ft. 0 in.	3 ft. 1 in.
Capacity of body	65 cu. ft.	110 cu. ft.	—
Turning circle	34 ft. 9 in.	36 ft.	36 ft.
Ground clearance	6 in.	8 in.	8 in.

single-leaf, elliptic springing. To power it there was what would be known as Ford's Essex V4 petrol engines or a Perkins for those who wanted a diesel.

Any detractors, especially as to the chassis design, were soon silenced – Ford's new commercial was simply a revelation, outperforming every comparable vehicle in every way, with its speed and general road-ability challenging not a few then-current cars.

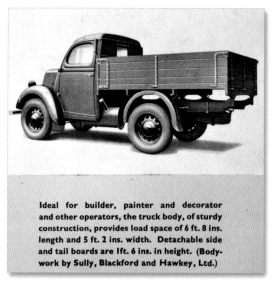

Ideal for builder, painter and decorator and other operators, the truck body, of sturdy construction, provides load space of 6 ft. 8 ins. length and 5 ft. 2 ins. width. Detachable side and tail boards are 1ft. 6 ins. in height. (Body-work by Sully, Blackford and Hawkey, Ltd.)

Chassis with Cab fittings, designed to suit purchasers who desire to make their own arrangements for bodywork, but wish to retain the advantages of the standard Fordson drivers compartment. This model is supplied with the following additions to the equipped chassis : windscreen, windscreen wiper, two doors (complete), header panel extended to rear door pillars and driver's seat. The 6.00 x 16 tyres fitted in lieu of standard 5.00 x 18 are an advantage on builder's trucks and other special body types, but do not increase the carrying capacity.

The standard 10-cwt. Chassis is equipped with cowl, instrument panel, header panel, engine bonnet, radiator grille front fenders, front bumper bar, off-side running board, cab floor and sill, wiring loom, combined head and side lamps.

These attributes quickly endeared it to all strata of society who required a fast load carrier – from rock groups to criminals, and most of all to the ordinary man who needed a vehicle for work.

Today the Transit is not far off its fiftieth birthday, and although the current version is far removed from the original it is still the Transit and made by Ford. Just a few days before writing this book, the following communiqué was released by Ford's News Centre: "Ford Motor Company today (20 June 2013) announced production of the seven millionth Transit, the popular commercial van launched in 1965 in Europe and now being extended

Martin Walter had done a few Utilecon conversions on Fords before the war, but here is the 1947 publicity flyer.

THE FORDSON 5-Cwt. "UTILECON" ALL PURPOSE VEHICLE (Regd.)

'Phone 3103 Martin Walter Ltd

UTILECON WORKS, FOLKESTONE, ENGLAND.

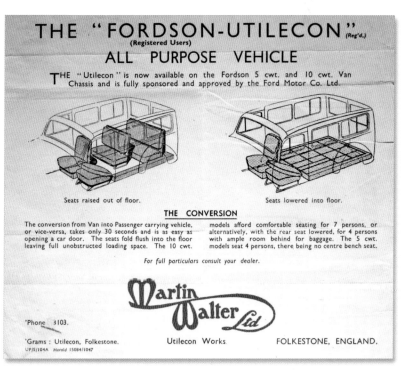

THE "FORDSON-UTILECON" (Reg'd.)
(Registered Users)
ALL PURPOSE VEHICLE

THE "Utilecon" is now available on the Fordson 5 cwt. and 10 cwt. Van Chassis and is fully sponsored and approved by the Ford Motor Co. Ltd.

Seats raised out of floor. Seats lowered into floor.

THE CONVERSION

The conversion from Van into Passenger carrying vehicle, or vice-versa, takes only 30 seconds and is as easy as opening a car door. The seats fold flush into the floor leaving full unobstructed loading space. The 10 cwt.

models afford comfortable seating for 7 persons, or alternatively, with the rear seat lowered, for 4 persons with ample room behind for baggage. The 5 cwt. models seat 4 persons, there being no centre bench seat.

For full particulars consult your dealer.

Martin Walter Ltd

'Phone 3103.

'Grams : Utilecon, Folkestone.
UP/S/104A Herald 15084/1047

Utilecon Works. FOLKESTONE, ENGLAND.

to 118 markets across six continents. The milestone was celebrated at the official opening today of a new Transit assembly plant in Nanchang, China, attended by Ford president and CEO Alan Mulally. The Jiangling Xiaolan facility is the result of a (US) $300 million investment by Ford's strategic partner Jiangling Motors Corp (JMC) and produces JMC-branded vehicles and Ford-branded vehicles for the growing Chinese market."

Lest your eyebrows go skywards, I should tell you that the Nanchang plant signalled the expansion of Transit production outside Europe back in 1997 and it will also be produced in North America for the first time at a facility in Kansas, Missouri.

For Britain, where the Transit began its life, there was not such good news. First made at Langley, Berkshire and then from 1972 at Swaythling near Southampton, the Transit had for some years been the sole remaining Ford vehicle still manufactured on British soil. Van production at Ford Otosan, the joint venture plant in Turkey, had meanwhile overtaken UK output and with the prevailing difference in overall manufacturing costs between the two economies, coupled with the current recession, there could only be one outcome.

By the time that this book is published, Transit manufacture will have ceased in Great Britain.

Ford had re-titled its commercials as Thames in 1948, and here is the cover of an October 1950 brochure.

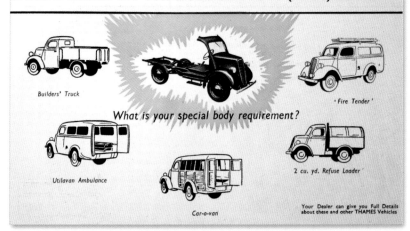

SPECIAL BODIES ON **THAMES 10 CWT.** (500 KG) CHASSIS

Builders' Truck

What is your special body requirement?

'Fire Tender'

Utilavan Ambulance

Car-o-van

2 cu. yd. Refuse Loader

Your Dealer can give you Full Details about these and other THAMES Vehicles

THE **THAMES** Seven Passenger **ESTATE CAR**

This US export flyer of February 1950 made no mention of Utilecon or Martin Walter, but this left-hand-drive estate car is one. At the time some American states were unhappy with the lights on certain English vehicles, so additional sidelights were provided beneath the headlamps. Around 1948, the rear wings on 10cwt vans had been given this rearward flair to reduce the amount of road dirt and spray thrown up.

The Thames ½-ton Pick-Up, based on the sturdy, well-tried 30 h.p. half-ton Truck, is the ideal vehicle for the operator who wants an economical, easy-to-handle light truck.

Another US flyer from February 1950. All 10cwt pick-ups had 16in wheels and 6.00-section tyres. This was the all-steel express body version by Anthony Hoists of Ruislip, Middlesex, whose publicity material stressed that, "The all metal construction makes it easy to clean and it will not retain odours from loads such as wet fish etc." The bed was 6ft long and had sockets on the sides so that a tilt could be fitted if required.

The rear seats were for five and could be folded flat in a matter of seconds to give 100 cubic feet of load area.

Thames vans get bouquets too...

A strangely proportioned but regal piece of fantasy architecture served as a backdrop to the 5cwt on the cover of the November 1951 brochure.

For the operator who requires a small but efficient vehicle, the Thames 5-cwt. van provides the best possible investment. It is designed for all-round economy, absolute reliability, and combines adequate carrying capacity with a smart and modern appearance.

Like its 5-cwt. counterpart, the Thames 10-cwt. van is designed to satisfy the requirements of the cost-conscious operator. Larger in capacity, more powerful in performance, it provides maximum efficiency for minimum outlay. It is easy to manoeuvre; compact in construction with good visibility for the driver, and has smart and attractive lines.

Anglia cars and 5cwt vans had been updated with this radiator grille and surround in the autumn of 1948; the petrol tank had been repositioned to the nearside at the same time. Headlamps were smaller than immediately post-war vans, and the eagle-eyed amongst you will doubtless have noticed that some vehicles had a single wiper mounted above the screen, which denoted an optional opening windscreen. At this point the EO4A became the E494A, and a total of just under 100,000 would be made before the latter was discontinued in 1954.

Both 5 and 10cwt Thames vans had a fabric panel in the roof but the artist forgot that the E83W had twin starting handle holes in the grille since the late '40s to facilitate construction of left- or right-hand-drive versions.

Owners of Thames vans are convinced they made the right choice by reason of:- low initial outlay, low running and maintenance costs, sturdiness of construction, ensuring long mileage life, and the incomparable Ford "after sales" service.

OWNERS

Drivers prefer Thames vans for a variety of reasons; their ease of handling, riding comfort which reduces fatigue, safety under all conditions, brilliant performance, and big carrying capacity coupled with low easy loading.

DRIVERS

Customers are pleased to see their goods delivered by Thames vans because of the dependability of the Ford vehicles; the promptness of the delivery service which they provide, the protection afforded, particularly for fragile merchandise, and their generally pleasing appearance.

CUSTOMERS

When this jolly-looking brochure was published in 1957 the 10cwt E83W was getting a bit long in the tooth. This would be its last year, and it was discontinued as total production neared 190,000.

Virtually unchanged from its birth in 1938, there was still a proper chassis of best Ford steel to mount the body on. As a rule of thumb, vans had 18in wheels whilst pick-ups wore 16in.

Here's the Refuse Loader by Eagle Engineering Co Ltd of Warwick.

How about the Laundry Van by Sully, Blackford & Hawkey Ltd of Leyton, East London.

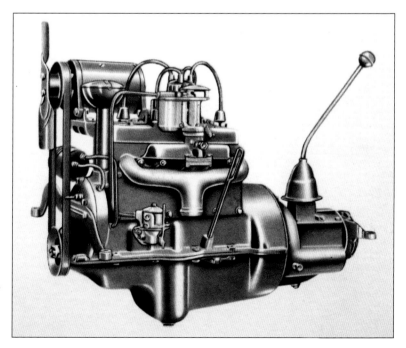

The 10cwt's 1172cc motor had a cylinder head-mounted dynamo from first to last but an externally plumbed bypass filter (seen above the timing cover) had been incorporated since the late '40s. The sump retained a recessed front portion to give clearance for the front axle.

A bit of sparkle and words alone on the cover of the September '54 glossy brochure were considered sufficient to whet the appetite for the brand-new Thames 5cwt 300E.

The 300E's looks belied its real dimensions, as its wheelbase was 3in shorter than its predecessor's. The 13in wheels were shod with 5.60-section tyres.

The unit-construction body/chassis had three longitudinal swages in the roof for extra strength and to prevent drumming. Two jacking points were provided beneath each sill.

The 66½ cubic feet was described as being a, "Useful capacity." There is no doubt, however, that it included the space beside the driver where the spare wheel lived. If a passenger seat was fitted the spare was then stowed vertically against the nearside of the body in front of the wheelarch.

The driver had a fuel gauge and ammeter to keep an eye on besides the speedometer, but he was kept aware of the oil pressure – or rather lack of it – by a light to the left of the speedo.

Bonnet was hinged at the front and gave good access to the spacious engine bay.

"An outstanding feature of the new Thames 5cwt is its 'Glide-Ride' suspension, affording maximum load protection and minimum driver fatigue." Then they called it, "The unique Ford independent front wheel suspension," but it was properly referred to as MacPherson strut type, which was first used by Ford of England on its 1951 Consuls and Zephyrs.

HYDRAULIC BRAKES FOR SAFETY

Previously Ford 5cwt van brakes had been operated by rod and cable, so Ford was understandably rather pleased with the system on its new model.

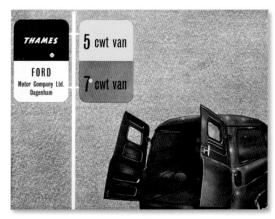

THAMES
FORD
Motor Company Ltd.
Dagenham

5 cwt van

7 cwt van

It wasn't long before a 7cwt version arrived. When new this model had chromium headlamp surrounds, whilst the 5cwt's were body colour.

The new Thames 5 cwt. van is fitted with the famous Ford 4 cylinder, 1,172 c.c., "L" shaped head engine. The excellent power to weight ratio, coupled with carefully selected gear and axle ratios, results in outstanding performance with traditional Ford economy of operation.

The trusty sidevalve Ford in updated 1172cc form, as fitted to the 300E. Compare this to the illustration page 89 and you will see several detail differences – notably the different sump fitted to engines used in conjunction with independent front suspension, "built-in" external oil filter, and that the dynamo was no longer mounted atop the cylinder head. Advertised output was 36bhp at 4400rpm. Gearbox was a three-speed with synchromesh on second and top.

Ford of Dagenham reliability

Drivers enjoy saloon comfort

The Thames 7 cwt. Van is outstanding value for such a low purchase price. Seating, instrument panel and controls are designed for comfort and convenience. The passenger seat is available at extra cost. Doors are tastefully panelled to match the durable upholstery. Windows wind up and down at a touch.

Reliable all speed gearbox

Extra strength rear springs carry 7 cwt. loads anywhere and everywhere in perfect safety. With Ford Glide-ride independent front suspension as well, every load is safer and drivers are more comfortable. With a full load, the van corners steadily.

Thames vans are famous for their excellent performance—it's the Ford of Dagenham tradition. The gear ratios for the three-speed gearbox ensure the best performance and economy in crowded traffic, on fast open stretches and up the steepest hills.

Low loading height and wide access to the roomy 66.5 cu. ft. load space

The 300E lasted until 1961 and here was the ultimate 7cwt version with chromium radiator grille, bumpers, windscreen surround and headlamp surround inserts. There was a flashy range of colours too: Black, Pompadour Blue, Ambassador Blue, Sapphire Blue, Morocco Beige, Chateau Grey, Regency Grey, Linden Green, Ming Yellow and Ermine White.

There's nothing parked nearby, so opening the door more should make things a little easier…

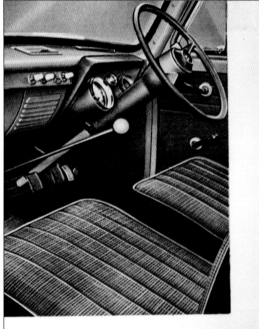

Hard to tell the difference between this and the first of the 5cwt 300Es but there were some – take a look at the badging on the front wing, for instance. Ford claimed to have squeezed another couple of horsepower and a hundred revs out of the engine too, as power was now advertised to be 38bhp at 4500rpm. From 1954 to 1961 just under 200,000 300Es were made.

The driver will praise the excellent all-round visibility, the comfortable seat, and in the 7 cwt. de luxe van the new facia panel incorporating a temperature guage, the new speedometer and the lockable glove box. Windows wind up and down at a touch.

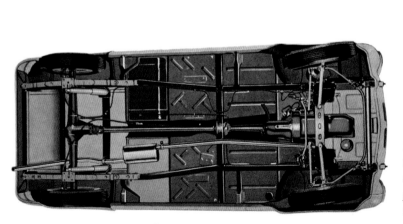

The manufacturer didn't paint the brake pipes and petrol tank red – this was for us to see their positioning. The rest, I believe, is self-explanatory.

CAR COMFORT...A great deal of thought and care have gone into planning, seating, and controls; a day behind the wheel becomes a pleasure, not a hardship.

MAXIMUM LOADABILITY...years of experience have conceived an interior layout to maximise every inch of the 66½ cubic feet of loadspace, including space beside driver.

Why show it with the optional passenger seat? Because it looks better.

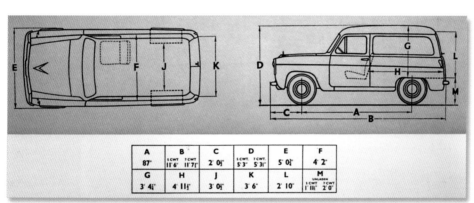

A	B		C	D		E	F
87"	5 CWT.	7 CWT.	2' 0½"	5 CWT.	7 CWT.	5' 0½"	4' 2"
	11'6"	11'7¼"		5'3"	5'3¼"		
G	H		J	K	L	M	
3' 4¼"	4' 11¼"		3' 0½"	3' 6"	2' 10"	UNLADEN	
						5 CWT. 7 CWT.	
						1' 11½" 2' 0"	

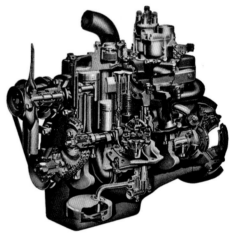

POWER WITH THRIFT OF 4 CYL. OVERSQUARE ENGINE!

LONG AND WIDE 8 CWT. LOAD-SPACE!

Consul COUPE UTILITY

The Consul Mk II was brought out in 1956, and before long there was this Coupe Utility for the Australian market.

ALL OF CONSUL'S FAMOUS PERFORMANCE AND ECONOMY — PLUS 8 CWT. CAPACITY!

A Great New Thames Range . . .

Thames' replacement for the lovable but geriatric E83W was the
forward-control 400E in late 1957, which could be had as
10/12cwt or 15cwt.

Wheelbase was 7ft irrespective of carrying capacity, indicated by a
number in the roundel between radiator grille and Thames badge –
this being a 15cwt. Independent front suspension was by coil and
wishbone because the use of Ford's preferred MacPherson strut
would have been problematic with the forward-control layout.

Unlike some similar-format commercials Ford didn't go for sliding front doors, and
if you wanted a side-loading door such as this it would set you back another £14.
Detachable side skirt panels simplified minor accident repair. No exotic names for the
colours in the brochure, however – just Green, Yellow, Blue, Grey, Black, Red, Ivory
or Fawn – and any of them cost you £12.10s for a van or £7.0 for a pick-up, as the
basic finish was what Ford described as Suede Grey Primer.

For the driver . . . wide curved windscreen,
controls coming easily to hand, and well-placed
instruments—incorporating a new-type
speedometer—seen at a glance. Behind this
wheel he'll feel confident in comfort.

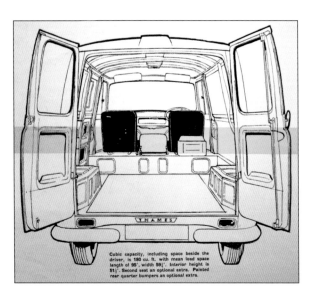

Cubic capacity, including space beside the
driver, is 180 cu. ft. with mean load space
length of 95", width 59½". Interior height is
51¼". Second seat an optional extra. Painted
rear quarter bumpers an optional extra.

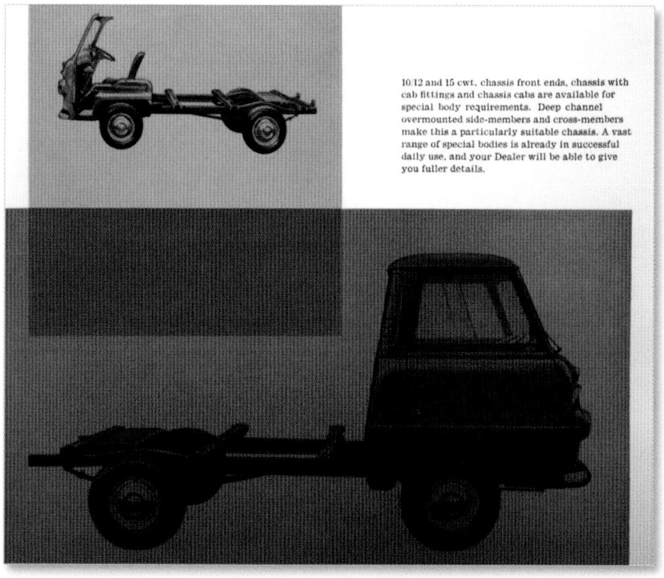
10/12 and 15 cwt. chassis front ends, chassis with cab fittings and chassis cabs are available for special body requirements. Deep channel overmounted side-members and cross-members make this a particularly suitable chassis. A vast range of special bodies is already in successful daily use, and your Dealer will be able to give you fuller details.

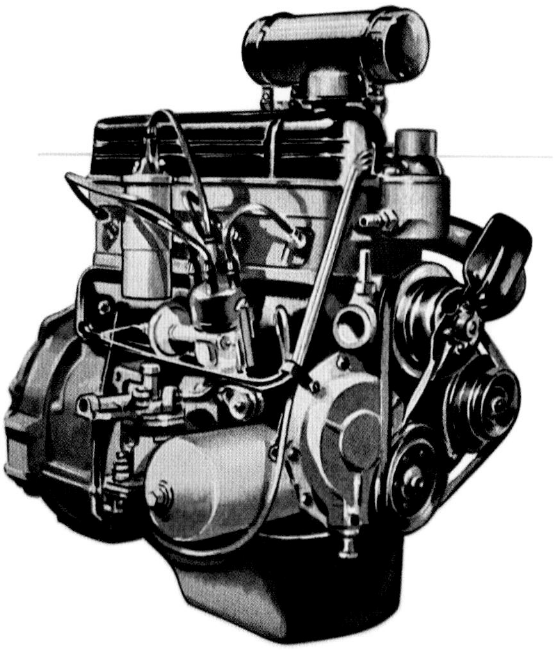

Typical of Ford's overhead-valve engines, the 1703cc Consul unit was over-square, with a bore and stroke of 82.55mm x 79.5mm. With the standard compression ratio of 6.9:1 it gave out 52bhp at 4400rpm but a 7.8:1 option was available for those who were prepared to use premium fuel. Gearbox was a three-speed with column change.

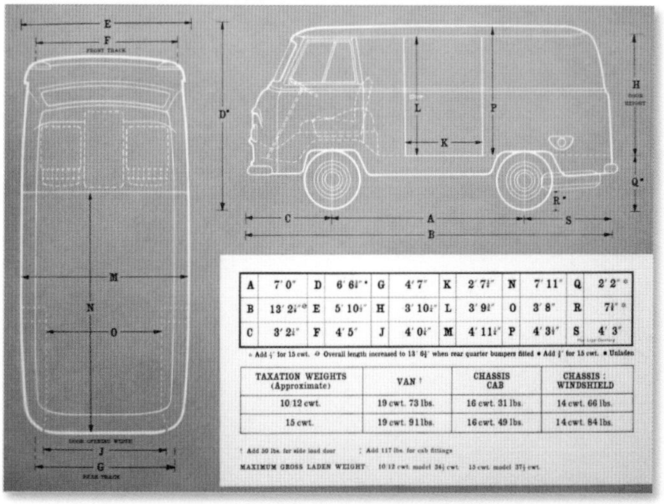

A	7′ 0″	D	6′ 6¼″ •	G	4′ 7″	K	2′ 7¼″	N	7′ 11″	Q	2′ 2″ *
B	13′ 2¼″ ⊖	E	5′ 10½″	H	3′ 10½″	L	3′ 9¼″	O	3′ 8″	R	7¼″ *
C	3′ 2¼″	F	4′ 5″	J	4′ 0¼″	M	4′ 11¼″	P	4′ 3¼″	S	4′ 3″

* Add ¼″ for 15 cwt. ⊖ Overall length increased to 13′ 6¾″ when rear quarter bumpers fitted • Add ½″ for 15 cwt. ▪ Unladen

TAXATION WEIGHTS (Approximate)	VAN †	CHASSIS CAB	CHASSIS : WINDSHIELD
10/12 cwt.	19 cwt. 73 lbs.	16 cwt. 31 lbs.	14 cwt. 66 lbs.
15 cwt.	19 cwt. 91 lbs.	16 cwt. 49 lbs.	14 cwt. 84 lbs.

† Add 30 lbs. for side load door ‡ Add 117 lbs. for cab fittings

MAXIMUM GROSS LADEN WEIGHT 10/12 cwt. model 34½ cwt. 15 cwt. model 37½ cwt.

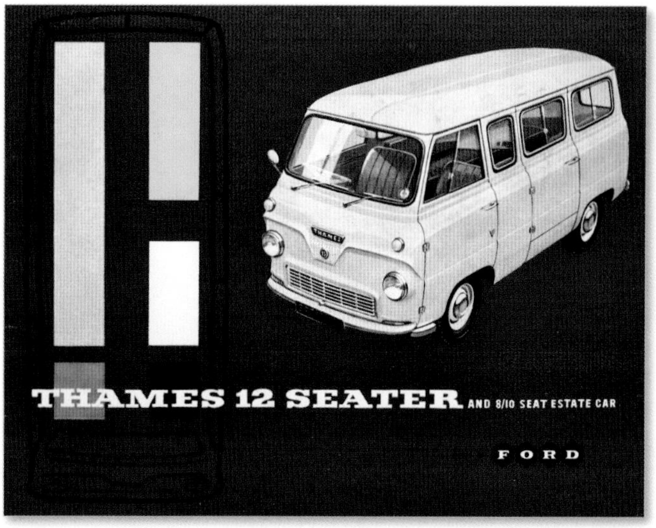
THAMES 12 SEATER AND 8/10 SEAT ESTATE CAR
FORD

There were 8/10- or 12-seater estate cars too. These and 15cwt vans had 6.40x15 tyres, whilst 10/12cwt versions had 5.90s.

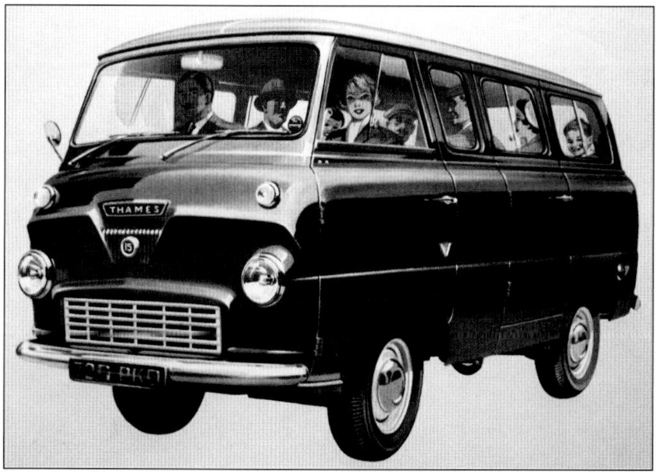
THAMES

I just love this bunch of passengers, starting with the driver and his upside down stick-on whip and lash, and what looks suspiciously like a syrup. I wonder where he's taking them… At first there had been a de luxe version of the 400E estate with a good deal of chrome, along with what was described as luxury trim and interior fittings, as well as a two-tone colour scheme of either Ivory above Red, Green or Fawn; or Grey above Red, Black or Blue.

Happy days: when you might be able to arrive for your flight in this fashion. Carry this picture in your head when next you travel by air.

Some on-site work for the 400E estate during the construction of the first length of the M5 motorway in Worcestershire.

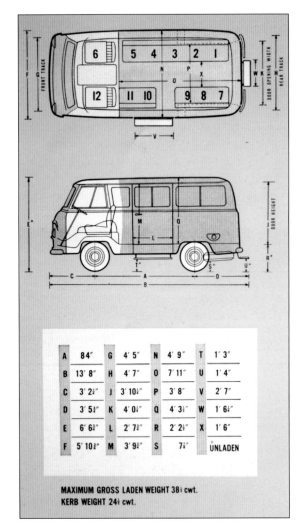

A	84"	G	4' 5"	N	4' 9"	T	1' 3"
B	13' 8"	H	4' 7"	O	7' 11"	U	1' 4"
C	3' 2¼"	J	3' 10¼"	P	3' 8"	V	2' 7"
D	3' 5¼"	K	4' 0¼"	Q	4' 3½"	W	1' 6¼"
E	6' 6¼"	L	2' 7¼"	R	2' 2½"	X	1' 6"
F	5' 10¼"	M	3' 9¼"	S	7½"		UNLADEN

MAXIMUM GROSS LADEN WEIGHT 38½ cwt.
KERB WEIGHT 24½ cwt.

Nothing like a spot of engine maintenance whilst you are waiting for your passengers.

The, "Powerful windscreen wipers," were unfortunately the vacuum devices beloved by Ford that slowed when you put your foot down and flailed away when you lifted off. Fitted as original equipment to its vehicles for so many years, this was about their last hurrah, and by the '60s the 400E would have electric wipers.

This is essentially a driver's vehicle. Forward control and a deep windscreen afford exceptional visibility; town manoeuvring is made easier still by a turning circle of only 35 feet.

ALL THAT A DRIVER WANTS

Instruments, including an arc-type speedometer, are grouped directly in front of the driver. Controls are ideally situated and pedals are well spaced. Other features include exterior and interior rear view mirrors, powerful windscreen wipers, and provision is made for fitting a heater and demister.

Thames *van range built by* FORD

Four years on from its launch, the November 1961 400E's brochure cover exuded self-assurance. It had a little more power too, with the uprated Consul engine now giving 55bhp. There was also the choice of a Perkins 4.99 diesel if you were prepared to stump up another £125. There'd be an optional four-speed gearbox as well, but that wouldn't be until the following year.

And what better way than with a Thames or — better still — a full fleet of Thames middleweights? There's a huge choice, comprising vans, pick-ups, 12-seaters, and, of course, chassis cab and chassis windshield versions ...

What a different place Soho was circa 1961 when the butchers Slater & Cooke, Bisney & Jones occupied 67 & 69 Brewer Street. Nowadays 67 is a health club and 69 is a health food shop, but a couple of nice lamb chops and a ride on a butcher's bike would probably do you a lot more good. There's no parking outside now, either.

ENGINE—Perkins 4/99 Four cylinder in line O.H.V. in-direct injection. Bore 3.0″ (76.2 mm.) stroke 3.5″ (88.9 mm.) Displacement 99 cu. in. (1621 c.c.) Compression ratio 20 : 1 Maximum B.H.P. 42 at 3,600 R.P.M. Maximum torque 72½ lb./ft. at 2,250 R.P.M. Detachable cast iron cylinder head, incorporating push rod operated valve gear. Fully balanced forged steel three bearing crankshaft. Aluminium alloy flat topped pistons with three compression and two oil control rings. Fully floating gudgeon pins. Engine suspension at three points on rubber. Firing order 1, 3, 4, 2.

ENGINE LUBRICATION—High efficiency rotor type pump with full pressure to main, big end, camshaft and rocker bearings. Cylinder walls lubricated by oil thrown from big ends, timing gears by direct spray. Full flow replaceable cartridge type filter. Capacity of sump including filter 7 pints.

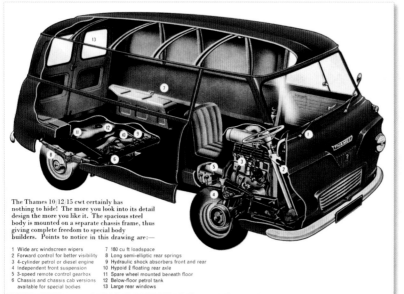

The Thames 10/12/15 cwt certainly has nothing to hide! The more you look into its detail design the more you like it. The spacious steel body is mounted on a separate chassis frame, thus giving complete freedom to special body builders. Points to notice in this drawing are:—

1 Wide arc windscreen wipers
2 Forward control for better visibility
3 4-cylinder petrol or diesel engine
4 Independent front suspension
5 3-speed remote control gearbox
6 Chassis and chassis cab versions available for special bodies
7 180 cu ft loadspace
8 Long semi-elliptic rear springs
9 Hydraulic shock absorbers front and rear
10 Hypoid ¾ floating rear axle
11 Spare wheel mounted beneath floor
12 Below-floor petrol tank
13 Large rear windows

We all played cricket then, and I can even remember travelling through the leafy lanes of Surrey on the way to an away school match in an identical Thames – except it was off-white. My bat was a Stuart Surridge; what was yours?

CHASSIS CAB

Ford planning pays off – and here's one of the reasons why. Unlike many similar vehicles, the 10/12 and 15 Cwts are built on a complete and independent frame (not integral construction). Three sturdy full-width body crossmembers are flanged at each end to take body uprights and provide solid support for a wide variety of special bodywork. They can also be used for mounting truck floats, pick-up bodies, box vans, etc. Note other advantages of Ford planning, too. No awkward engine or gearbox sticking out behind the chassis cab. No fuel tank or spare wheel wasting valuable body space. Everything is housed below the level of the crossmembers and bodywork mounting is simple in the extreme.

Versatility, strength of construction, maximum use of freight space – you'd be hard put to find anything to match this vehicle.

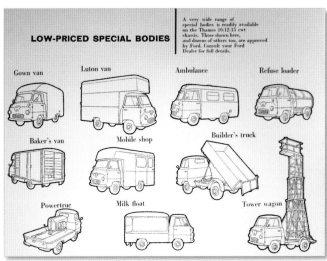

LOW-PRICED SPECIAL BODIES

A very wide range of special bodies is readily available on the Thames 10/12,15 cwt chassis. Those shown here, and dozens of others too, are approved by Ford. Consult your Ford Dealer for full details.

Gown van — Luton van — Ambulance — Refuse loader — Baker's van — Mobile shop — Builder's truck — Powertruc — Milk float — Tower wagon

What would be the last incarnation of Ford's long line of Anglia passenger cars was launched in 1959, but it was not until the last part of 1961 that the 307E van version became available. Apart from the badge on the front you can tell this was the 7cwt model on account of its chrome bumpers, headlamp peaks, exterior mirrors and radiator grille, which on the 5cwt were painted.

NEW THAMES 5&7 CWT VANS

built by FORD

Stock colours were Green, Yellow, Blue, Grey, Black, Red, Ivory or Fawn, and all meant an addition of £10 to the June 1961 list price of £459. If you really wanted to push the boat out, another £9 2s would equip your purchase with a passenger seat and extra sun visor, an extra floor mat and rear quarter bumpers, but if you wanted to go for a fresh air heater and demister too, that would bring the grand total to £488 2s.

"TV rental and radio dealers will like it for its high rear door lintel (console sets can be loaded without tilting), and its smooth, protecting "glide ride suspension," said the caption. The front suspension was by MacPherson strut and the rear by conventional semi-elliptics. Tyres and wheels were 5.40x13 with four-plies on the 5cwt and six-plies on the 7cwt.

"The driver on door-to-door delivery jobs will be delighted with the wide opening side doors and the convenient height of the seat – slipping in and out is quick and simple," read the caption.

1. One-piece curved windscreen.
2. Exterior mirrors and an interior mirror.
3. Electric windscreen wipers.
4. Air-intake grille for the fresh air heater and demister.
5. Forward sloping bonnet for good visibility.
6. Functional and attractive grille.

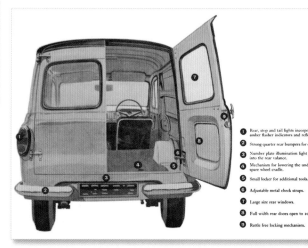

1. Rear, stop and tail lights incorporating amber flasher indicators and reflectors.
2. Strong quarter rear bumpers for extra safety.
3. Number plate illumination light is built into the rear valance.
4. Mechanism for lowering the under floor spare wheel cradle.
5. Small locker for additional tools.
6. Adjustable metal check straps.
7. Large size rear windows.
8. Full width rear doors open to 100°.
9. Rattle free locking mechanism.

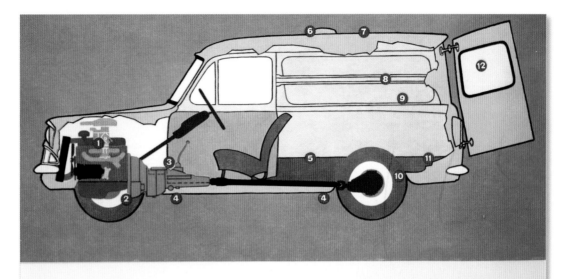

The 300E's forward-hinged bonnet had been a popular design feature that was carried through to its 307E replacement.

① "Over Square" 997 cc O.H.V. engine.

② Independent front suspension.

③ 4-speed gearbox.

④ 4 conveniently located jacking points.

⑤ Removable ¾" thick resin bonded plywood floor.

⑥ Roof ventilator.

⑦ Swaging for roof rigidity.

⑧ 2 internal side cross members and 1 adjustable roof cross member for extra body strength.

⑨ Maximum load space of 73 cu ft.

⑩ Long semi-elliptical rear springs.

⑪ 6 gallon fuel tank completely insulated from loadspace.

⑫ Full size rear windows.

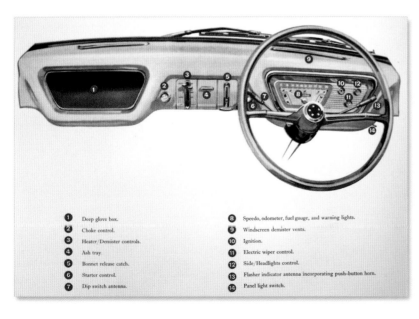

① Deep glove box.

② Choke control.

③ Heater/Demister controls.

④ Ash tray.

⑤ Bonnet release catch.

⑥ Starter control.

⑦ Dip switch antenna.

⑧ Speedo, odometer, fuel gauge, and warning lights.

⑨ Windscreen demister vents.

⑩ Ignition.

⑪ Electric wiper control.

⑫ Side/Headlights control.

⑬ Flasher indicator antenna incorporating push-button horn.

⑭ Panel light switch.

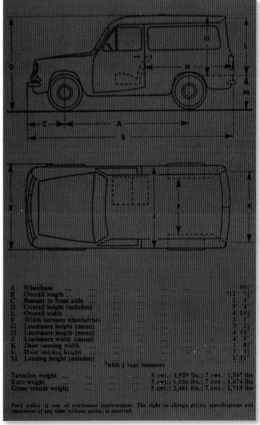

A	Wheelbase	90
B	Overall length	*12 7
C	Bumper to front axle	2 7
D	Overall height (unladen)	5 4
E	Overall width	4 11
F	Width between wheelarches	3 3
G	Loadspace height (mean)	4 3
H	Loadspace length (mean)	4 10
J	Loadspace width (mean)	4 3
K	Door opening width	3 1
L	Door opening height	3 8
M	Loading height (unladen)	1 11

*with ½ rear bumpers

Taxation weight		5 cwt.: 1,529 lbs.; 7 cwt.: 1,567 lbs.
Kerb weight		5 cwt.: 1,636 lbs.; 7 cwt.: 1,674 lbs.
Gross vehicle weight		5 cwt.: 2,481 lbs.; 7 cwt.: 2,715 lbs.

Ford policy is one of continuous improvement. The right to change prices, specifications and equipment at any time without notice, is reserved.

The 997cc 105E engine was wildly over-square, with a bore and stroke of 80.96mm x 48.4mm. On the van's compression ratio of 7.5:1 it gave 34bhp at 4400rpm but Cosworth-tuned versions that went into then-current Lotus Formula Juniors made 85bhp.

PINT SIZE RUNNING COSTS!

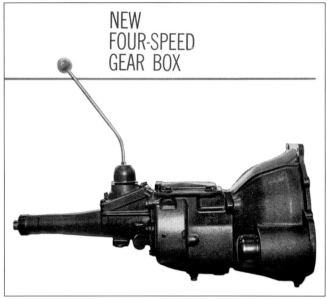

NEW
FOUR-SPEED
GEAR BOX

THAMES 5/7 CWT VAN

For as long as anyone could remember Ford had favoured three-speed gearboxes for passenger cars and light commercials but its new four-speeds were very good 'boxes indeed.

Nothing too unconventional about the cover of this 1964 brochure that depicted a smiling flat-cap-and-overalls tradesman on his way to work. The reason for his pleasure could be that he had the extra power of the optional high-compression 8.9:1 engine (41bhp at 5000rpm) that was now available, or the even more powerful 1198cc version with 58.17mm stroke, which put out 53bhp at 4800rpm. If it had this motor it was known as the 307E.

All kinds of scenarios possible here, but he looks a little apprehensive whilst the popsie is giving him the eye and applying more lipstick so what are we to suppose? Whatever is going on, they are both out of luck, as that antique French boule clock is over 6ft high and there's only 4ft 10in behind the seats. Even without his lady friend and the optional passenger seat it would be a squeeze, although there would then be 73 cubic feet of load space.

Camels or Tigers, Ptarmigans or clocks . . . room for every kind of load with the versatile and ever-willing 5/7 cwt.

The spare wheel, positioned in an under floor cradle, can be lowered quickly and conveniently with the wheel brace. The lowering mechanism, located in the floor at the rear of the van, does not encroach upon the load space in any way, and it is a simple matter to insert the brace in a hole set into the rear door sill.

Well, I bet you didn't expect that outcome! You don't think, do you… No, you don't think that whoever dreamt this up had access to some kind of illegal substances? The copywriter must have been indulging himself too, as his animal identification capabilities were sadly lacking and his expectations as to what our friend might be able to get into, or even want try and get into, the Thames were rather wide of the mark.

Amusing though the advertising department's flights of fancy may have been, the average potential customer most likely found this load more instructive. As the caption says, it is a simple matter to insert the brace…but in common with all systems of this kind there can be all sorts of fun and games if you need to extract the spare when Anno Domini and a bit of rust set in. A total of, I am told, 205,001 Anglia vans had been made by the time they were discontinued in November 1967. The Escort passenger car followed on from Anglias and a van version was available in the spring of 1968.

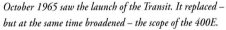

October 1965 saw the launch of the Transit. It replaced – but at the same time broadened – the scope of the 400E.

The first Transit I owned was a well-used Ambassador Blue, '66 12cwt. Its wide track and beam axles gave it roadholding and a feeling of security, empty or loaded, that was a revelation compared with the lollopy old J2s and Commers that I'd used before. Other colour options were Fiord Blue, Galleon Green, Ermine White, Highway Yellow, Merchant Fawn, Cargo Grey and Monaco Red.

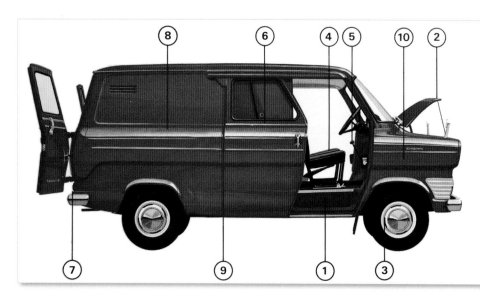

1/**Unrivalled access** with clear walk through to nearside and loadspace.

2/**Easiest maintenance** for forward placed, quickly accessible V4 engine.

3/**Highest safety standards**. Large area drum brakes. Servo-assisted braking system optional. Robust all-steel construction.

4/**First-class comfort** from high quality seating and car-like driving position.

5/**Floor-mounted gearchange** with lever clear of walk through.

6/**Widest choice of door options**. Cab doors – hinged or sliding, hinged side loading doors, double rear doors or tailgate.

7/**Ideal loading height** of 26 inches standard throughout van range.

8/**Big loadspace** shaped for optimum carrying capacity.

9/**Built and tested to last** – heavy duty construction throughout. Corrosion stopped by new electrocoating process.

10/**Good power-with-economy** guaranteed by exceptional power/weight ratio.

Ideal loading height

Loading height of a mere 26 in. means you can carry out loading and unloading quickly, efficiently, and with the minimum of effort. The same loading height applies to all Transit vans so that loading can easily be carried out from the same level for all models in the range, irrespective of payload. On LWB models Ford are able to maintain this significantly low loading height by fitting dual rear wheels and 14 in. tyres.

Big loadspace

Designed to take advantage of every available inch, the Transit gives you all the room you want and more. The SWB model is highly competitive with 178 cubic feet, while for that bulkier load the LWB with 261 cubic feet is your van. Not only the whole of the van body but the space alongside the driver can be utilised – giving an extra 21 cubic feet. On SWB models, the width between wheel-arches is no less than 50 in. – greater than any other van of comparable size.

The floor is the same level throughout so that articles can be stacked flat for the entire length. Metal floor is swaged for strength.

Interior dimensions have been calculated to accommodate standard sizes, for example you can put 8 ft. hardboard sheets into SWB models. The spare wheel housing tucked away under-floor increases the usable cargo space.

Full or half bulkhead behind driver can be obtained as optional equipment.

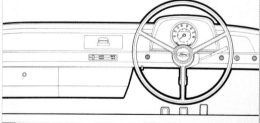

A variety of sliding and hinged doors or a combination of both was available.

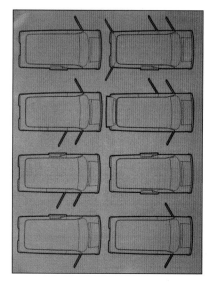

You may have heard this before, and I can assure you it is true, but they really did drive as well as – or better, and faster than – some of the cars around at the time. Fuel economy wasn't their strong point, however.

You could have a pick-up like this on any of the chassis, or if you preferred a steel version, Walkers made one. Wheels on all Transits were 14in with 6.50-, 7.00- or 7.50-section tyres depending on the capacity.

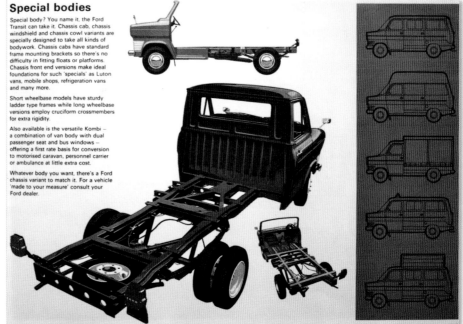

Special bodies

Special body? You name it, the Ford Transit can take it. Chassis cab, chassis windshield and chassis cowl variants are specially designed to take all kinds of bodywork. Chassis cabs have standard frame mounting brackets so there's no difficulty in fitting floats or platforms. Chassis front end versions make ideal foundations for such 'specials' as Luton vans, mobile shops, refrigeration vans and many more.

Short wheelbase models have sturdy ladder type frames while long wheelbase versions employ cruciform crossmembers for extra rigidity.

Also available is the versatile Kombi — a combination of van body with dual passenger seat and bus windows — offering a first rate basis for conversion to motorised caravan, personnel carrier or ambulance at little extra cost.

Whatever body you want, there's a Ford chassis variant to match it. For a vehicle 'made to your measure' consult your Ford dealer.

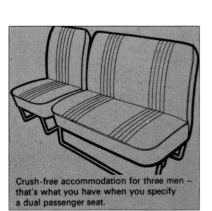

Crush-free accommodation for three men — that's what you have when you specify a dual passenger seat.

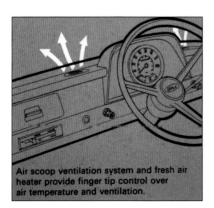

Air scoop ventilation system and fresh air heater provide finger tip control over air temperature and ventilation.

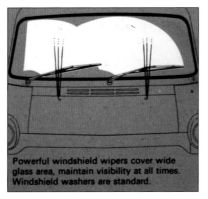

Powerful windshield wipers cover wide glass area, maintain visibility at all times. Windshield washers are standard.

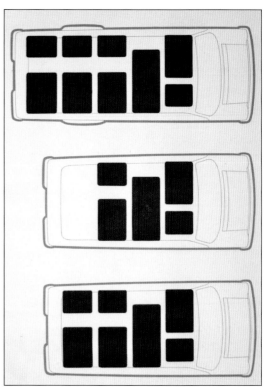

Here's the long-wheelbase (LWB) 15-seater bus, and the Custom version to boot, with chrome bumpers, dual horns, two interior sun visors, lockable glovebox, dashboard crash pad, PVC body side and door trim with de luxe Cirrus seat trim. The short-wheelbase (SWB) 9- and 12-seat (11 if it was a diesel) buses could also be supplied with Custom trim and extras.

Diesel engine

If you prefer diesel, the efficient Perkins 4/99 engine is at your service (on SWB models only). This smooth running engine will provide trustworthy performance for many years, responding to your demand every moment of the time. Its excellent fuel economy with resulting lower running costs, makes the 4/99 ideal for town work and stop-start operations. The highly efficient injection equipment assures accurate fuel metering at all speeds, under all loads.

Like the petrol engine, the diesel does not intrude into the cab compartment and to accommodate this in-line unit the van front end is extended slightly.

Good power with economy

Compact, power-packing V4 engine puts real punch into the Ford Transit.

The V4's compactness – it's no longer than a briefcase – means more space for driver and passengers, free access into cab and no transmission tunnel to interrupt walk through. Servicing is made easy too, with complete access to the engine from the front.

The exceptional power/weight ratio gives sparkling performance with outstanding load carrying power and economy – you get more miles to the gallon from the V4. Lively acceleration through the gears gives that extra urge for safe overtaking, makes the Transit a pleasure to drive. Deliveries will always be on time with this unique power unit.

Ever trustworthy, the V4 has been evolved as a result of Ford's long-standing know-how of V engines, plus lengthy and critical testing of the V4 in particular.

Two versions of the V4 are available, 1·7 litre for SWB models and 2 litre for LWB models. The smaller engine achieves a maximum of 73 bhp, while the 2 litre version packs a tremendous 85·5 bhp at 4750 rpm. Compression ratio is 7·7:1 in each case.

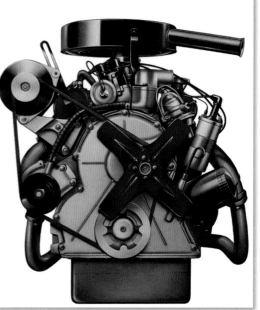

Despite being a big fan of the early Transits and doing many, many miles with them at home and abroad, I have to take issue with Ford's appraisal of the V4 motor in that it had a very definite Achilles heel. The fibre camshaft drive gear can shear its teeth, and if you're unlucky valves hit pistons. I had it happen twice – the second time on the Hammersmith flyover, but got away without the nasty bit. My travelling companion Pauline was a member of the AA, which insisted on towing the Transit to the nearest garage. Anyway, I bought another gear and popped it in by the side of the road – someone tells me they're difficult to get hold of now.

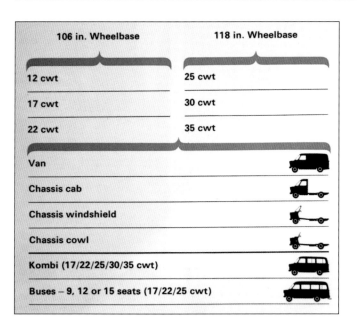

106 in. Wheelbase	118 in. Wheelbase
12 cwt	25 cwt
17 cwt	30 cwt
22 cwt	35 cwt

Van

Chassis cab

Chassis windshield

Chassis cowl

Kombi (17/22/25/30/35 cwt)

Buses – 9, 12 or 15 seats (17/22/25 cwt)

Built and tested to last

A revolutionary new electric paint process which gives every square inch of body a hard corrosion-resistant coat of primer has been developed by Ford and is now applied to the Transit. Instead of the conventional method of dipping and spraying, each body is completely submerged in a primer-filled tank and paint electrolytically deposited. In this way a uniform coating is built up over every surface, even such normally inaccessible places as door interiors and box sections.

Electrocoating successfully armour plates the vehicle against rust and provides an excellent base for top enamel coats. The full protection and longer vehicle life achieved by this remarkable process add up to your getting better value than ever with the Transit.

Some of the early ones I owned must have missed this process!

Dimensions SWB

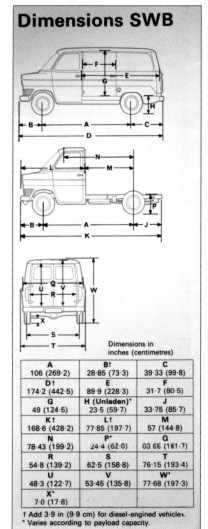

A	B†	C
106 (269·2)	28·85 (73·3)	39·33 (99·8)
D†	E	F
174·2 (442·5)	89·9 (228·3)	31·7 (80·5)
G	H (Unladen)*	J
49 (124·5)	23·5 (59·7)	33·75 (85·7)
K†	L†	M
168·6 (428·2)	77·85 (197·7)	57 (144·8)
N	P*	Q
78·43 (199·2)	24·4 (62·0)	60·66 (161·7)
R	S	T
54·8 (139·2)	62·5 (158·8)	76·15 (193·4)
U	V	W*
48·3 (122·7)	53·45 (135·8)	77·68 (197·3)
X*		
7·0 (17·8)		

Dimensions in inches (centimetres)

† Add 3·9 in (9·9 cm) for diesel-engined vehicles.
* Varies according to payload capacity.

Dimensions LWB

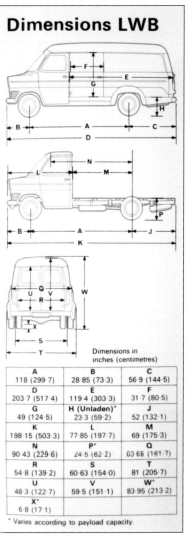

A	B	C
118 (299·7)	28·85 (73·3)	56·9 (144·5)
D	E	F
203·7 (517·4)	119·4 (303·3)	31·7 (80·5)
G	H (Unladen)*	J
49 (124·5)	23·3 (59·2)	52 (132·1)
K	L	M
198·15 (503·3)	77·85 (197·7)	69 (175·3)
N	P*	Q
90·43 (229·6)	24·5 (62·2)	60·66 (161·7)
R	S	T
54·8 (139·2)	60·63 (154·0)	81 (205·7)
U	V	W*
48·3 (122·7)	59·5 (151·1)	83·95 (213·2)
X*		
6·8 (17·1)		

Dimensions in inches (centimetres)

* Varies according to payload capacity.

Gearbox

Ford leads the field in gearbox design and the Transit four speed box is no exception. Synchromesh on *all* forward gears and floor-mounted gearchange ensure you always obtain smooth positive gearchanging – enabling you to go up or down through the gears quickly and confidently. Ratios are ideally spaced for maximum gradeability, first class acceleration and great flexibility in heavy traffic.

No exaggeration – it really was a lovely gearbox to use, and clutchless gear changes were easy in the higher ratios once one was out on the open road.

JOWETT

The Jowett brothers William and Benjamin went into business as motor manufacturers in the early 1900s but several years were to elapse until they produced a car of their own, with just a few dozen examples leaving their small factory before the First World War dictated a switch to the manufacture of munitions.

The money generated prompted a move to nearby Idle on the outskirts of Bradford, Yorkshire, where a fresh company named Jowett Cars Ltd soon had an improved version of the pre-war utility car on sale. Named the Seven, this robust little two-seater tourer, with a torquey flat-twin engine of just over 900cc, had been designed with the hilly Yorkshire terrain in mind but soon gained wider acceptance; by 1923 four-seater and light commercial versions had become available.

Having created what would nowadays be referred to as a niche market the firm saw little need for radical changes, and up until 1929 braking was on the rear wheels only; it would be a further five years until a four-speed gearbox was deemed necessary to cope with the increasing weight of more up-to-the minute bodywork. Two years later an 1166cc flat-four Ten was added to the range, but any commercials still employed the twin that were now known as the Eight due to a small increase in capacity to 946cc.

During the Second World War the government had no use for Jowett vehicles but versions of the flat-twin motor were used to power fire pumps and generators, and the works were also sub-contracted to produce aircraft components.

In 1945 the company was sold to the financier Charles Clore, who sold it on again to investment bankers Lazzard two years later. By then, post-war vehicle production had recommenced in the form of the Jowett Bradford van, with a mildly revolutionary new passenger car in the pipeline.

For the Bradford, the firm's management had seen no need to deviate from the old well-tried powerplant, so a flat-twin was used, albeit now enlarged to 1.1-litres, in conjunction with a three-speed gearbox.

In 1947 Jowett launched its advanced Javelin four-

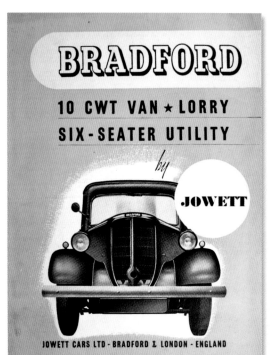

THE BRADFORD VAN
Designed for a 10 cwt. payload with a capacity of 93 cubic feet, yet to give all the economy of an 8 h.p. engine. With low unladen weight, yet extremely strong with bonded metal body. For light bulky loads 8 cwt. springs may be specified when ordering. Extras: Painting in green, blue or grey; passenger's seat.

THE BRADFORD 10 CWT. VAN

A Bradford van was no speed queen, and acceleration through the three gears was pretty sluggish – its 1-litre engine gave a stingy 19bhp at 3500rpm. But there was plentiful torque at low revs, and anyone who has driven one will testify that it pulled like a train to the mesmeric beat of its horizontally-opposed twin.

door aerodynamic saloon, with rack-and-pinion steering, torsion-bar independent suspension all round and a forward-mounted 1½-litre flat-four engine that was powerful enough to give excellent performance. Three years later Jowett took one of its prototype tubular-framed, aluminium-bodied sports two-seaters, with much the same mechanicals, to Le Mans, where it won its class. By autumn the 90mph Jupiter went into full-scale production.

As well as a van the Bradford was by then additionally available as a pick-up or estate car, but the firm was aware that it was rapidly dating, so work on a replacement began. With the project ongoing, plus the Javelin and the new Jupiter (which went on to win its class at Le Mans again in 1951 and '52), on the face of it Jowett's future was looking rosy.

But interest in the Javelin, in particular export sales, began to fall; a home-market lag, as the public awaited a forthcoming reduction in purchase tax due in April 1953, exacerbated the situation. Furthermore, Briggs Motor Bodies, which supplied Jowett with Javelin and Bradford van bodies, was in the process of being bought by Ford, who retained the main factory that abutted its own Dagenham plant, and passed on the Doncaster branch to another body manufacturer Fisher and Ludlow – which in turn was soon taken over by the recently-created British Motor Corporation.

Thus with vastly reduced sales, Javelin production suspended since mid-'53, depleted capital and the new commercial looking increasingly likely to be stillborn, it was impossible for the Jupiter to tide over the entire firm, and the decision to close was made. During 1954 the Idle factory was sold to International Harvester, which manufactured tractors at the site until the early 1980s.

Jowett itself moved a few miles down the road to a former woollen mill at Birstall, where it produced parts

THE BRADFORD LORRY
The ideal Builders' or Merchants' open truck with 27 square feet of loading space, drop sides and rear panel. Immensely strong. Extras: Painting in green, blue or grey; passenger's seat.

THE BRADFORD 18 CWT. LORRY

for Blackburn and General Aircraft, as well as continuing to supply parts for its own cars.

In 1956 Jowett became part of Blackburn, which kept the Jowett parts department operational until the British aircraft industry shake-up of 1963. In turn, Blackburn was split and absorbed by Hawker Siddeley, with its engine division going to Bristol Siddeley.

The front wings had the appearance of being designed for another vehicle and then chopped off short at the rear, but that was how they were made to give the necessary clearance for front-hinged doors. In the event of a customer wishing to fit bodywork of their own, the makers would supply the vehicle as a cab chassis (with complete cab) or drive-away chassis (fitted with temporary box seat).

ENGINE AND CHASSIS			VAN AND UTILITY		
Bore	3⅛ in.	(79·4 mm.)	Width inside	4 ft. 6 in.	137 cm.
Stroke	4 in.	(101·6 mm.)	Width between arches	3 ft. 3¼ in.	99·7 cm.
Swept volume	1,005 c.c.		Length inside behind		
Licensing weight	14 cwt.	723 Kg.	driver's seat	4 ft. 9⅛ in.	146 cm.
Power output	19 b.h.p. at 3,500 r.p.m.		Length of floor	5 ft. 3½ in.	161·3 cm.
Wheelbase	7 ft. 6 in.	228·5 cm.	Max. inside length	9 ft. 0 in.	274 cm.
Track	4 ft. 0½ in.	123·2 cm.	Max. height inside	3 ft. 9½ in.	115·6 cm.
Gear-box	3-speed and Reverse		Loading height	22½ in.	57·1 cm.
	Ratios—Top	4·89 : 1	Width door opening	3 ft. 11 in.	119·4 cm.
	2nd	9·3 : 1	Height door opening	3 ft. 4 in.	101·6 cm.
	1st	18·1 : 1	Capacity behind seat	78 cu. ft.	2·152 cu. m.
	Rev.	24·7 : 1	Capacity driver's cab	15 cu. ft.	·368 cu. m.
Turning circle	34 ft.	10·35 m.	Floor space	20 sq. ft.	1·87 sq. m.
Ignition	Coil, 6 volt battery		Overall length	12 ft. 0 in.	365·7 cm.
Petrol tank capacity	5½ gallons	25 litres	Overall width	5 ft. 0 in.	152·4 cm.
Tyres	5·00 × 16 in.		Overall height (loaded)	5 ft. 9 in.	175·2 cm.
Wheels	2·75 × 16 in.				
Ground clearance	7½ in.	19 cm.	**LORRY BODY**		
			Platform	5 ft. 6 in.	168 cm.
				× 4 ft. 11 in.	× 150 cm.
			Platform area	27 sq. ft.	2·52 sq. m.

NEW PRICES AS FROM 1/7/47			EXTRAS ON CHASSIS		EXTRAS ON VANS AND LORRIES	
Bradford Van	...	£310	Driver's Seat	£4 0s. 0d.	Passenger Seat	£4 0s. 0d.
Bradford Lorry	...	£300	Additional Seat	£4 0s. 0d.	Painting in one of the 3	£8 0s. 0d.
Bradford Drive-away			Pair Doors	£15 0s. 0d.	standard colours, Grey,	
Chassis	...	£250			Blue or Green	
Bradford Six-seater Utility		£340				
Bradford De Luxe Utility		£415				

THE BRADFORD SIX-SEATER UTILITY

THE BRADFORD 6-LIGHT VAN

As from August 1st, 1947, the BRADFORD 6-seater Utility described below has been discontinued and substituted by the 6-Light Van priced at £335, painted in green, blue or grey; or in primer, £327. It has the same equipment as the standard van but in addition is fitted with a passenger's seat and has three windows in each body-side and larger windows in the rear doors. Thus, the outside appearance is identical with the illustration of the Utility on the left.

Pre-empting the people carrier by many years, yet insufficient demand saw it dropped – but what a useful vehicle! All models had rod-operated Girling brakes that were, if the linkages and pivots were in good condition and correctly adjusted, more efficient than some other vehicles that utilised the same system.

THE BRADFORD SIX-SEATER UTILITY

To meet the needs of those requiring extra passenger accommodation—as a station wagon, shooting brake or personnel car—the Six-Seater Utility has been introduced. The body of the Utility—which has four windows in each side—is of the same spacious dimensions as the Van (93 cubic feet) and has the four extra passenger seats staggered at each side of the wide centre aisle for maximum leg room. They are quickly detachable for carrying bulky loads. The wide opening rear doors give easy access to these seats. The 8 cwt. springs are fitted. Price includes painting in grey, blue or green.

MORRIS

ithin ten years of its foundation in 1913, William Morris' car manufacturing company had become the largest in Great Britain. And so with ample funds for expansion he took steps to embrace commercial vehicles in his repertoire.

Determined that his existing factory at Cowley, near Oxford, should devote itself solely to the manufacture of cars, he set about locating a suitable premises for this new venture.

In years gone by he had relied upon outside suppliers for a good number of components, and had bought axles and steering boxes from the Birmingham firm of EG Wrigley. Since losing the Morris contract and then being let down by other customers, Wrigley had become short of money and needed to sell.

As Morris had recently bought Hotchkiss, the Coventry-based firm that supplied his engines, it made sense to acquire the relatively-nearby Wrigley premises too. By the beginning of January, Morris had moved in, and a month later the new firm of Morris Commercial Cars Ltd was up and running.

Morris chose a 1-tonner to start the ball rolling, available as either a lorry or a van, which was fitted with virtually the same four-cylinder, sidevalve,

This austere little brochure took Lord Nuffield's light commercials into the early post-war years.

1.8-litre engine as his Morris Oxfords. At first sales were sluggish, but after a while they picked up and Morris Commercials was on its way.

By 1926 a 30cwt Z-type lorry was catalogued and a half-track version of the 1-tonner was being experimented with, as well as a 6x4 with military use in mind. A little later, even larger vehicles would be in production (including single- and double-deck buses) but by then Morris was catering for the tradesman and shopkeeper. Cowley-based 8 and 10cwt vans had proved to very popular, and from the autumn of 1929 Minor-based 5cwt vans, complete with diminutive overhead-cam (OHC) engine, took to the road.

A couple of years later the OHC motor was phased out on account of cost and replaced with a sidevalve in Morris' Minors. Naturally the vans followed suit, then in 1935, with the advent of the Morris Eight, the little commercial was given the latter's slightly larger engine.

Morris Commercials was now based on a 17-acre site at Adderly Park, Birmingham, which it had moved to in 1932 when the original premises had been outgrown. By then, the bulk of the firm's output consisted of vehicles between 1½- and 5-ton capacity, although an 8/10cwt van had recently been introduced.

During the late-1930s, with the prospect of another European war increasingly likely, various vehicles were developed for the military. But before the inevitable happened in September 1939, a more modern range of civilian commercials was coming onto the market, including the 1-ton forward-control PV van and the little 5cwt Z-type; most would last into the 1950s.

Meanwhile, Viscount Nuffield's (as he had become in 1938, after being made Lord Nuffield in 1934 and Sir William Morris in 1929) Morris Motors had been engaged upon a significant part of the country's re-armament programme, insomuch as it had been charged by the Air Ministry to develop and manage, with government funding, a shadow factory that would manufacture Spitfires at a large site adjacent to Castle Bromwich Aerodrome.

Sadly, the efficiency that had taken his companies to the forefront of the British motor industry did not extend to this project, and by May 1940 not a single aircraft had been completed. On the tenth of the month Winston Churchill took over as prime minister, and within a week his newly appointed minister of aircraft production, Lord Beaverbrook, had instigated the facility's handover to Vickers-Armstrong. By the end of the war, more than 12,000 Spitfires had left Castle Bromwich.

From then on, Morris' main contribution to aircraft production was the manufacture of some 2000 Tiger Moths at Cowley, but the military vehicles it had developed were made in their thousands – as were Morris 10 Tillies and huge amounts of other miscellaneous munitions.

After the war Morris' civilian production virtually recommenced where it had left off, and by 1946, in addition to its larger commercials, the PV 1-ton, Y-type 10cwt and Z-type 5cwt were in production.

The first entirely new peacetime light commercial would be the 10cwt forward-control J-type of 1948, but work was already well under way on the design and development of two cars, the smaller of which was referred to as the Mosquito.

Both models would be launched at the 1948 motor show: the Mosquito now titled the Morris Minor MM, and its larger sibling the Morris Oxford MO; each was the work of an engineer-designer by the name of Alec Issigonis, who had worked for Morris since the mid-1930s. It would be some time before either was produced as a commercial, but by 1950 van and pick-up versions of the Oxford were on the market as the Cowley MCV, whereas the Minor would have to wait until 1953 to be accorded the same treatment.

By that time the merger between the Nuffield companies and Austin had taken place, creating the British Motor Corporation. It might have happened earlier than 1952 (talks had taken place several years before) but long-standing and irreparable differences between Viscount Nuffield and his old general manager Leonard Lord, who had defected to Austin not long before the war and was now its chairman (Herbert Austin having died in 1941), scuppered the scheme. For the first year of its existence BMC was chaired by Viscount Nuffield, with Leonard Lord taking over in 1953 and officially remaining in that

5-cwt. model

CAPACITY: 70 cubic feet with an additional 9 cubic feet beside driver

The Y-type van was, like the smaller Z, new for 1940 but had to wait until the end of the war until production – for the civilian market, certainly – got into full swing. It was powered by a sidevalve four-cylinder engine of 1547cc that produced 34bhp at 3400rpm and had a three-speed gearbox with synchromesh on second and top. Its 18in diameter pressed-steel wheels had 5.25-section tyres.

position until his retirement in 1961.

During 1952 the old PV was replaced by the LD but the first wholly BMC-produced light commercial was unveiled during 1956 in the form of the unitary-construction, forward-control Morris J2 (or Omnivan if it was an Austin). New, too, were the Series III ½-ton vans and pick-ups that replaced the 10cwt Cowley and were based on then-current Cowley/Oxford saloons. Morris 1000s now became Series IIIs too, but the only visual change was the ditching of the split-screen for a one-piece. All three would enjoy a long lifespan via a few changes along the way – the J2 until 1967 and the others until 1972.

Next came Alec Issigonis' magnificent Mini and the Morris/Austin vans and pick-ups that it begat. Magnificent not in size, but in some respects it marked the apogee of what had become the British motor industry. The industry in reality (or leastways as it was then) is gone but the modern version of the Mini lives on in the hands of BMW – an irony that will not be lost on those who know that BMW got into car production during 1928 with the purchase of fellow German firm Dixi, which was making Austin Sevens under licence; from 1929 the cars became known as BMWs.

The Austin/Morris forward-control, the 10cwt J4, came along in 1960, and would be the last light commercial that BMC designed from scratch. In 1968

The Z-type van was based on the Series E saloon. Its sidevalve four-cylinder engine had a capacity of 918cc that gave a healthy 29.6bhp (later sales material reduced the figure to 27.5) at 4400rpm and was mated to a three-speed gearbox with synchromesh on second and top. The pressed-steel wheels were 17in diameter and shod with 4.00-section tyres. Catalogued from 1940 it was made until 1954, with over 50,000 produced; those of you who are old enough may remember the little green Post Office Telephones versions with roof-mounted ladders and un-damageable matt-black rubber wings.

10-cwt. model

CAPACITY: 120 cubic feet with an additional 11 cubic feet beside driver

it was excused its split-personality role when it became simply the BMC J4, and in 1974 it underwent a frontal lobotomy that transformed it into the Sherpa.

The Sherpa lasted until 1982, when it proceeded through a series of identity changes and makeovers to become the Leyland DAF 200 Series and then the

LDV Pilot from 1993 to 2006 – at which point it finally came to the end of the road. I have already touched on the tragic demise of what was once one of Britain's highest-profile industries in the Austin preamble, and as Morris ended in the same way we will leave it here.

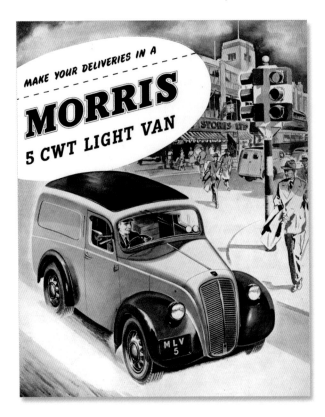

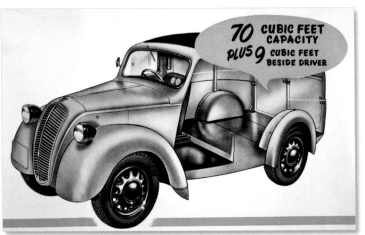

By 1952 England is getting back on its feet and the little Morris 5cwt speeds down a busy street lined by modern shops with affluently-attired gentlemen going about their business. All Z-types had Lockheed hydraulic brakes but later on – from chassis number 41707, if you really want to know – they were fitted with more the more powerful Morris Minor type with twin leading shoes on the front.

OPERATING ECONOMY

Even when used for house-to-house delivery, operating costs of the Morris Light Van are remarkably low. The sturdy Morris engine has been specially designed to give economical results on every kind of delivery work in town or in country.

LOW MAINTENANCE COSTS

Simplicity of design keeps maintenance costs low. All maintenance points are readily accessible. It is easy to service a Morris Van—and cheap, too! A short stop for routine servicing and the Morris Van is soon on the road again without waste of time.

ADVERTISING—GOOD BUSINESS

Good van-advertising is very effective. It will carry your name or your sales message into every street on the delivery round and attract valuable attention. That is why Morris Vans are provided with generous panel space. Let a Morris Van be YOUR silent salesman.

EASY IN TRAFFIC

Short over-all length, easy handling and small turning circle allow the Morris Van to slip with ease through the busiest streets. The goods delivered, it is quickly away on the return journey to be loaded once more. It saves time—it saves money—it gives quicker service.

EASY LOADING AND UNLOADING

Rear doors opening to the full width of the Van and a low floor, help to speed up loading and off-loading. Goods can be handled with ease and without risk of damage. Big savings of time and fuel are made daily.

SAVES TIME AND MONEY

With its short wheel base and excellent view through the two rear windows, the Van can be manœuvred with ease into confined spaces and close to loading decks. The doors of the cab are hinged at the front to assist the driver when reversing.

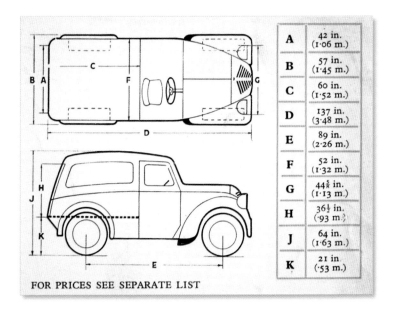

A	42 in. (1·06 m.)
B	57 in. (1·45 m.)
C	60 in. (1·52 m.)
D	137 in. (3·48 m.)
E	89 in. (2·26 m.)
F	52 in. (1·32 m.)
G	44⅝ in. (1·13 m.)
H	36½ in. (·93 m.)
J	64 in. (1·63 m.)
K	21 in. (·53 m.)

FOR PRICES SEE SEPARATE LIST

COMFORTABLE CAB

The driver's seat is well upholstered and correctly shaped to avoid driving fatigue. Ventilation of the cab and additional ventilation of the interior of the van are regulated by a single winding control for the windscreen.

LONG LIFE CHASSIS

The frame, specially designed to give lightness with strength, is of the double box type. Construction is simple, yet gives a good safety margin. It will give long service with freedom from wear.

Despite being launched in 1939 the Morris Commercial PV didn't go into serious production until 1946. Its purpose, so said the sales material, was to undertake, "Close radius deliveries – to speed them up and lower their cost." The sliding doors were said to save time by, "Rapid getting in and out of the body." Somewhat surprising, but strictly to be taken in the context of the time, were other virtues such as its, "Agility," the, "quickly accelerating engine," and, "that feeling of security so often lacking in large-capacity vans." The gawky but capacious PV lasted into the BMC era and was replaced by the Morris LD in 1954 (see Austin section for the almost identical LD).

If, for whatever reason, you didn't want the standard body you could purchase just the running chassis. But were the stipulations that went with it always adhered to? The overhead-valve motor, along with its four speed gearbox, first saw the light of day pre-war and the 18in wheels also gave away the chassis' 1930s' origins, although braking was by Lockheed's impressively named Phase II two-leading-shoe system.

"Comfortable seating and handy controls make driving this van a pleasure." Hmm – ex-Royal Tank Regiment drivers might have thought so, but I'm not sure Mr Average would have found the experience one of life's pleasures.

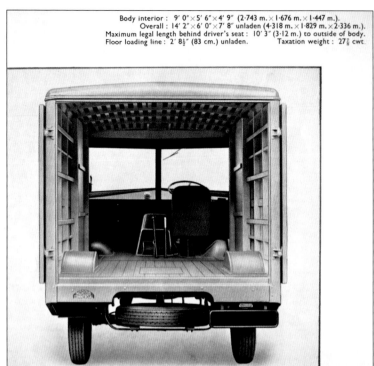

Body interior : 9' 0" × 5' 6" × 4' 9" (2·743 m. × 1·676 m. × 1·447 m.).
Overall : 14' 2" × 6' 0" × 7' 8" unladen (4·318 m. × 1·829 m. ×2·336 m.).
Maximum legal length behind driver's seat : 10' 3" (3·12 m.) to outside of body.
Floor loading line : 2' 8½" (83 cm.) unladen.   Taxation weight : 27½ cwt.

"Body is framed up in good-quality hardwood, reinforced where necessary with steel plates, and the sides are suitably panelled." Was this a suitably vague description that allowed the use of whatever wood or metal was available in those times?

"The front panel complete with grille can be detached, thus giving access to the radiator." Very useful, considering you couldn't even replenish it by way of this procedure – the filler protruded from the top of the panel behind the windscreen!

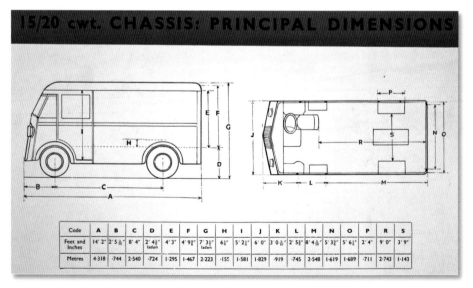

15/20 cwt. CHASSIS: PRINCIPAL DIMENSIONS

Code	A	B	C	D	E	F	G	H	I	J	K	L	M	N	O	P	R	S
Feet and Inches	14' 2"	2' 5⅜"	8' 4"	2' 4½" laden	4' 3"	4' 9¾" laden	7' 3½" laden	6⅛"	5' 2¼"	6' 0"	3' 0 3/16"	2' 5⅜"	8' 4 3/16"	5' 3¾"	5' 6¼"	2' 4"	9' 0"	3' 9"
Metres	4·318	·744	2·540	·724	1·295	1·467	2·223	·155	1·581	1·829	·919	·745	2·548	1·619	1·689	·711	2·743	1·143

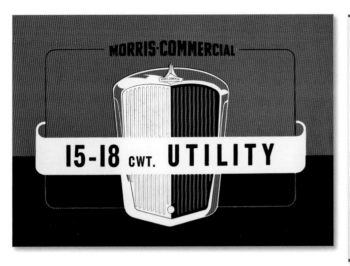

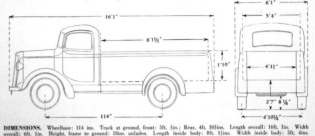

A MONEY-SAVER EVERY MILE!

Its 4-cylinder, O.H.V. engine develops ample power (42 b.h.p.) — but its fuel-thrift keeps petrol bills down!

Its characteristic reliability saves expensive service "lay-ups". Its extreme accessibility cuts maintenance time and costs. Its "equi-load" design means maximum payload space. Its

short overall length saves time in traffic. Its low loading height saves time on "turn-arounds".

Its "comfort-cab", with conveniently-positioned controls and bench-type "Dunlopillo" seating, saves driver-fatigue — in fact, this MORRIS-COMMERCIAL money-saver can save *you* money every mile!

DIMENSIONS. Wheelbase: 114 ins. Track at ground, front: 5ft. ½in.; Rear, 4ft. 10½ins. Length overall: 16ft. 1in. Width overall: 6ft. 1in. Height, frame to ground: 18ins. unladen. Length inside body: 8ft. 1½ins. Width inside body: 5ft. 4ins. Height inside body: 1ft. 10ins. Loading width of tailboard: 4ft. 3½ins. Loading height: 2ft. 7ins. Weight: 1 ton, 13 cwt., 3 qrs., 14 lbs. (unladen). Ground clearance: 8½ins. under rear axle. Turning circle: 42ft. 9ins.

Utes were an antipodean speciality, and York Motors PTY of Sydney was the New South Wales distributor in 1951 for the 15-18cwt.

Its overhead-valve engine was the same pre-war 2050cc unit as fitted to Morris' PV van, along with its gearbox. But with some off-road use in mind, the rear axle had a 5.7:1 differential.

I'd like to be kind but this Utility's body is not too elegant; however, at over 8ft long it'd nearly hold a small flock of jumbucks, and to cope with the outback it had 16in wheels shod with 7.70-section heavy-duty tyres.

The September 1948 launch brochure for the Morris J-type van depicted it with Easiclean wheels, without separate sidelights and, if you were able to see the front, slightly different styling detail.

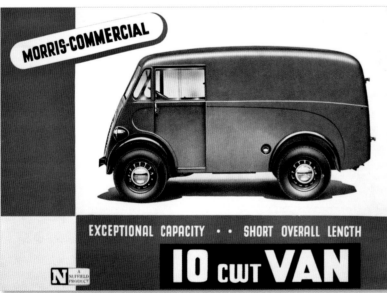

From this viewpoint, the van looked very much as it did during full-scale production. The all-metal body had a capacity of 150 cubic feet, with slats to secure loads as well as to prevent damage to side panels. Outrigged hinges on rear doors allowed them to fold back against the body sides for ease of access when loading.

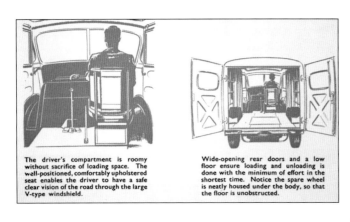

The driver's compartment is roomy without sacrifice of loading space. The well-positioned, comfortably upholstered seat enables the driver to have a safe clear vision of the road through the large V-type windshield.

Wide-opening rear doors and a low floor ensure loading and unloading is done with the minimum of effort in the shortest time. Notice the spare wheel is neatly housed under the body, so that the floor is unobstructed.

Under the rectangular engine cover with protruding air filter lurked a detuned version of the sidevalve four-cylinder motor used in the current Morris Oxford. Its 1476cc, fuelled by a Solex carburettor whose sibilant tones from the aforementioned filter would accompany you on your journeys, managed a conservative power output of 36bhp at an equally conservative 3500rpm. The gearbox had three speeds, and the brakes were Lockheed hydraulic on all four wheels.

The chassis is designed with simple, clean lines, yet is exceedingly strong and rigid. The powerful cross-members give a wide safety margin under all normal conditions.

Only very early J-types had the rectangular sidelights, as seen on this example. The sliding front doors were suspended on ball bearing tracks – as in fact were most, if not all, door mechanisms of this type (regardless of manufacturer) throughout this book. Many of these vans were supplied to the Post Office for mail delivery or telephone work and these, like their diminutive siblings, were equipped with rubber mudguards all round.

In 1957 the J-type was given an uplift and from then on known as the JB, when the aged sidevalve engine was replaced by the 1496cc version of BMC's B-series engine, along with a four-speed gearbox. At the same time a badge-engineered Austin version known as the 101 was put on the market. Production of the J in both guises was brought to an end in 1961 after nearly 50,000 had been made. It was replaced by the J2.

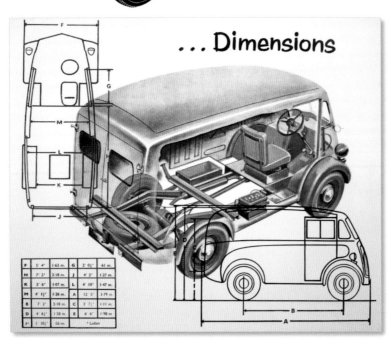

... Dimensions

F	5' 4"	1·63 m.	G	2' 0½"	·61 m.
H	7' 2"	2·18 m.	J	4' 2"	1·27 m.
K	3' 6"	1·07 m.	L	4' 10"	1·47 m.
M	4' 1½"	1·26 m.	A	12' 5"	3·79 m.
B	7' 2"	2·18 m.	C	3' 7½"	1·11 m.
D	4' 6½"	1·38 m.	E	6' 6"	1·98 m.
I*	1' 10½"	·56 m.		* Laden	

Doors open wide – low floor for easy loading!

Ample unobstructed floor space—wide-opening rear doors and a low floor facilitate speedy loading and unloading with the minimum of effort—smoothly operating sliding doors, all help to speed the job. Similar care is apparent in the construction of the body, which gains in strength and safety from being made of steel. Such characteristics make Morris vans popular for all types of business. Rear doors have outrigger hinges enabling them to fold flat against the body sides.

150 CUBIC FEET (4·25 m.³)

The Morris JB van with its 150 cu. ft. (4·25 m.³) of body space and sleek manoeuvrability is admirably suited to the door-to-door delivery of light yet bulky goods. It is sound business economy to operate JB.

Great for tight-corner manoeuvres

Turning circle 35 ft. (10·668 m.), width 64 in. (1·625 m.), length 149 in. (3·79 m.), floor loading line 22½ in. (·56 m.), all-round visibility excellent. No wonder the JB is so quick on jobs.

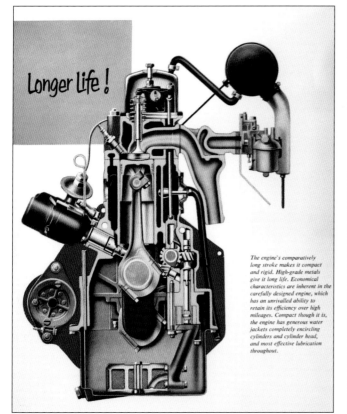

Longer Life!

The engine's comparatively long stroke makes it compact and rigid. High-grade metals give it long life. Economical characteristics are inherent in the carefully designed engine, which has an unrivalled ability to retain its efficiency over high mileages. Compact though it is, the engine has generous water jackets completely encircling cylinders and cylinder head, and most effective lubrication throughout.

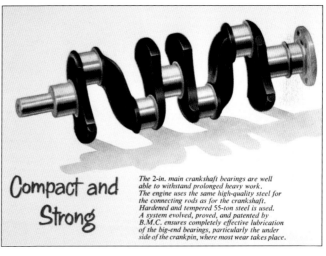

Compact and Strong

The 2-in. main crankshaft bearings are well able to withstand prolonged heavy work. The engine uses the same high-quality steel for the connecting rods as for the crankshaft. Hardened and tempered 55-ton steel is used. A system evolved, proved, and patented by B.M.C. ensures completely effective lubrication of the big-end bearings, particularly the under side of the crankpin, where most wear takes place.

Some unusual and informative illustrations of the ubiquitous B-series used in so many BMC products, both car and commercial. This is the 1496cc version with Solex carburettor that, with a 7.15:1 compression ratio, gave 42bhp at 4000rpm.

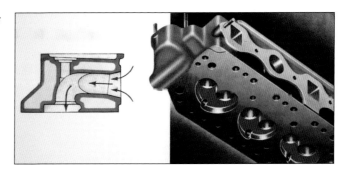

What a happy pair indeed! The Victor Mature-lookalike and Mr Happy himself imagining he's relaxing at the wheel of a luxury limousine – blissfully unaware that when he got dressed he put his right shoe on his left foot!

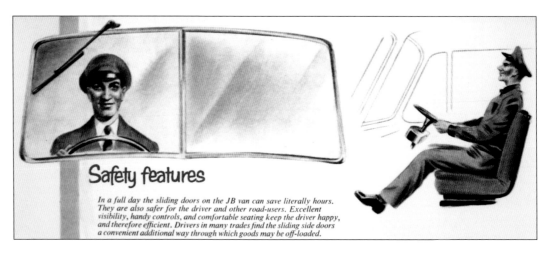

Safety features

In a full day the sliding doors on the JB van can save literally hours. They are also safer for the driver and other road-users. Excellent visibility, handy controls, and comfortable seating keep the driver happy, and therefore efficient. Drivers in many trades find the sliding side doors a convenient additional way through which goods may be off-loaded.

The JB chassis was available in this form for those who wanted bodywork of their own choice. The engine cowling had been redesigned (along with an induction system that lived underneath) in 1954, well before the 1957 change to an overhead-valve engine.

Which is the secret agent here? The two suits in the background or the fellow posing as a television repair man who has a somewhat clandestine look about him?

In 1950 Morris reintroduced the Cowley title for its Oxford MO-based light commercials that replaced the ageing Y-series 10cwt van. The 120 cubic feet of load space could be stretched to 138 if the optional passenger seat was not fitted.

These were the days of the working pick-up and, with a fraction under 6ft behind the cab, the Cowley makes a nonsense of foolishly-named modern lifestyle vehicles such as the Warrior or Animal.

With a wheelbase of 97in – 11in longer than the J-type van – the Cowley was a more sizeable vehicle than a photo suggests due to having similar styling to the smaller and more common Morris Quarter-Ton van (colloquially referred to as the 1000 van) that came later. From the side the slightly more bulbous wing moulding on the door, elongated rear wing moulding, gently curving swage line that almost meets the latter and the Cowley's lack of a visible B-post tell them apart.

A domed interior light with push-and-pull switch is mounted in the centre of the roof and immediately in front of the rear doors. It is simple to operate in the dark as it can easily be reached when one door is opened. The lamp is frosted to prevent glare.

Lurking in the shadow were the spare wheel (forward of the nearside wheelarch), and jack and tool roll on the offside.

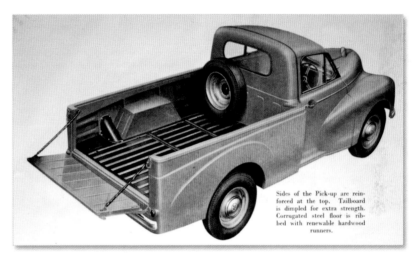

Sides of the Pick-up are reinforced at the top. Tailboard is dimpled for extra strength. Corrugated steel floor is ribbed with renewable hardwood runners.

Why they chose to tint this illustration beats me, as the standard colours were Beige, Azure Blue (early models Railly Blue), Dark Green or Platinum Grey.

CHASSIS
and All-Steel Body

The chassis is deliberately designed for the single purpose of goods carrying. Frame side-members are of generous box section joined together with cross-members of heavy channel construction.

For coachbuilders who wish to build specially designed bodies, the chassis, with open or closed cab, is available.

The all-steel driver's cab is beautifully appointed with handsome facia and steering column gear shift. A single driver's seat is fitted as standard; a second seat or a full-width bench-type seat is available as an optional extra. These alternative seating arrangements can be easily and rapidly changed by the operator.

Normally I allow manufacturers' captions to speak for themselves but in this case I must pose the question, does it really look as though this gentlemen is having an easy time of his entry and exit? And he's no heavyweight either…

Wide-opening all-steel cab doors of generous width and a low floor allow easy entry and exit, add to driver comfort and safety, speed up work on the delivery round. Cab doors are hinged forward for safe, easy reversing.

Engine and all components are readily accessible— service is simpler and cheaper.

Both van and pick-up utilised the 1476cc four-cylinder sidevalve motor that was fitted to the Oxford and in less powerful form to the J-type van. Like its passenger car counterpart it used an SU carburettor, which no doubt assisted peak power to nearly 41bhp at 4000rpm against the J's 36bhp at 500rpm less. It was mated to a four-speed gearbox with synchromesh on the three upper gears.

Front suspension is by long torsion bars, double-acting hydraulic dampers, and auxiliary telescopic shock absorbers.

Rear suspension is by semi-elliptic springs mounted on flexing rubber bushes controlled by telescopic hydraulic dampers. Goods carried are completely insulated from road shock.

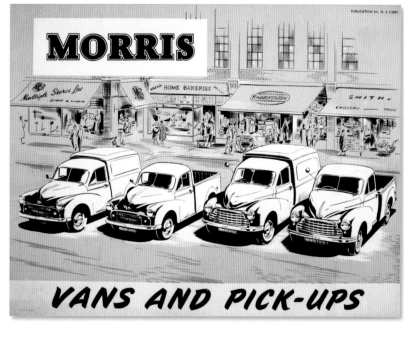

MORRIS

PUBLICATION No. H. 9 E.52H

VANS AND PICK-UPS

The Morris Minor (MM) had been launched at the 1948 motor show. Retrospectively known as the lowlight model (due to the headlamps being situated either side of the radiator grille), the little unitary-construction saloon or convertible was equipped with torsion bar front suspension and rack-and-pinion steering. It soon became a best-seller, even though its performance was limited by the maker's adherence to the same 918cc sidevalve engine as its predecessor the Eight. By the time commercial versions came along in 1953, the headlights were up on the wings (changed in 1950 largely due to the American market) and the formation of BMC had given access to the little overhead-valve A-series motor.

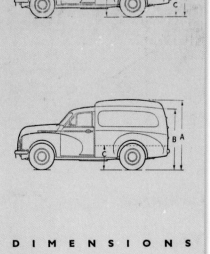

Minor commercials shared features such as the two-piece vee-windscreens with their Series II saloon and convertible counterparts but under the skin had a separate chassis. Like Morris Eight Z-type vans they were popular with the Post Office, and for the first couple of years or so its Minors were equipped with rubber front wings of the same shape as early lowlight cars but having separate headlamps perched on top.

D I M E N S I O N S

A	B	C	D
75 in. 1·90 m.	66 in. 1·67 m.	28½ in. 72·4 cm.	45 in. 1·14 m.
E	**F**	**G**	**H**
68 in. 1·72 m.	97 in. 2·46 m.	169 in. 4·29 m.	52½ in. 1·33 m.
J*	**K**	**L**	**M**
77 in. 1·95 m.	44 in. 1·11 m.	65 in. 1·65 m.	69 in. 1·75 m.

* Pick-up 71½ in. (1·81 m.)

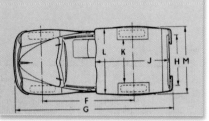

Only export vehicles had two front seats as standard, in which case the capacity was 78 cubic feet. But an extra 12 cubic feet could be squeezed into a home-market model if the optional passenger seat was dispensed with.

Series II Minor commercials had this type of radiator grille until February 1955, at which point they were given a new design with horizontal slats that had been introduced on the passenger cars during the previous October; at the same time the sidelights were repositioned beneath the headlights. Neither van nor pick-up, unlike their passenger equivalents, had trafficators, even though it appears they were on the B-post in this picture. It was simply a moulding that gave that impression of trafficators, and if you wanted them you had to make your own arrangements. Another anomalous feature that Morris Minor buffs will almost certainly be aware of is that van and pick-up bonnets were without badges or side mouldings, whilst the doors were the same as those on the four-door saloon. All passenger Minors had a side moulding that ran from bonnet to boot, thus the commercials' side view, with a moulding on just the door, was rendered somewhat incongruous.

Factory colours for the Series II pick-up and van up until February 1955 were Beige, Azure Blue, Dark Green or Platinum Grey. Thenceforth they were Azure Blue, Sandy Beige, Clarendon Grey and Empire Green; seats were brown throughout. A chassis with cab (with or without back panel) was also available for customers wanting to fit their own bodywork, and would normally be supplied in primer but could also be finished in one of the standard colours.

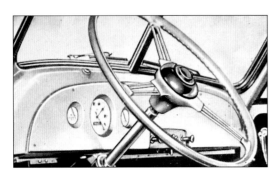

This is the wood-effect painted dashboard with speedo flanked by petrol and oil pressure gauges, all with cream dials, fitted to early vans and pick-ups. Within a year the dash and gauges were standardised for the entire passenger and commercial range, with a large central silver/bronze-faced speedo (incorporating a petrol gauge and oil warning light) flanked by large glove compartments.

Originally designed for Austin's A30, the 803cc four-cylinder overhead-valve engine was mated to a four-speed gearbox with central change. Morris neglected to provide horsepower figures in sales literature, but as the A30's figures were 28bhp at 4800rpm it should be somewhere between those numbers and a period road test that credited the 803cc-engined Minor with 30bhp.

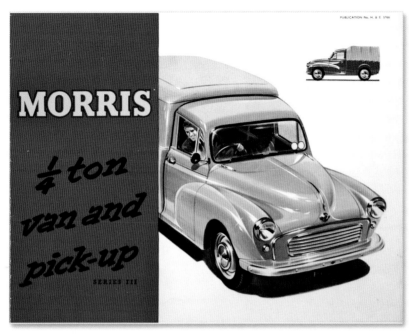

PUBLICATION No. H. & S. 1766

MORRIS

¼ ton van and pick-up

SERIES III

Named Series IIs simply because they joined the Morris Minor range some time after that series had commenced with passenger cars, the van and pick-up were in fact the first of their type. Launch of the next series was synchronised in the autumn of 1956, so the third manifestation of passenger cars and second of commercials became the Series III. Gone was the old split-screen in favour of a single curved windscreen. Yellow or red were never standard colours, by the way – this July 1957 brochure listed Clarendon Grey, Birch Grey, Dark Grey or primer for Morris' light commercials.

All this was new for the Series III except for the large central speedo and dash layout that had come in during February 1955.

New safety features include the one-piece curved windshield with more slender side pillars. A deep-sunk-centre steering wheel is fitted for driver safety. The horn control is carried on a side extension to the steering column and can be operated by the finger-tips with both hands on the wheel. The attractive facia includes two handy gloveboxes, and a full-width parcel shelf is provided.

The two-tone colour scheme would have been the customer's own but over the years van and pick-up brochures specified various standard colours. In 1959 you were offered Dark Grey, Light Grey or Dark Green whilst in 1962 you could have had Rose Taupe (I had one of these and of course she ended up being called Rosie), Dove Grey or Almond Green.

This suspension and steering setup featured on all Minors – no mention of worn trunnions, however, as the cars were yet young. Whenever I witnessed the phenomena – and fortunately it never happened to me – it was always as the unfortunate driver was pulling away, and down would go the front as the worn trunnion bush on one side or the other cried, "Enough!" and the suspension collapsed. Ignorance is bliss, they say, and in this case the reward for disregarding rattles and clunks was a bottom wishbone cutting a groove in the tarmac and the relevant wheel assuming a funny angle. I never heard of it happening at speed or causing a dreadful accident, but I suppose the law of averages would dictate it probably did.

Hydraulic fully compensated two-leading-shoe brakes, direct-acting rack and pinion steering and torsion bar independent front suspension with hydraulic piston-type shock absorbers are features that instil confidence in drivers and operators alike.

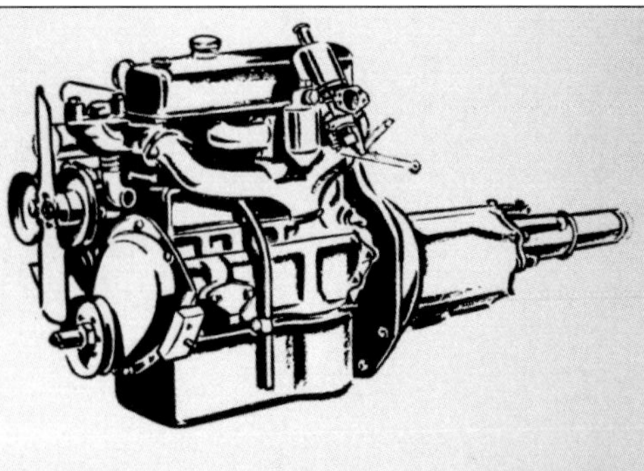

The brilliant new engine of 950 c.c. capacity gives extra performance for brisk house-to-house deliveries. Embodying many of the proved features of the well-known Morris Minor engine, this bigger o.h.v. unit has many new ones too. Power is stepped up to 37 b.h.p. at 4,800 r.p.m. . . . and greater reserves of power mean longer engine life.

The A-series engine had been enlarged by increasing the bore from 58mm to 63mm, but it was not as simple as that – importantly, it had an improved block casting, enlarged big end bearings and other fundamental improvements.

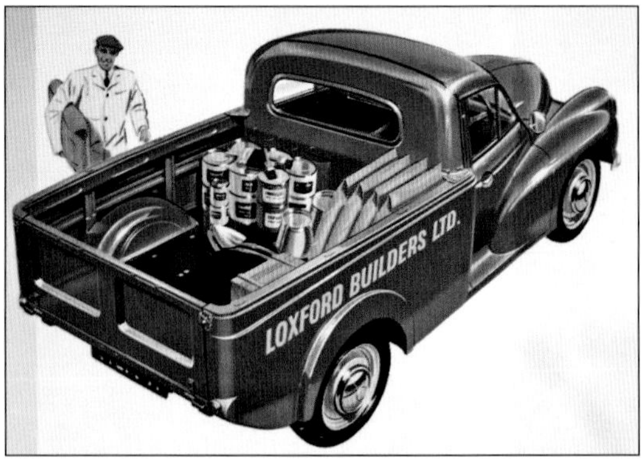

September 1962 saw the final hike in the Minor's engine size when it was given the 1098cc A-series, along with an improved four-speed gearbox with stronger ribbed outer casing. Output was in the region of 45bhp at around 5100rpm.

From then on the vans and pick-ups were known as Series Vs (whatever happened to IV I have no idea) and in this form carried on past our dateline until early in 1968 when the 6cwt capacity Series Cs were introduced, followed by 8cwt versions a short while later. When the end came in February 1972 over 325,000, of all types, had been produced.

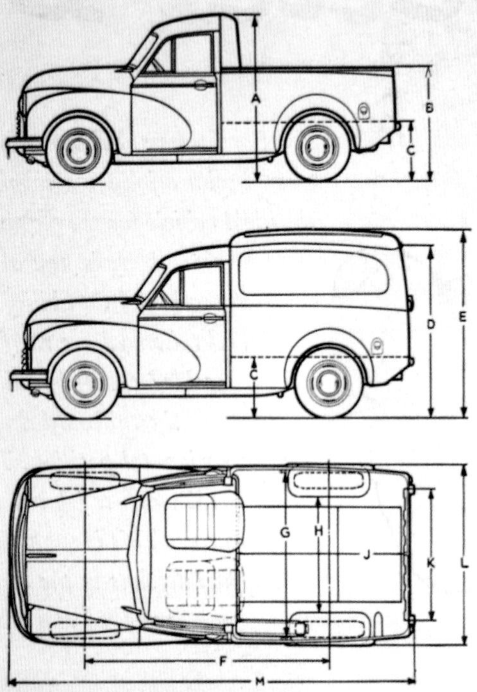

DIMENSIONS

A 5 ft. $0\frac{3}{4}$ in. (1·54 m.)	**B** 3 ft. $5\frac{13}{16}$ in. (1·06 m.)	**C** 1 ft. $10\frac{3}{4}$ in. (58 cm.)	**D** 5 ft. $0\frac{1}{2}$ in. (1·54 m.)
E 5 ft. $5\frac{7}{8}$ in. (1·67 m.)	**F** 7 ft. 2 in. (2·18 m.)	**G** 4 ft. $7\frac{1}{2}$ in. (1·41 m.)	**H** 3 ft. $3\frac{1}{8}$ in. (99 cm.)
J 4 ft. $11\frac{1}{4}$ in. (1·5 m.)	**K** 3 ft. $9\frac{1}{8}$ in. (1·15 m.)	**L** 5 ft. $0\frac{1}{2}$ in. (1·54 m.)	**M** 11 ft. $10\frac{5}{8}$ in. (3·62 m.)

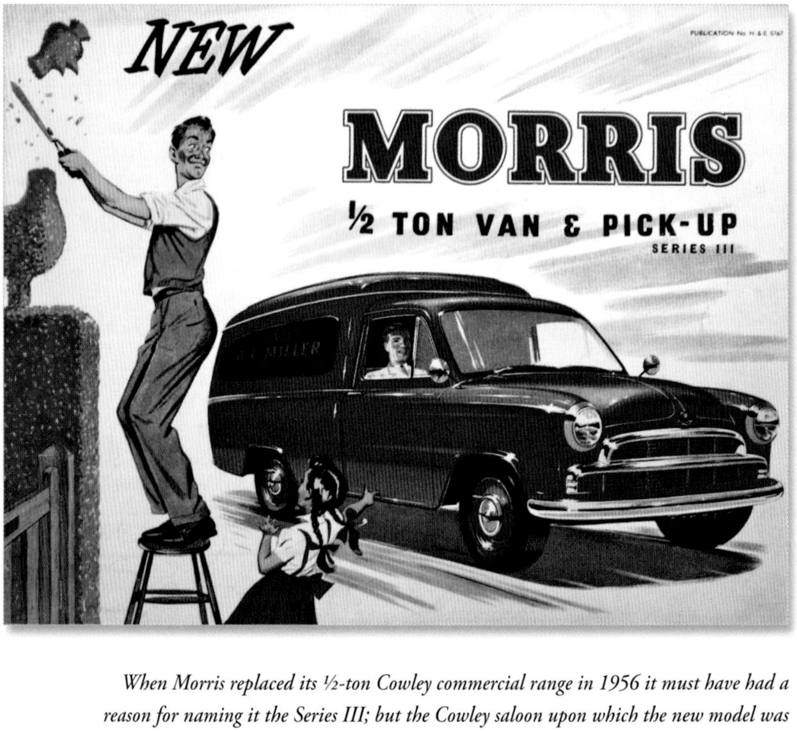

When Morris replaced its ½-ton Cowley commercial range in 1956 it must have had a reason for naming it the Series III; but the Cowley saloon upon which the new model was based was just making the change from Series I to II, and the now-defunct (and totally different) Cowley vans and pick-ups had but one manifestation. Maybe it was to slot in with the Series III Minor commercials that were also new to the market. Why did manufacturers illustrate their brochures with non-standard colours? If the van looked better in red, why not offer the shade in addition to Dark Grey, Light Grey or Dark Green?

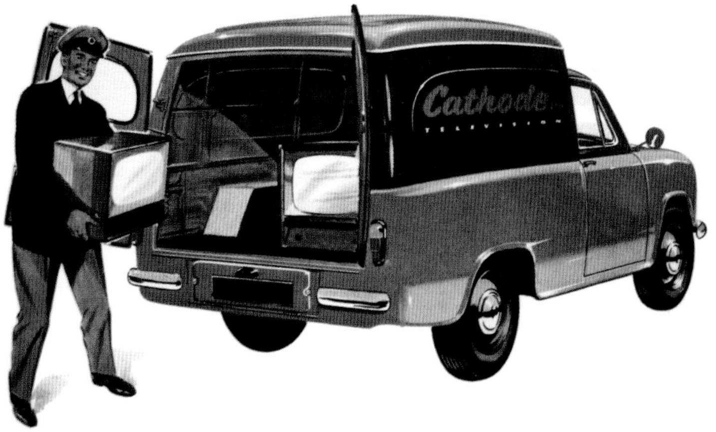

Television was all the rage for any thoroughly modern family back in the mid-'50s but back then a good number were rental sets, and it was very likely a Bush, Pye or Ferguson that would be delivered by a Morris, Austin or a Commer. Nearly 60 years on, sad to say, they are virtually pandemic and many households in the UK have several of the things – but they'll be branded Samsung, Sony or suchlike and you'll very likely be driving to your nearest superstore to buy one.

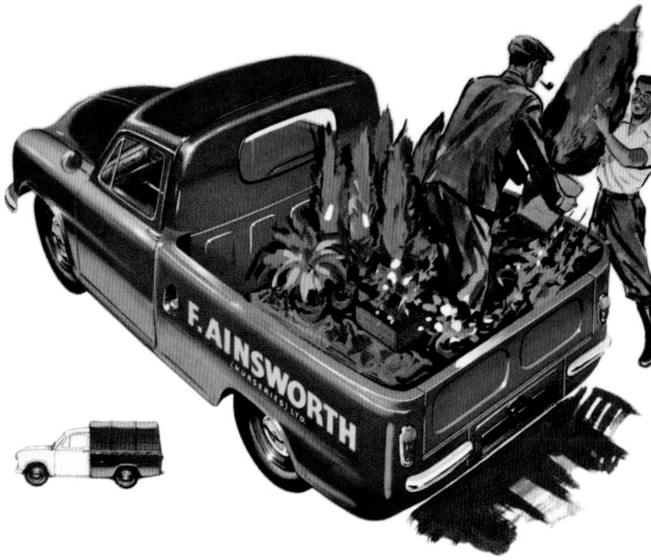

The BMC conglomerate was well entrenched and badge-engineering had already been embarked upon by the time the Series III Morris ½-tonner came about – but it was very different from its Austin counterpart, with the B-series 1489cc powerplant being about all they had in common. There was even a discrepancy there, as the Morris brochure claimed 50bhp at 4200rpm and Austin only laid claim to 47bhp at 4100rpm. The Morris had a sporty four-on-the-floor, whilst Austin's four was on the column. Morris also had a slightly shorter wheelbase (2¼in), rack-and-pinion steering against cam-and-peg, as well as Lockheed brakes to the Austin's Girling (both hydraulic). Partially thanks to its raised roof, the Morris van also had 120 cubic feet of load space against the Austin's 110, with 18 more available if you dispensed with the optional passenger seat. The pick-up, too, had a single seat as standard, so if you wanted one for a passenger or a bench seat on either model – or even a heater come to that – it would mean an increase to the basic purchase price.

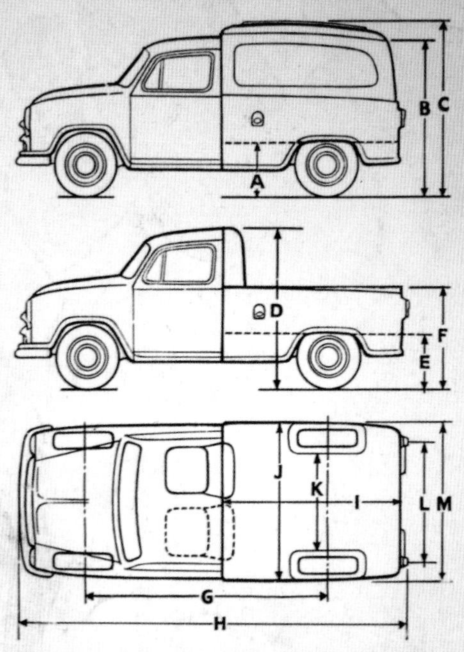

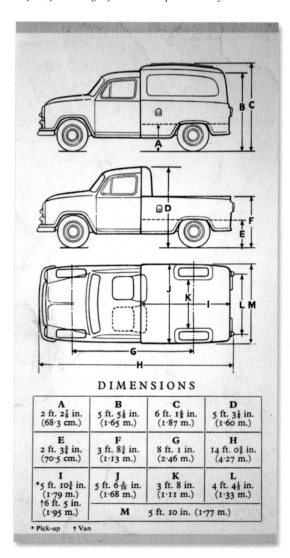

DIMENSIONS

A 2 ft. $2\frac{7}{8}$ in. (68·3 cm.)	**B** 5 ft. $5\frac{5}{8}$ in. (1·65 m.)	**C** 6 ft. $1\frac{5}{8}$ in. (1·87 m.)	**D** 5 ft. $3\frac{1}{8}$ in. (1·60 m.)
E 2 ft. $3\frac{3}{4}$ in. (70·5 cm.)	**F** 3 ft. $8\frac{3}{4}$ in. (1·13 m.)	**G** 8 ft. 1 in. (2·46 m.)	**H** 14 ft. $0\frac{3}{8}$ in. (4·27 m.)
I *5 ft. $10\frac{3}{4}$ in. (1·79 m.) †6 ft. 5 in. (1·95 m.)	**J** 5 ft. $6\frac{5}{16}$ in. (1·68 m.)	**K** 3 ft. 8 in. (1·11 m.)	**L** 4 ft. $4\frac{1}{2}$ in. (1·33 m.)
	M	5 ft. 10 in. (1·77 m.)	

* Pick-up † Van

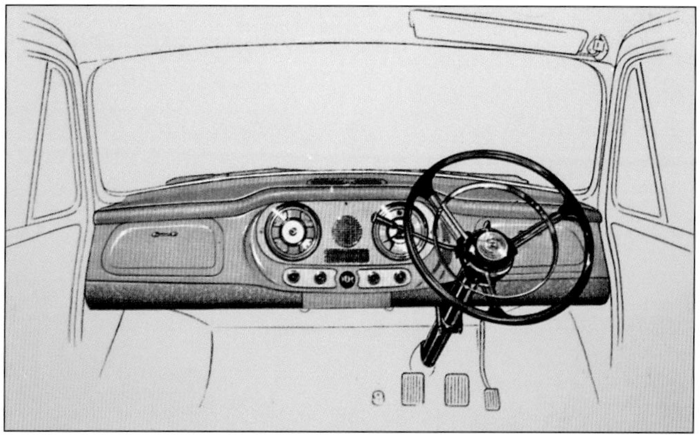

Occupant safety was beginning to be addressed by manufacturers and the ½-tonner had a foam rubber protection pad along the top rail of its stylish dash, as well a steering wheel with deep-sunk centre – although in the event of a real pile-up neither would offer much more than token protection. In common with many of its contemporaries the dashboard layout facilitated the choice of left- or right-hand drive.

NEW! TOUGH! VERSATILE!

MORRIS
½ TON
VAN & PICK·UP

You could have your '62 Morris ½-ton van or pick-up in Horizon Blue, Farina Grey, Tweed Grey or Willow Green; all came trimmed in black with seats piped in Dove Grey. From the time of their introduction all Morris ½-tonners, in common with Austins, had 15in wheels shod with 6.00 cross-ply tyres but when both varieties changed over to the larger 1622cc engine in '63 the wheel size was reduced to 14in combined with larger 6.40-section tyres. Morris ½-ton vans and pick-ups, like their Austin counterparts, continued to be built until the beginning of the '70s.

"New! Tough! Versatile!" New to Morris maybe, but the 1962 edition of its ½-tonner simply featured the corporate badge and insignificant elements of frontal styling to differentiate it from the "new" Austin ½-ton – itself just a facelifted version of a six-year-old design. Steering, brakes and gearchange were now to Austin spec and even the motor no longer claimed three extra horsepower. By consulting the dimensional charts you'll find one or two tiny discrepancies but I'm pretty sure they were nothing more than a lack of interdepartmental cohesion when arriving at the figures.

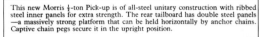

This new Morris ½-ton Pick-up is of all-steel unitary construction with ribbed steel inner panels for extra strength. The rear tailboard has double steel panels —a massively strong platform that can be held horizontally by anchor chains. Captive chain pegs secure it in the upright position.

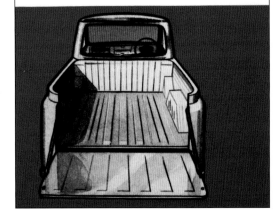

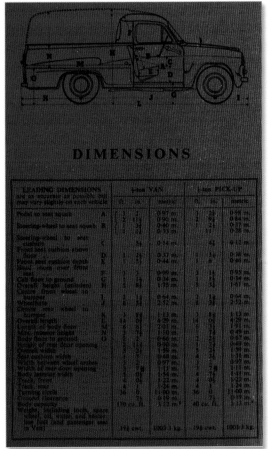

DIMENSIONS

Cab interior. All the comfort of a car with instruments and controls to match. The driving seat can be adjusted for maximum driving ease and controllability. At slight extra cost fresh-air heater and passenger seat can be installed if desired.

Here is the Morris version of BMC's first jointly designed and produced light commercial. To my eyes the Austin radiator grille harmonised with the overall design more successfully than the Morris type, but you may not agree.

The accentuated perspective of this artwork suggested a long-wheelbase version but all J2s were 7ft 6in. Sliding doors were standard on the van but hinged could be ordered by special request. Other extras listed were heater and demister, "mate's seat" (standard on pick-up, minibus and export vehicles), radio, sun visors and – would you believe it – spare wheel and tyre (the skinflints!).

Later pick-ups would be given triangulated extensions behind the cab to add some strength and obviate any tendency for the body to flex at this point.

The J2 was available with either a single-hinged side-loading door or a double as shown here. Capacity was 200 cubic feet whatever the layout.

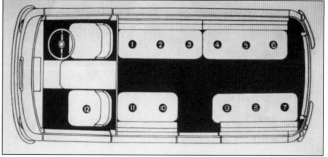

If it was an Austin it would be the Omnicoach but – hey presto – it's a Morris, so it's the Minibus. Seating was for ten including the driver in the model shown here, or 12 in the alternative version that had the seats arranged lengthwise with passengers facing one another.

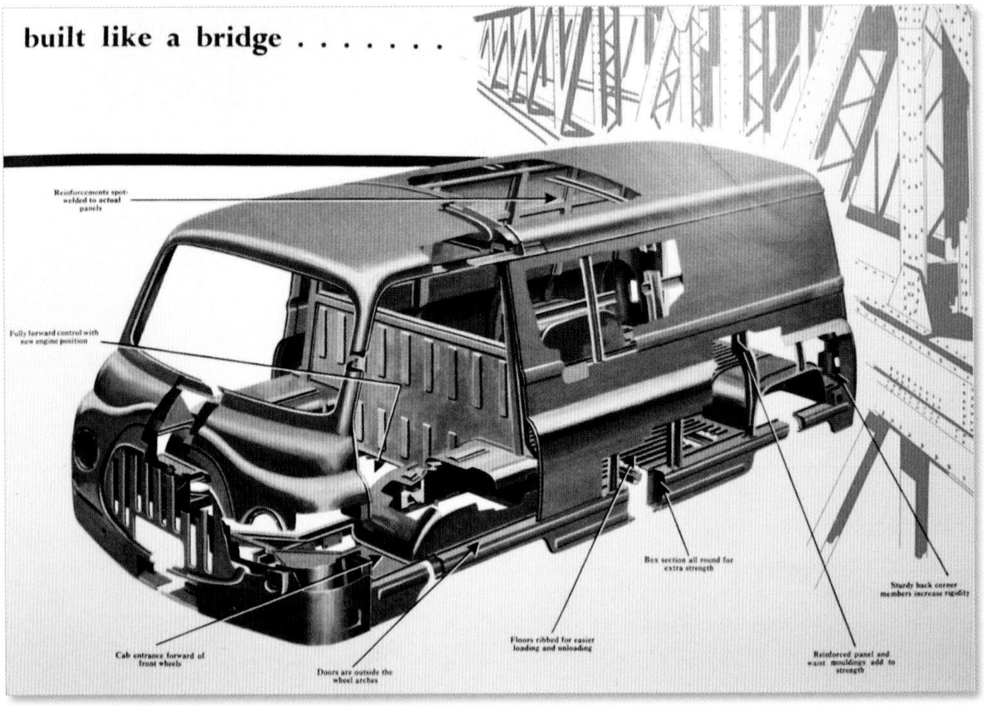
built like a bridge . . . .
Reinforcements spot-welded to actual panels
Fully forward control with new engine position
Box section all round for extra strength
Sturdy back corner members increase rigidity
Cab entrance forward of front wheels
Doors are outside the wheel arches
Floors ribbed for easier loading and unloading
Reinforced panel and waist mouldings add to strength

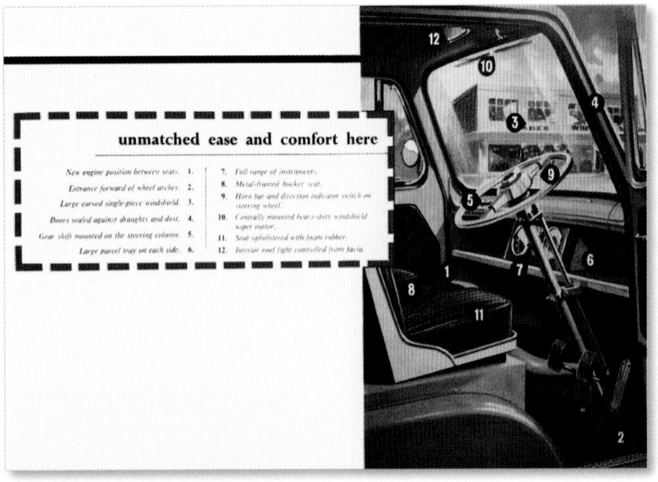
unmatched ease and comfort here
New engine position between seats. 1.
Entrance forward of wheel arches. 2.
Large curved single-piece windshield. 3.
Doors sealed against draughts and dust. 4.
Gear shift mounted on the steering column. 5.
Large parcel tray on each side. 6.
7. Full range of instruments.
8. Metal-framed bucket seat.
9. Horn bar and direction indicator switch on steering wheel.
10. Centrally mounted heavy-duty windshield wiper motor.
11. Seat upholstered with foam rubber.
12. Interior roof light controlled from facia.
12
10
3
4
9
5
1
7
6
8
11
2

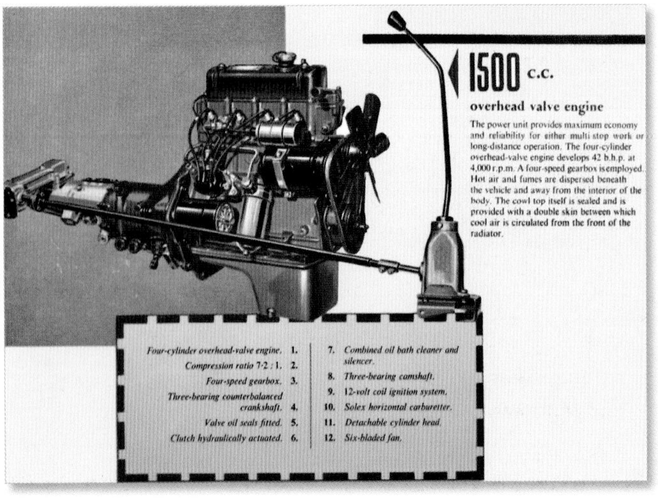
1500 c.c.
overhead valve engine
The power unit provides maximum economy and reliability for either multi-stop work or long-distance operation. The four-cylinder overhead-valve engine develops 42 b.h.p. at 4,000 r.p.m. A four-speed gearbox is employed. Hot air and fumes are dispersed beneath the vehicle and away from the interior of the body. The cowl top itself is sealed and is provided with a double skin between which cool air is circulated from the front of the radiator.
Four-cylinder overhead-valve engine. 1.
Compression ratio 7·2 : 1. 2.
Four-speed gearbox. 3.
Three-bearing counterbalanced crankshaft. 4.
Valve oil seals fitted. 5.
Clutch hydraulically actuated. 6.
7. Combined oil bath cleaner and silencer.
8. Three-bearing camshaft.
9. 12-volt coil ignition system.
10. Solex horizontal carburetter.
11. Detachable cylinder head.
12. Six-bladed fan.

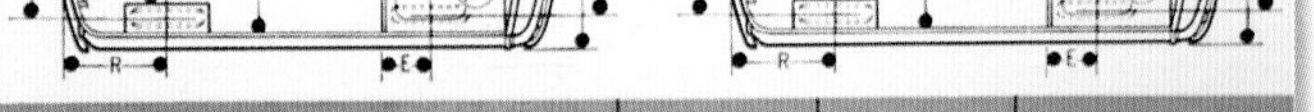
A
B
C
F
H
M
S1
S2
CM
J
K
N
T
P
D
R
E

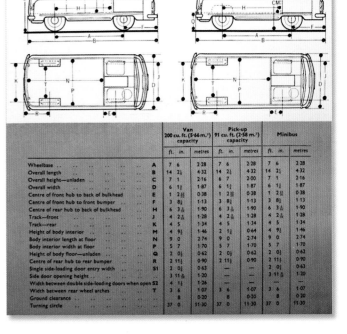

		Van 200 cu. ft. (5·66 m.³) capacity		Pick-up 91 cu. ft. (2·58 m.³) capacity		Minibus	
		ft. in.	metres	ft. in.	metres	ft. in.	metres
Wheelbase	A	7 6	2·28	7 6	2·28	7 6	2·28
Overall length	B	14 2¼	4·32	14 2¼	4·32	14 2¼	4·32
Overall height—unladen	C	7 1	2·16	6 7	2·00	7 1	2·16
Overall width	D	6 1⅝	1·87	6 1⅝	1·87	6 1⅝	1·87
Centre of front hub to back of bulkhead ..	E	1 2 15/16	0·38	1 2 15/16	0·38	1 2 15/16	0·38
Centre of front hub to front bumper	F	3 8½	1·13	3 8½	1·13	3 8½	1·13
Centre of rear hub to back of bulkhead ..	H	6 3 1/16	1·90	6 3 1/16	1·90	6 3 1/16	1·90
Track—front	J	4 2 5/16	1·28	4 2 5/16	1·28	4 2 5/16	1·28
Track—rear	K	4 5	1·34	4 5	1·34	4 5	1·34
Height of body interior	M	4 9½	1·46	2 1¼	0·64	4 9½	1·46
Body interior length at floor	N	9 0	2·74	9 0	2·74	9 0	2·74
Body interior width at floor	P	5 7	1·70	5 7	1·70	5 7	1·70
Height of body floor—unladen	Q	2 0⅜	0·62	2 0⅜	0·62	2 0⅜	0·62
Centre of rear hub to rear bumper	R	2 11½	0·90	2 11½	0·90	2 11½	0·90
Single side-loading door entry width	S1	2 0¾	0·63	—	—	2 0¾	0·63
Side door opening height	..	3 11 3/16	1·20	—	—	3 11 3/16	1·20
Width between double side-loading doors when open	S2	4 1½	1·26	—	—	—	—
Width between rear wheel arches	T	3 6	1·07	3 6	1·07	3 6	1·07
Ground clearance	..	8	0·20	8	0·20	8	0·20
Turning circle	..	37 0	11·30	37 0	11·30	37 0	11·30

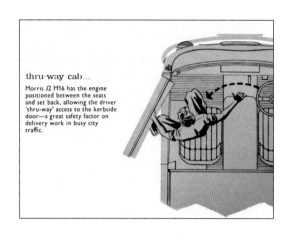

thru-way cab...

Morris J2 M16 has the engine positioned between the seats and set back, allowing the driver 'thru-way' access to the kerbside door—a great safety factor on delivery work in busy city traffic.

This feature was old hat and, besides, you can take it from me even for the young and spritely it was not that easy to cross from side to side.

In 1961/62 the J2 became the J2M16. The new model had been given a floor-change gearbox along with the option of BMC's 1500 diesel engine. By '63 the standard petrol model was equipped with the larger 1622cc edition of the B-series motor.

Alternative is the B.M.C. 1·5-litre diesel engine for even greater economy in running. This too is a 1489 c.c. capacity o.h.v. unit. It develops 40 b.h.p. (maximum) at 4,000 r.p.m. A Ricardo Comet V combustion system with heater plugs is fitted.

In both petrol and diesel units the cowl top is sealed and double-skinned to carry cool air from the front of the radiator.

1.5 litre diesel engine

J2 pick-ups had these abbreviated side extensions behind the cab for several years, and they were unaltered for the M16.

J2s were also available in chassis cab form but doors were an extra. Road wheels were 15in with 5.90-section tubeless tyres or 6.40s if you intended to carry extra-heavy loads.

There was nothing except badge and radiator grille to choose between BMC's J4s. This was yet another brochure that failed to reproduce one of the standard colours on its cover – or inside, come to that. For the record, they were Light Blue, Charcoal Grey, Light Grey or Mid Green.

You could have your J4 with either sliding or what this brochure called "slam doors" – although I remember the former whooshing shut with quite a crash. Here's one with sliding doors and optional side door to ease access to its 160 cubic feet of load space; but that would cost you extra.

At first J4s had the 42bhp petrol or 40bhp diesel; each developed these figures at 4000rpm, had the same bore and stroke of 73.02mm x 88.9mm and, obviously, the same cubic capacity of 1489cc. Later on, the petrol version was endowed with a little more oomph by way of the 49bhp 1622cc motor. All versions had a four-speed floor-change gearbox.

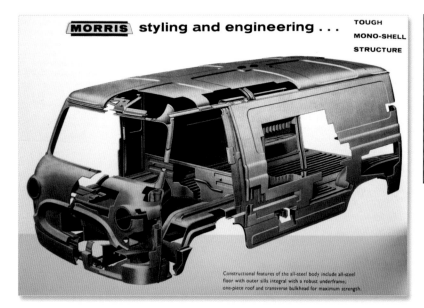

MORRIS styling and engineering . . . TOUGH MONO-SHELL STRUCTURE

Constructional features of the all-steel body include all-steel floor with outer sills integral with a robust underframe; one-piece roof and transverse bulkhead for maximum strength.

A tilt for your pick-up was an extra, and BMC still kept its stingy policy of charging extra if you wanted a seat for your mate, chum, wife or a hitchhiker. You could build your own body on the chassis/cab unit but the brochure carried the ominous rider: "Subject to approval."

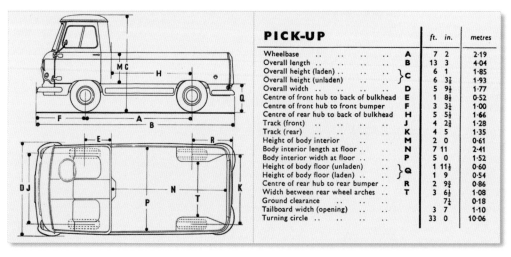

PICK-UP		ft.	in.	metres
Wheelbase	A	7	2	2·19
Overall length	B	13	3	4·04
Overall height (laden)	}C	6	1	1·85
Overall height (unladen)		6	3⅞	1·93
Overall width	D	5	9¼	1·77
Centre of front hub to back of bulkhead	E	1	8½	0·52
Centre of front hub to front bumper	F	3	3½	1·00
Centre of rear hub to back of bulkhead	H	5	5½	1·66
Track (front)	J	4	2⅜	1·28
Track (rear)	K	4	5	1·35
Height of body interior	M	2	0	0·61
Body interior length at floor	N	7	11	2·41
Body interior width at floor	P	5	0	1·52
Height of body floor (unladen) ..	}Q	1	11½	0·60
Height of body floor (laden) ..		1	9	0·54
Centre of rear hub to rear bumper ..	R	2	9½	0·86
Width between rear wheel arches ..	T	3	6½	1·08
Ground clearance			7¼	0·18
Tailboard width (opening)		3	7	1·10
Turning circle		33	0	10·06

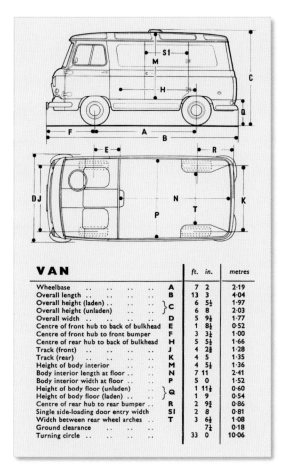

VAN		ft.	in.	metres
Wheelbase	A	7	2	2·19
Overall length	B	13	3	4·04
Overall height (laden)	} C	6	5½	1·97
Overall height (unladen)		6	8	2·03
Overall width	D	5	9½	1·77
Centre of front hub to back of bulkhead	E	1	8½	0·52
Centre of front hub to front bumper	F	3	3½	1·00
Centre of rear hub to back of bulkhead	H	5	5½	1·66
Track (front)	J	4	2½	1·28
Track (rear)	K	4	5	1·35
Height of body interior	M	4	5½	1·36
Body interior length at floor ..	N	7	11	2·41
Body interior width at floor ..	P	5	0	1·52
Height of body floor (unladen) ..	} Q	1	11½	0·60
Height of body floor (laden) ..		1	9	0·54
Centre of rear hub to rear bumper ..	R	2	9½	0·86
Single side-loading door entry width	S1	2	8	0·81
Width between rear wheel arches ..	T	3	6¼	1·08
Ground clearance			7½	0·18
Turning circle		33	0	10·06

For once BMC's publicity people had no need to talk the company's product up with this March 1960 brochure. The Mini, in any form, was most certainly revolutionary and delivery costs could be slashed – providing, of course, you didn't have too much to deliver. For the first of the vans there were just two in-house colour options – Whitehall Beige or Smoke Grey, both with tan upholstery.

The only excuse I can think of for this lurid artwork was that it highlighted the 46-cubic-feet interior – there'd have been 12 more had the artist left out the optional, as ever, passenger seat.

Once the word got around, for every Mini van being driven by a man in a shirt and tie, sports jacket and flat cap doing light delivery work, there'd be another zooming about the place with a youngster at the wheel (or youngish at any rate). If you could run to the HP payments for a purchase tax-free van, £360 was about the cheapest brand-new four-wheeler around – and most certainly the cheapest that would give you instant kudos. It was amazing how would-be Helen Shapiros or Cilla Blacks would risk their stockings and their dignity to catch a ride somewhere – anywhere!

FRONT WHEEL DRIVE

Gives you EXTRA DRIVING CONTROL AND SAFETY

Driving is safer, control is greater, with direct transmission to the front wheels. And it's another space-saver—eliminating long transmission shaft and back axle 'hump'!

Gives you FAR MORE PAYLOAD SPACE

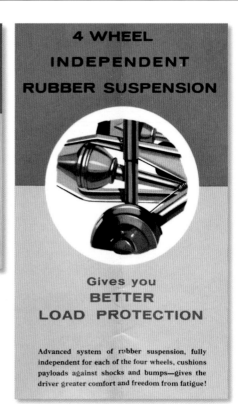

4 WHEEL INDEPENDENT RUBBER SUSPENSION

Gives you BETTER LOAD PROTECTION

Advanced system of rubber suspension, fully independent for each of the four wheels, cushions payloads against shocks and bumps—gives the driver greater comfort and freedom from fatigue!

Servicing is three times as easy—the same oil and filler are used for engine, gears, and axle.

Ample room for driver's legs. Seat is easily adjustable.

Driver's seat is adjustable. Tips forward for easy access to rear compartment. Battery is stowed behind seat. Spare wheel has special compartment below load space floor.

'East–West' engine combined with clutch, gears, and drive axle in one unit.

All instruments centred in a single group with switches and controls mounted below.

The front subframe complete with entire drive train, suspension and ancillaries viewed from the rear.

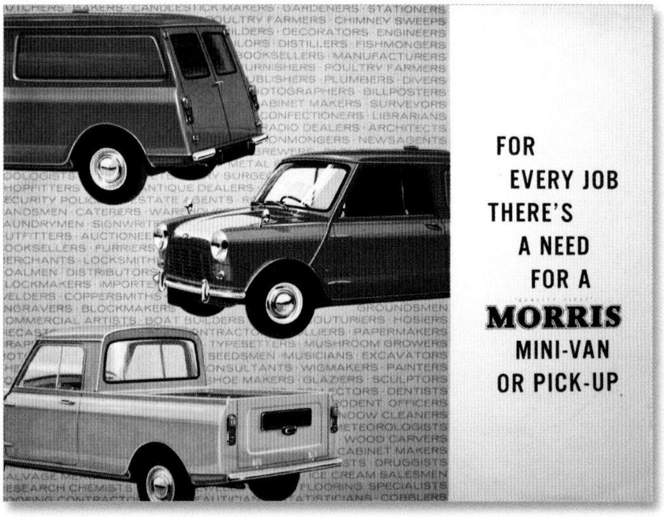
FOR
EVERY JOB
THERE'S
A NEED
FOR A
MORRIS
MINI-VAN
OR PICK-UP

A little optimistic but that's advertising. The 1964 brochure's claim was right on the mark however – "Whether you need a single van or a whole fleet the Morris Mini-Van and Pick-up are ready and willing to cope with a thousand and one jobs". No idle boast with over a million Minis of all types sold by that time.

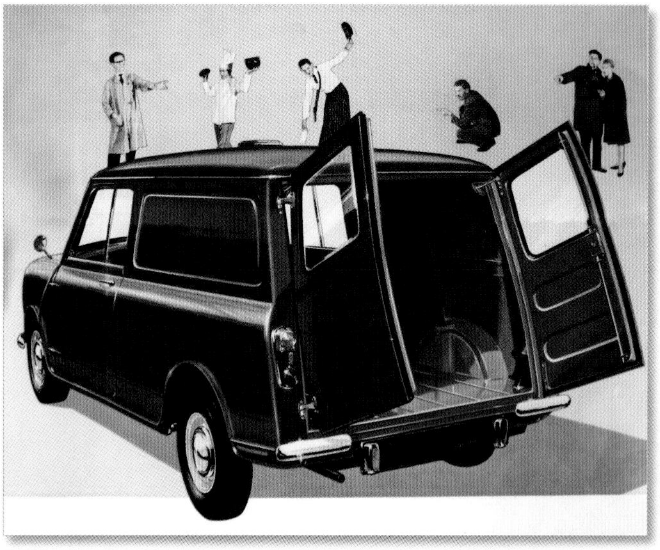

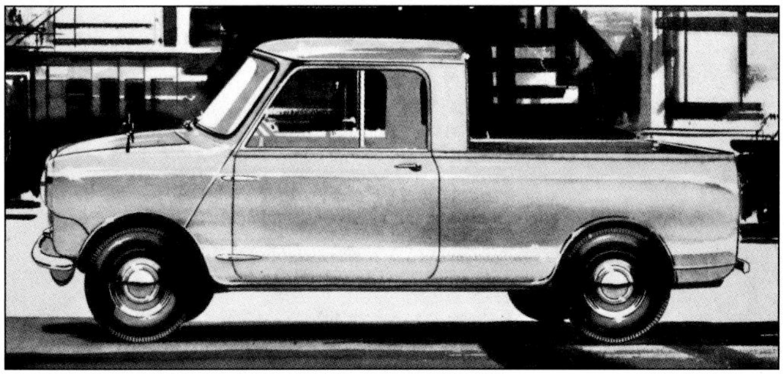

No mention of an optional tilt in the brochure, but the pick-up's bed had sockets for the hoops and provision to secure it at the rear of the cab. Rear number plate hinged for running with the tail gate down.

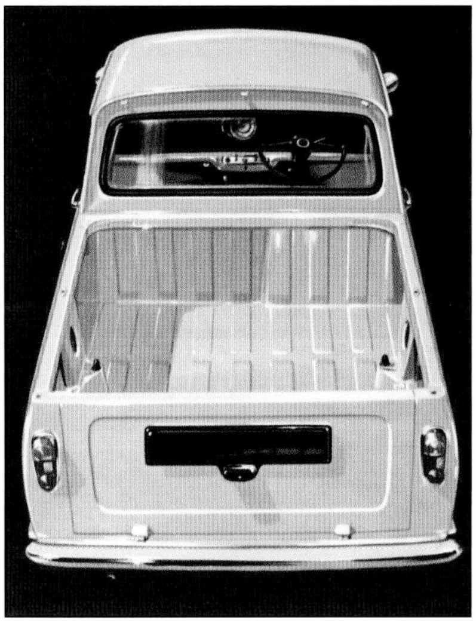

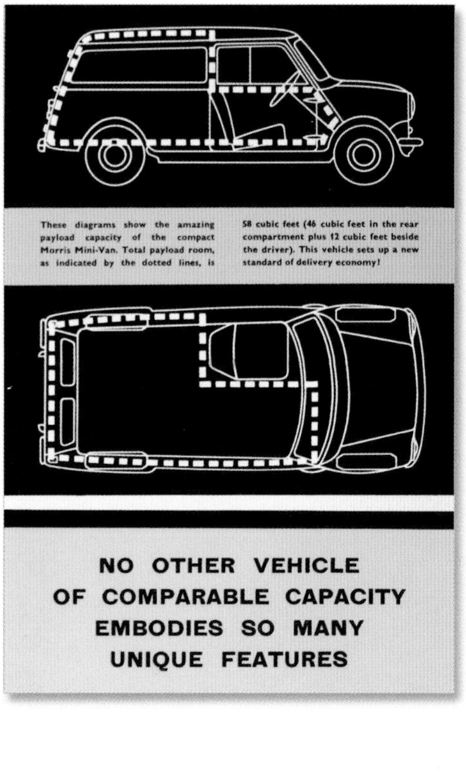
These diagrams show the amazing payload capacity of the compact Morris Mini-Van. Total payload room, as indicated by the dotted lines, is 58 cubic feet (46 cubic feet in the rear compartment plus 12 cubic feet beside the driver). This vehicle sets up a new standard of delivery economy!
NO OTHER VEHICLE
OF COMPARABLE CAPACITY
EMBODIES SO MANY
UNIQUE FEATURES

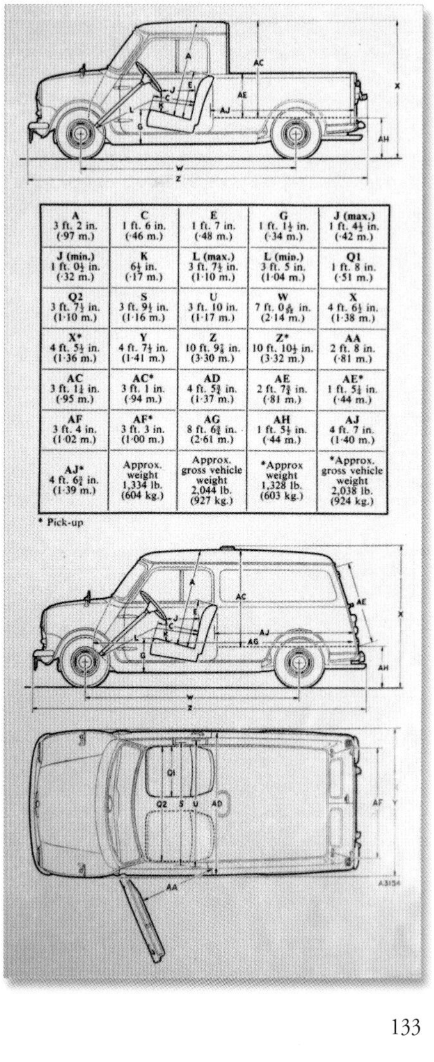

A 3 ft. 2 in. (·97 m.)	C 1 ft. 6 in. (·46 m.)	E 1 ft. 7 in. (·48 m.)	G 1 ft. 1½ in. (·34 m.)	J (max.) 1 ft. 4½ in. (·42 m.)
J (min.) 1 ft. 0½ in. (·32 m.)	K 6½ in. (·17 m.)	L (max.) 3 ft. 7½ in. (1·10 m.)	L (min.) 3 ft. 5 in. (1·04 m.)	Q1 1 ft. 8 in. (·51 m.)
Q2 3 ft. 7½ in. (1·10 m.)	S 3 ft. 9½ in. (1·16 m.)	U 3 ft. 10 in. (1·17 m.)	W 7 ft. 0 $\frac{8}{32}$ in. (2·14 m.)	X 4 ft. 6½ in. (1·38 m.)
X* 4 ft. 5½ in. (1·36 m.)	Y 4 ft. 7½ in. (1·41 m.)	Z 10 ft. 9⅞ in. (3·30 m.)	Z* 10 ft. 10½ in. (3·32 m.)	AA 2 ft. 8 in. (·81 m.)
AC 3 ft. 1¼ in. (·95 m.)	AC* 3 ft. 1 in. (·94 m.)	AD 4 ft. 5⅞ in. (1·37 m.)	AE 2 ft. 7⅞ in. (·81 m.)	AE* 1 ft. 5¼ in. (·44 m.)
AF 3 ft. 4 in. (1·02 m.)	AF* 3 ft. 3 in. (1·00 m.)	AG 8 ft. 6¾ in. (2·61 m.)	AH 1 ft. 5½ in. (·44 m.)	AJ 4 ft. 7 in. (1·40 m.)
AJ* 4 ft. 6¾ in. (1·39 m.)	Approx. weight 1,334 lb. (604 kg.)	Approx. gross vehicle weight 2,044 lb. (927 kg.)	*Approx weight 1,328 lb. (603 kg.)	*Approx. gross vehicle weight 2,038 lb. (924 kg.)

* Pick-up

MORRISON-ELECTRICAR

Crompton Parkinson had been formed in 1927 by the merger of two of the country's longest-established electrical manufacturers: Crompton & Co (which specialised in lamps and electrical installations) and F&A Parkinson, which made electric motors.

While the forthcoming recession left some of Crompton Parkinson's rivals and other electrical companies in a parlous state, it started the 1930s in a strong enough position to establish factories in India and Australia, as well as make various takeover bids, which continued throughout the decade.

Events of 1939 brought numerous government contracts for the supply of all manner of electrical equipment and for the manufacture of light-calibre weapons ammunition. One wartime acquisition was the Young Accumulator Company, which also owned the controlling interest in the Associated Electric Vehicle Manufacturers Ltd that had been formed in 1936 and comprised AE Morrison & Sons, Leicester, Electricars of Birmingham and the Hants Electric Chassis Co – all users of Young's batteries.

Under its new ownership the conglomerate was renamed Morrison-Electricar but production of the current range of battery-electrics that were capable of coping with payloads of up to 2 tons or more continued until the after the war, when the line-up was reduced to just a 1-tonner.

A joint venture in 1946 between Austin Motor Company and Crompton Parkinson brought about the foundation of Austin Crompton Parkinson Electric Vehicles Ltd. Under this arrangement Austin acquired 50 per cent of ME shares, and henceforth vehicles would be marketed as Morrison-Electricar in the UK and Austin-Electricar abroad.

The existing South Wigston factory on the outskirts of Leicester was supplemented by a new one in Birmingham to cope with a new range that would encompass vehicles of up to 3-ton capacity, which became available during 1948. Despite the limitations imposed by battery capacity and recharging times they found a ready market at home and abroad, so the 1950s were good years; and when milk float manufacturer TH Lewis ceased to manufacture its Electruk in 1960, Morrison-Electricar took over the business.

In the mid-'60s the manufacturing base was transferred to a purpose-built factory at Tredegar in South Wales. Then in 1968, upon the merger of BMC and Leyland, the latter inherited Austin's 50 per cent share and the firm's name was changed to Compton Leyland Electricars Ltd.

Early in 1972 the company exhibited a futuristic Michelotti-styled electric microcar at the Geneva motor show. It was based on a shortened Mini but 40 years ago, in spite of the Arab oil crisis, it was destined to go nowhere. In the same year, the business was absorbed into the vast Hawker Siddeley empire when Crompton, which had been taken over four years earlier, bought back from Leyland the half share it had relinquished to Austin just after the war. Within just a few years the Hawker Siddeley group was broken up, and by the early 1980s what remained of Crompton Electricars was acquired by M&M Electric Vehicles, which is still in business at Atherstone in Warwickshire.

A little shapelier than the Douglas 20cwt electric van, if that is an apt word in this case. Larger too, with both body and wheelbase nearly 6in longer. It also featured a removable front panel for maintenance but doors were an optional extra. Bodywork was steel (rather than the Douglas' laminate) and, ready to go complete with batteries, this Morrison tipped the scales at just about 2 tons.

MORRISON-ELECTRICARS

20-CWT VAN

Mobile Confectionery Shop

"This mobile confectionery shop will meet the varied needs of the confectionery trade and maintain earning capacity throughout the year," read this brochure printed in September 1949. Unfortunate timing, as sweet rationing had just been reintroduced after being experimentally relaxed earlier in the year, and would not finally be abandoned until 1953. The jolly little vehicle was also innocently said to, "Combine gay attractiveness with quality," a turn of phrase that could well have people popping their heads over the fence in the stifling PC of the twenty-first century – especially in view of the brochure's colour scheme.

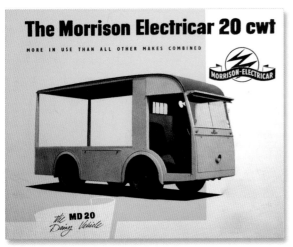

The SD20 (short deck) and MD20 (medium deck) of 1954 had a redesigned chassis with 82in wheelbase. Turning circle was 5ft less than the old 20cwt van and the brakes were now Girling hydraulic. It could be had with either standard or high-speed axles, the latter increasing maximum speed from about 16 to 20mph unladen.

At 15ft the special aluminium-panelled confectionery body by Transport Electrics of Bristol was a good deal larger than the regular 20cwt chassis upon which it was based.

The large capacity battery operated refrigerated conservator is flanked by a wash basin which has a hot water supply.

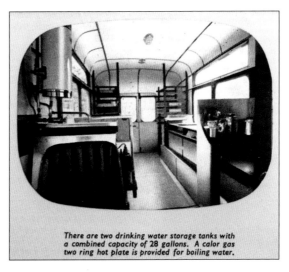

There are two drinking water storage tanks with a combined capacity of 28 gallons. A calor gas two ring hot plate is provided for boiling water.

The interior is very roomy and conveniently arranged for customer entry. Large storage racks and cabinets are provided.

10 CWT. VAN

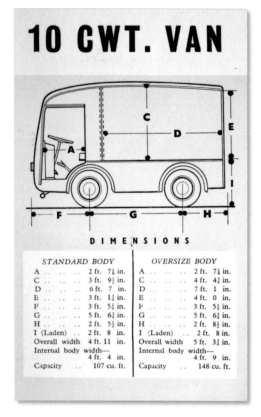

DIMENSIONS

	STANDARD BODY	OVERSIZE BODY
A	2 ft. 7¼ in.	2 ft. 7¼ in.
C	3 ft. 9½ in.	4 ft. 4¾ in.
D	6 ft. 7 in.	7 ft. 1 in.
E	3 ft. 1¼ in.	4 ft. 0 in.
F	3 ft. 5¼ in.	3 ft. 5½ in.
G	5 ft. 6½ in.	5 ft. 6½ in.
H	2 ft. 5½ in.	2 ft. 8½ in.
I (Laden)	2 ft. 8 in.	2 ft. 8 in.
Overall width	4 ft. 11 in.	5 ft. 3¾ in.
Internal body width—	4 ft. 4 in.	4 ft. 9 in.
Capacity	107 cu. ft.	148 cu. ft.

Like all Morrisons the 10cwt had three forward speeds and reverse operated by way of solenoid contactors, and a foot switch with hand control for reverse. Weighing in at just under 30cwt it would run for about 50 miles between charges if fitted with the largest (240Ah) capacity battery of the two available for this model. Empty, it would do 18mph but loaded only 16mph. In common with other Morrisons, doors cost you extra.

General Purpose Delivery Vehicle

THE MORRISON-ELECTRICAR | 10 CWT. VAN

MORRISON ELECTRICAR

Morrisons were also built for specialised tasks, such as an ambulance and this tower wagon for London street-light maintenance.

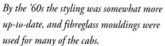

By the '60s the styling was somewhat more up-to-date, and fibreglass mouldings were used for many of the cabs.

RELIANT

Reliant's three-wheeler commercials carried on almost unchanged from the pre-war versions, as this 1947 sales leaflet shows.

Raleigh was one of the oldest established and most successful bicycle companies to expand into the manufacture of motorcycles and cars, but unlike its peers the firm left it until after the First World War to do so. During the 1920s it produced a range of unremarkable but workmanlike two-wheelers and then, in 1930, acquired the rights from Ivy motorcycles for a little three-wheeler delivery machine named the Karryall.

Looking for all the world like the front of a motorcycle, including the petrol tank, with a rudimentary van

body perched on the back, it was renamed the Raleigh LDV (light delivery) and the firm proceeded to make refinements, such as doing away with the handlebars in favour of a steering wheel.

Next came another three-wheeler – an extraordinary device called the Safety Seven and marketed as a sports tourer, but resembling a small car shorn of its front axle, wheels and wings, with a single wheel propping it up in lieu of replacements. It would have been all but inexplicable for either of Raleigh's vehicles to find buyers were it not for the lower rate of road tax enjoyed by three-wheelers, which gave their owners the chance to do the chancellor out of a few quid – but what a price to pay!

There was not a complete lack of sales but, due to concern that the firm was straying in ill-advised directions from the ethos that had created one of the world's largest bicycle manufacturers, Raleigh's management was prompted to curtail the company's motor vehicle endeavours and return to its roots.

Undismayed, and soon to be out of a job anyway, the head designer of the motor department, Tom Williams, decided to further the light van venture and began work on improved designs in the garden shed of his home at Tamworth, Staffordshire. Aided by a handful of ex-Raleigh employees, a prototype was put together over the winter of 1934. After some alterations, the first production Reliants – as Williams christened them – started to leave the newly-rented factory premises at nearby Two Gates in the summer of 1935.

Although still fairly motorcycle-like, with the driver (or perhaps one should say rider) sitting astride a single-cylinder sidevalve JAP engine with kick start and a chain-driven rear axle, they were capable of carrying 7cwt and sold in reasonable numbers. The following year a much-improved 10cwt model had been developed and was on the market with water-cooled JAP vee-twin, shaft drive and an optional electric starter, as well as a conventional driving position to the right of the engine; this model sold even better.

By 1938 the Reliant van's capacity had been upped to either 8cwt or 12cwt, and what would be a short-lived arrangement had been made with Austin for supplies of its Seven engine/gearbox for power – despite being informed that the unit would soon be discontinued.

THE FOLLOWING ARE FEATURES COMMON TO ALL "RELIANT" VEHICLES

ENGINE—Four-cylinder water-cooled; 56 m.m. bore; 76 m.m. stroke; 747.5 c.c. capacity. Crankshaft (mounted on three bearings), nickel chrome steel; connecting rods, nickel alloy steel; camshaft, case hardened steel. Thermo syphon cooling with film radiator (Serck) and fan.

FUEL—3½-gallon Tank, fuel supplied to engine by A.C. petrol pump. Solex carburettor.

CLUTCH—Borg and Beck.

GEARBOX—Three-speed and reverse.

TRANSMISSION—Hardy Spicer prop. shaft.

BRAKES—Girling on all wheels — interconnected—hand and foot operated.

AXLE—Spiral bevel rear axle—differential—large bearings and shafts.

STEERING—Burman Douglas.

TYRES and WHEELS—4.00 x 18, on 8 cwt. model; 5.00 x 16 on 12 cwt. model.

BODY—Large capacity bodies — steel panels on ash frame.

FRAME—Heavy channel section with tubular and channel cross-members.

SPRINGS—Long semi-elliptic underslung rear springs. Front suspension by massive coil spring.

ELECTRICAL EQUIPMENT—Horn, starter, screen wiper, four lamps—with dip beam.

GENERAL EQUIPMENT—Tools, spare wheel, speedo, jack, hand-starter.

We reserve the right to alter specification and prices without notice.

Insurance, from £4/1/- per annum third party
£8/1/6 ,, comprehensive

The Reliant Eng. Co. (Tamworth) Ltd., Watling Street, TWO GATES TAMWORTH, Staffs.
Telephone : TAMWORTH 336. Telegrams : RELIANT, TAMWORTH 336

As well as the 8cwt there was the larger 12cwt model. A longer load space meant that capacity was up to 104 cubic feet and, sensibly, it was fitted with fatter 5.00x16 tyres whilst the 8cwt rode on skinny 4.00x18s. The thought of such a vehicle taking to the roads fully-laden gives one food for thought; maybe the manufacturer was already having doubts when it wrote in sales material, "If anything, the vehicle is steadier on the road (which may be very difficult to accept by those who have experience of the 8cwt model)." For whatever reason, however, it was quietly dropped before too long.

Undeterred, Reliant set about the manufacture of its own version, and on the eve of the war had one on test.

I'm sure the Reliant Engineering Company (Tamworth) Ltd would have been happy to make as many three-wheeled commercials for the armed forces as it was able, but it should come as no surprise that the firm was not asked to do so; instead it was more usefully employed in the manufacture of a diverse range of products for the duration, from Norton motorcycle frames to components for Power Jets.

Post-war production commenced pretty much as it had left off, and by 1947 both 6cwt and 8cwt in van or pick-up form were once again available; production capacity was boosted by the erection of a new body shop on the Two Gates site that Reliant now owned. The company's engineering facilities were soon to be improved, too, when Morson Engineering of Coventry was purchased and its machinery installed, enabling gearboxes to be made in-house.

For the next few years sales were buoyant, despite the 1948 list price of Reliant's van being just £10 less than a Morris 5cwt, for example. Little need was felt to deviate from the staple product, apart from minor improvements and the introduction of the Regent and Prince Regent as time went on.

In 1952, contrary to the established practice of using a car as a base for a small commercial, Reliant launched a private car version of its Regent van. Primarily aimed at the family sidecar man who wanted to move onto a car, but at a lesser expense, it was a four-seater tourer. And with a coronation in the offing the royal connotation was continued, so the new model was named the Regal.

From then on, car and van production increasingly converged until in 1956 the last Regent van left the factory, and the Regal MkIII was announced along with a 5cwt van version. For some time Reliant had been experimenting with fibreglass panels, and the MkIII had a wooden-framed fibreglass body – a method of construction that was used until the Regal MkVI of 1961. The following year the new 3/25 (Regal MkVII) car and 5cwt van were launched with a restyled fibreglass body comprising a bonded inner and outer shell, as well as Reliant's own 600cc overhead-valve aluminium engine.

Defying logic (mine at any rate), the Regal lasted until 1968 – plus a further five years more as the 3/30, with an extra 100cc added to its engine capacity. Although 1973 saw the last of the Supervans (as they were now named) the cars went on as Robins, then Rialtos, and back to Robins again until 2001, when the rights to their manufacture were sold to B&N Plastics.

Starting in 1958 with an arrangement for the manufacture of vans with Autocars of Israel, Reliant went on to be involved in the manufacture of numerous fibre-

Reliant had started to fit Austin's 747cc sidevalve engine to its three-wheelers during 1938. So when the Austin Seven was discontinued a year later, Reliant set about manufacturing a virtual carbon copy – one must presume with the nod from Longbridge. By this time Reliant had made some improvements to the lubrication system and was also making its own gearboxes – facilitated by their acquisition of a Midlands gear-cutting company.

glass-bodied four-wheeled cars. These included the Sabre sports car (also with Autocars) that led to the entirely UK-made and marketed Sabre Six, from which was evolved the Scimitar and then the GTE that ran from 1968 until 1986; all were Ford engined. Along the way Reliant also made some less-fondly remembered vehicles such as the little Kitten saloon and the Scimitar SS1, with its German-made chassis, which took the place of the GTE.

For most of the '60s and '70s the Hodge group of companies was the majority shareholder, and in 1969 Bond was bought (out of which came the ridiculous Bug). Then, in the same year as part of a shakeup, it – and another member of the group, Hodgkinson Bennis – emerged as the Reliant Motor Group.

In 1973 the Standard Chartered bank bought the entire Hodge empire, and in 1977 disposed of its controlling Reliant shares to JF Nash Securities. Things really started to go downhill in the later 1980s, and the firm emerged from a 1990 spell in receivership owned by Beans Industries. Another bout followed in '94, with Avonex taking up the baton for a year until the hammer fell once again and, with just a skeleton staff left, ex-Jaguar executive Jonathan Heynes thought he could wave a magic wand. A move was made from the Two Gates Tamworth factory to a brand-new plant at Burntwood early in 1999, after which Heynes upped and left; production there ceased in 2000. Another move to Cannock was made, but the end of the road had come for Reliant as a car producer.

"RELIANT" 4-CYLINDER ENGINE
with 3 Bearing Crankshaft, 3 Speed and Reverse Gearbox, Borg and Beck Clutch Solex Carburetter. A.C. Petrol Pump, Lucas Electrical Equipment.

CHASSIS
Note the Burman Douglas Steering fitted to the very neat chassis layout—defining compactness and strength.

"REGENT" 10-cwt. Model
PRICE: VAN or TRUCK
£295
ex works
Plus £82 13 11 Purchase Tax
ANNUAL TAX **£10**

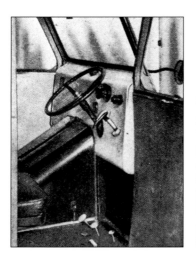

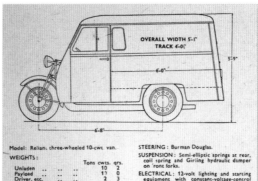

OVERALL WIDTH 5'-1" TRACK 4'-0"

Model: Reliant three-wheeled 10-cwt. van.
WEIGHTS:

	Tons	cwts.	qrs.
Unladen	10	2	
Payload	11	0	
Driver, etc.	2	3	
	1	3	1

ENGINE: Reliant four-cylindered side-valve petrol engine; bore 56 mm.; stroke 76 mm.; swept volume 747 c.c.; maximum output 14 b.h.p. at 3,500 r.p.m.; R.A.C. rating 7.5 h.p.; maximum torque 28.5 lb.-ft. at 2,000 r.p.m.

TRANSMISSION: Through Borg and Beck single-dry-plate clutch to three-speed gearbox, thence by Hardy Spicer open propeller shaft to spiral-bevel drive of the semi-floating rear axle.

GEAR RATIOS: 3.65, 1.77 and 1 to 1 forward; reverse 4.77 to 1; back-axle ratio 6.5 to 1.

BRAKES: Pedal connected to Girling wedge-operated units at all wheels; hand brake interconnected with foot brake; diameter of drums, front 7 ins., rear 9 ins.; width of shoes 1¼ ins.; frictional area 52 sq. ins. per ton gross weight as tested.

FRAME: Channel-section side members with tubular and channel-section cross-members, all bolted in position.

STEERING: Burman Douglas.
SUSPENSION: Semi-elliptic springs at rear, coil spring and Girling hydraulic damper on 'ront forks.
ELECTRICAL: 12-volt lighting and starting equipment with constant-voltage-control dynamo. Battery capacity 58 amp.-hrs. at 10-hr. rating.
FUEL CONSUMPTION: (a) Straight running 38.1 m.p.g. at 28 m.p.h. average speed; (b) one stop per mile 35.5 m.p.g.; (c) four stops per mile 26.7 m.p.g.; that is, 44.9 gross ton-m.p.g. as tested (a), 41.8 gross ton-m.p.g. (b) and 31.4 gross ton-m.p.g. (c), giving a time-load-mileage factor of 1,254.
TANK CAPACITY: 3½ gallons, range 90-130 miles according to service.
ACCELERATION: 0-20 m.p.h. through gears, 9.3 secs.; 0-30 m.p.h., 18.9 secs.; top-gear acceleration, 10-20 m.p.h., 11.4 secs.; 10-30 m.p.h., 24.4 secs.
BRAKING: From 20 m.p.h., 28.5 ft. (15.1 ft. per sec. per sec.); from 30 m.p.h., 61 ft. (15.8 ft. per sec per sec.).
WEIGHT RATIOS: 0.603 b.h.p. per cwt. gross weight as tested. Payload 43 per cent. of gross load.
TURNING CIRCLE: Right lock 26 ft., Left lock 31 ft.
MAKER: The Reliant Engineering Co. (Tamworth), Ltd., Tamworth, Staffs.

The Regent's slightly more modern lines were set off by 16in pressed-steel Easiclean wheels and chromium hubcaps (often referred to as nave plates in those days). When The Commercial Motor *magazine tested a Regent in 1952 it was impressed by the 0-30mph time of 19 seconds and fuel consumption of slightly more than 26mpg during a standard test of a fully-laden delivery run with four stops per mile. To come to a halt from 30mph required 61ft. All in all, the magazine found little fault and closed with the comment that it could offer no suggestions for improving the Regent.*

There had been criticism of visibility whilst manoeuvring, so both the traditional 6cwt and new Regent were endowed with extra side windows. During 1952 the small Reliant could be had with 16in Easiclean wheels (£7 or so) and in September of the same year an upgraded 6cwt with the styling of the Regent, which was rather charmingly named the Prince Regent.

The last of the girder-fork Reliants had been made in 1956, and by the end of 1958 the firm offered not only the new Reliant 5cwt van but a four-wheeler too – the Regent Four.

Three wheels aside, the looks of the 5cwt were, by 1958 standards, fairly up-to-the-minute. For small manufacturers like Reliant – which could ill afford the cost of tooling for pressed-steel body panels – the relatively new medium of fibreglass provided the perfect solution, and the firm had begun to use it for all bodywork in 1956.

The van that never was! Although this home-market brochure listed the Regent Four at a basic price of £435 it was, so far as I am aware, never released on the English market. The reference to it being, "Produced in response to an overseas demand," referred to Autocars of Israel, for which the little creature was made. Regent Fours were shipped in semi-kit form and assembled at Autocars' Haifa plant. No mention of it in this brochure but there was a pick-up version too. The, "Well known 36bhp engine," that powered it was none other than Ford's trusty 1172cc sidevalve.

Reliant appeared to have a compulsion to present its wares as new when very often they weren't – or not to any appreciable extent. This late-1961 brochure was the last hurrah for the sidevalve-engined cars, and very little had changed over the last few years except for some of the fibreglass mouldings – to wit the doors and lower body front and rear, which were redesigned to incorporate bumpers. The vehicles were the last Reliants to have wooden floors and wooden framing incorporated in the body.

No big changes to the chassis and running gear, unless you count a three-spoke wheel instead of the two-spoke version fitted previously or that the tyre/wheel size had gone down from 4.50x14 to 5.20x13in; until then the latter had been for export only.

The bonded two-piece fibreglass mouldings used for doors gave rigidity – fine at the rear but those at the front, combined with the moulded dashboard, made for a spartan interior. A passenger seat was an extra.

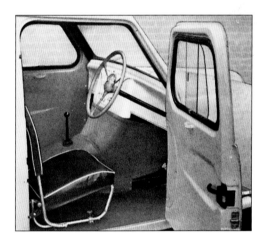

A charming scene, but with an absolutely flat floor and no passenger seat I can just picture our friend Mr Baylis making an emergency stop and watching as a cascade of pork chops ends up in the nearside footwell.

No innovations chassis-wise but a brand-new, short-stroke, overhead-valve, 600cc engine. Although the bore was the same as the old engine it was much more than a rehash and had an aluminium cylinder block with wet liners. For years the Reliant owner had to be content with 17.5bhp at 4000rpm, so the prospect of 25 horses at 5250rpm was an appealing one – especially if one of your friends, enemies or business rivals had one of the not-altogether-dissimilar Bond 250Gs to mount his challenge.

This really was a new model – the 3/25. Still with a diminutive bonnet, however, which was used for checking the fluids and one or two other tasks. To carry out more serious work the centre console would have to be removed, and if the engine and gearbox had to come out it was dropped onto the floor.

Externally, internally and mechanically Reliant's three-wheeler van, as well as its passenger car sibling, had very much come of age. The bonded fibreglass mouldings that made up the bodyshell included the floors, and the complete structure was bolted to the chassis. Winding windows and opening quarterlights were a luxurious touch but if you wanted a passenger seat, heater and demister – or even a spare wheel – any or all were extras.

The well proved 600 c.c., o.h.v. lightweight engine

"Big-load capacity, outstanding fuel economy," boasted the brochure. Translated into numbers this meant 50 cubic feet of space behind the seats and up to 65mpg.

STANDARD

Prior to the Second World War – when it was called upon to manufacture light utility trucks for the armed forces – the Standard Motor Company had, with a single exception, left the manufacture of commercial vehicles to others during its all-but-40 years of existence that had begun in 1903.

It was then that Reginald Maudslay, great grandson of the renowned engineer Henry (whose achievements included the invention of the micrometer and the screw-cutting lathe) had set up in business at small premises in Coventry. Starting with a humble single-cylinder car, the company soon progressed to medium or large six-cylinders, which remained a speciality for a while before settling on smaller fours a couple of years before the First War.

Smallest of these was the 9.5hp (1087cc) Model S, which was also available as a light commercial with the choice of a High Van or Canvas Top. Shortly after hostilities commenced, the company ran an ad in *The Autocar* magazine suggesting you would need one of its light vans if your horses were commandeered.

Having outgrown more than one building and relocated into the large canal-side Cunard Works in 1913, the volume of government contracts soon led to the opening of yet another plant at Canley, to the south west of Coventry, in 1916. This would eventually become Standard's main factory and headquarters, although hundreds of aircraft were built there during the remaining years of the war.

The post-war boom saw Standard rivalling Austin's market share, and over 10,000 of its middle-range saloons and tourers were sold during 1924; but it was too good to last, and the late '20s saw sales in decline.

Salvation came in the form of Captain John Black, who became joint managing director in 1929, having left the same position at Hillman when it was taken over by Rootes. Under his guidance the company rode out the depression and entered the '30s with a concise and reasonably-priced range of a 9hp four-cylinder and 16hp or 20hp sixes. He also entered into agreements for the supply of Standard running chassis to

The **STANDARD** *12 cwt. Delivery Van*

THE new Standard Delivery Van is fitted with the same chassis and powered by the same engine as the famous Vanguard saloon. With a payload capacity of 12 cwt., the clean, sweeping lines of the Standard Delivery Van give it an unusually attractive appearance, while its many refinements such as the fine quality upholstery, convenient grouping of controls, anti-draught ventilation and the adjustable bucket type driver's seat add comfort to sturdy utility.

Hard on the heels of Standard's 1948 Vanguard saloon, patriotically named after what would would be the last of the British Navy's battleships that had been launched four years earlier, came a van version built on the same 7ft 10in wheelbase chassis as the car. Most went for export at first but by 1950 it became easier to for home-market customers to acquire one. Early examples such as this had a plain bonnet but from the autumn of 1950 there was a chrome motif on the front and parking lights below the headlights.

In common with the majority of light commercials of the period only a driver's seat was provided, but the Standard 12cwt came with a steel parcel platform alongside it. If you needed a passenger seat it would cost you extra; obviously, more wanted one than not, and for 1950 the van was catalogued to have two seats as standard. The ad men appear to have got themselves in a muddle with its carrying capacity, however, and the initial brochure gave the cubic capacity as 85 cubic feet (without utilising the parcel shelf), whilst the 1950 publication suggested 105 cubic feet or 125 with passenger seat removed. All internal measurements being identical, my maths tells me that the second calculation was nearer the mark.

was there for all to see but the English Government was in denial and the country was getting back on its feet, so there seemed little reason to take too much notice. With production now centred at Canley an entirely new range was launched in 1936; and by the time Germany's invasion of Poland brought an end to the uneasy peace, the so-called Flying Standards were made in varying sizes from the Eight to Twenty, and even a none-too-successful V8 Twenty.

Light Utility Trucks, or "Tillies", were in immediate demand and to construct theirs, Standard first used the independent-front-suspension Twelve as a base and later the longer-wheelbase (9ft) beam-axle Fourteen chassis fitted with 1607cc Twelve motors. A large number of militarised Twelve saloons were also produced, as well as a fairly ineffective little armoured car named the Beaverette, but it was the company's contribution to the nation's aircraft production that in all probability had the most far-reaching effects on the war's outcome. Standard is officially credited with the manufacture of 1066 examples of what was arguably Britain's most effective warplane, the Mosquito, as

The ritzy steering wheel with large chromium horn ring, along with right-hand column change (it changed to the left towards the end of 1949) that controlled the three-speed synchromesh gearbox were the same as the Vanguard saloon's.

other manufacturers or coachbuilders – most famously with William Lyons, who used them to create his SS cars that by the end of the decade led to Jaguar.

From the mid-1930s the likelihood of another war

well as 750 Airspeed Oxford trainers. In addition a large number of Bristol Beaufighter fuselages and thousands of radial engines were turned out.

John Black had been made Sir John in 1943 for his work as chairman of the Aero Engine Committee, and as the war was drawing to a close he added what remained of the Triumph Motor Company to his own. It had lain moribund after passing through the hands of the official receiver in 1939, and then its factory and entire contents had been destroyed during the Coventry blitz – so he didn't get much. But all he wanted was the name, which cost him next to nothing after the old site was sold on, because any future Triumphs would be made at Canley.

The first cars to go on sale post-war were the old Flying Eight and the Twelve, the former now with a four-speed gearbox. The first new models were Triumphs – the 1800 Roadster and saloon – which, due to pertaining exigencies had tubular chassis and aluminium bodies, the latter being easier to obtain than sheet steel at the time.

Had Black not become involved with Harry Ferguson (which admittedly ended in a lucrative contract to build his tractors), the design and development of Standard's Vanguard would likely have been completed earlier, but it was not until 1948 that it went on the market to replace the Eights and Twelves in accord with a one-model policy.

This process of rationalisation soon applied to all Standard-Triumph's products, and the 2088cc four-cylinder engine that had been designed for the Vanguard – but which had first been fitted to Ferguson tractors – ended up in Triumph's Roadster and what now became the 2000 saloon, replacing the pre-war Standard Fourteen engine. The tubular chassis, too, would shortly be replaced by lengthened versions of the pressed-steel Vanguard's, complete with its suspension.

To cater for a reawakening light commercial market the Vanguard was the obvious choice, even though both Triumphs had a longer wheelbase, and it came to fruition with 12cwt delivery vans and pick-ups. Although not strictly a commercial, there was also an estate car.

Energies were then turned to the development of a small Standard in place of the recently-discontinued pre-war models and a sports car for the Triumph brand – one of the main reasons for Black's acquisition of the name, as he'd promised himself he would one day produce such a machine ever since his offer to buy SS Cars had been turned down by William Lyons in the '30s.

In the latter part of 1953 the first of what would be a long line of Triumph sports cars, the TR2, went into

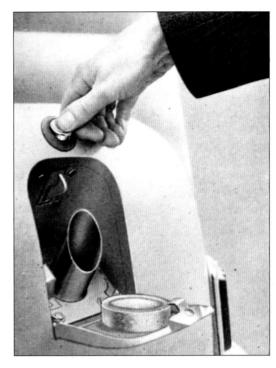

The press button that operated the fuel filler cap could be locked with a key that was provided.

production and a completely new Standard Eight was announced. By the following summer the Ten was in production, with a van and pick-up version soon to come. But the man who had made Standard what it now was and rescued Triumph from the abyss was gone. Injuries sustained in a car accident gave the rest of the board, who were increasingly at odds with his autocratic behaviour, the chance to force Black into retirement at the beginning of January.

Standard-Triumph didn't roll over and die, however, and although the ageing Renown would be discontinued at the end of the year the new TR would go from strength to strength, while the Vanguard would potter along aided by occasional updates.

In 1958 the forward-control Atlas commercials were introduced. As it was an entirely new design it could have been equipped with any of the company's existing engines, but the chosen unit was too small, and then delayed for more than a year before the situation was remedied.

A replacement for the Standard Eight and Ten saloons was in the pipeline too, but when it came to naming – as a result of the sports cars that Black had known would be good for the marque's image – Triumph was considered to be the more marketable brand, and the new model ended up as the Herald.

A year after its introduction, in 1959, Standard-Triumph was bought by Leyland Motors; but Standard light commercials continued to be made and a none-too-successful van version of the Herald was marketed from 1962 until '65. In 1968 Leyland

In addition to the van Standard offered a pick-up, but here is the special version with rather more shapely hind quarters specially for the antipodean market – which continued to be catered for with later Vanguard utes through the '50s.

became the British Leyland Motor Corporation and in 1970 the name Standard was dropped, whilst the Triumph brand continued through the ramifications that led the main players of the British motor industry through the melting pot to absorption and virtual extinction.

By 1994 BMW had become the owner of the Standard and Triumph names upon its purchase of

the Rover Group, but relinquished the Standard name to British Motor Heritage when it was bought by its management.

A legacy of Sir John Black's glory days lasted on in the form of Standard Motor Products of India, however. Set up in the late 1940s, it had disassociated itself from British Leyland around 1970 and continued to make cars and light commercials until 1988.

The STANDARD Pick-Up Utility

The large amount of space available in the Standard Pick-up Utility for both goods and passengers will be seen in the above illustration.

Right: Passengers can easily gain access to the seats in the rear by means of the step on the bumper.

THE Standard Pick-up Utility has the same engine and chassis as the famous Standard Vanguard saloon and it has been designed as a general utility vehicle for town, city or farm use.

Bench seats are provided in the rear for passengers, while high ground clearance, sturdy suspension and powerful engine make it the ideal vehicle for carrying out a variety of tasks.

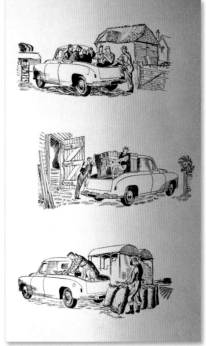

I wonder: could these endearing little sketches truly be said to epitomise Australian farm life circa 1950?

SPECIFICATION

BODY FEATURES

Pick up utility truck body with 2 passenger door cab. Steel panelled, rust proofed. Vee front screen and windows fitted with Triplex toughened glass. Door handles flush fitting, pull-out type, easy-close doors. Low level flat floor. Fine quality upholstery. **Effective body dimensions.** Length 58" (147 cm.). Width of floor 42" (107 cm.). Height of floor above ground 21" (53 cm.). **Carrying capacity :** 9 persons (3 in Cab) or 3 persons in Cab and 8 cwt. (400 kgs.) of goods.

Equipment includes: Instruments grouped in front of driver on fascia panel include: speedometer with trip, electric clock, fuel, water temperature and oil pressure gauges. Concealed lighting, ignition warning light, twin windscreen wipers. Anti-draught ventilation, hinged deflector lights in front doors. Window winders to both doors. Locks to both doors. An additional lock is provided for the fuel filler orifice. One piece bonnet arranged with lock-release control operated from inside body, to prevent the bonnet being opened when doors are locked. Self-cancelling trafficators controlled from centre of steering wheel. Ample protection provided by substantial chromium plated bumpers at front and rear. Large diameter horn operating ring concentric with steering wheel. Sun visors, flush fitting when not in use.

Extra Equipment. Accommodation provided for fitting heater and de-mister with controls, also car radio, controls and aerial.

GENERAL DIMENSIONS AND PERFORMANCE

Length 13' 8" (417 cm.). Width 5' 9" (175 cm.). Height (laden) 5' 4" (163 cm.). Wheelbase 7' 10" (239 cm.). Track (front) 4' 3" (130 cm.). Track (rear) 4' 6" (137 cm.). Tyre Size 6.00—16". Ground clearance—rear axle (laden) 8" (21 cm.). Turning circle 35 ft. (11 metres). Weight (excluding extra equipment): Dry, 22 cwt. (1,170 kg.); complete with fuel, tools, oil and water, 23½ cwt. (1,250 kg.). Acceleration (2 up) 10-30 m.p.h. (16-48 km.) 11 secs. fully laden 14 seconds. Maximum climbable gradient (3 up), no payload, 1 in 2½. Maximum climbable gradient fully laden 1 in 3. Petrol consumption 22/24 m.p.g.

ENGINE AND CHASSIS DETAILS

Four cylinders. 85 mm. bore × 92 mm. stroke. Capacity 2088 c.c. Compression ratio 6.7. Centrifugally chill cast re-placeable cylinder sleeves, fitted in direct contact with cooling water. Aluminium alloy split skirt pistons. 60 ton steel connecting rods. Precision bearings. Three bearing counter-balanced crankshaft. Overhead valves push rod operation. Patented design ensuring silence. Thermostatically controlled cooling system. A.C. mechanically operated fuel pump. Solex down-draught carburettor. Combined air cleaner and silencer. "Buoyant Power" flexible mounting for engine and gearbox unit. **Transmission:** Borg and Beck 9" diameter dry plate clutch. Light action pedal with balanced control linkage. **Gearbox:** Three forward ratios and reverse. Remote control gear change on steering column. Silent helical gears with positive synchromesh on all forward gears. Drive by hypoid bevel gears. **Suspension:** Low periodicity, coil springs for independent suspension at front, long semi-elliptic rear springs. Controlled by hydraulic dampers. Anti-roll bar at rear. **Brakes:** Lockheed hydraulic. **Frame:** Exceptionally rigid, formed by opposed channel steel pressings welded together, producing tubular side members of rectangular form and boxed cross-members, the whole braced by a cruciform member. Completely rust-proofed. **Steering:** Cam and roller type. Three spoke 17" diameter wheel, spring type arranged to provide maximum vision of instruments. **Electrical Equipment:** 12 volt, 51 amp./hr. battery under bonnet. Head lamps, tail lamps, and stop light. Concealed wind-tone horns.

The STANDARD Pick-Up Truck

Some users had found the original pick-up's bed too short, so although the wheelbase remained 7ft 10in the rear of the 1952 model's body was given considerably more overhang, which allowed a generous load length of 5ft 8in with the tailgate up.

The practical pick-up type truck body, high ground clearance, sturdy suspension and powerful engine combine to make the Standard 12 cwt. Pick-Up Truck an ideal vehicle for carrying out a variety of tasks. It has the same engine and chassis as the famous Vanguard Saloon. Stout lashing hooks and sockets for hood poles are provided and there is a built-in bracket at the rear to take a towing attachment.

The rear panel of the Standard Pick-Up Truck is supported in the loading position by chains. The number plate being hinged remains visible when the tail board is in the lowered position. The petrol filler cap is secured by a lock. The extra wide rear window and additional corner windows ensure all round vision from the driver's cab. The low level flat floor of the 1953 model has been lengthened by ten inches to give additional space for pay load.

The Standard Vanguard range had a frontal facelift for 1952 that gave it a chunky die-cast plated grille and an enlarged bonnet motif that one could almost say was a mascot. Under the skin it was all but unchanged, with the four-cylinder 2088cc overhead-valve engine still catalogued to put out at 68bhp at 4200rpm despite a mild increase in its compression ratio from 6.7:1 to 7:1. Petrol consumption, the manufacturer told the prospective purchaser, could be expected to be between 22 and 24mpg, and the top speed, "Over 70."

THE STANDARD 12 CWT DELIVERY VAN & PICK-UP TRUCK

the 12 cwt. Delivery Van

The clean, handsome lines of the Standard Delivery Van will be a worthy salesman for your business, promoting goodwill and adding prestige to your name. Fitted with the same powerful 2 litre engine as the famous Standard Vanguard saloon, the 12 cwt. Delivery Van can tackle every kind of gradient smoothly and easily and will maintain a high performance under a variety of conditions. Its interior is extremely roomy, with a cubic capacity of 105 ft. (3 cu. metres). With the passenger seat removed a total capacity of 125 cu. ft. (3.5 cu. metres) is available. The driver's compartment is arranged with saloon car comfort with adjustable bucket-type seats. (A bench type seat can be fitted as an extra if required.)

The 1954 commercial motor show had the diesel-engined version of the Phase II Vanguard commercials on display. A completely different, longer-stroke design from the petrol engine, it had a capacity of 2092cc and was Britain's first production diesel-engined car. Standard also took the opportunity to unveil its Ten-based vans and pick-ups.

PICK-UP TRUCK

BREAKDOWN TRUCK

FASHION HOUSE VAN

DROPSIDE TRUCK

NO FINER ASSET TO ANY BUSINESS

For the person who needed something that would cope with a lot more weight than the 6cwt, Standard offered this in 1958 to fill the void left when the original Vanguard-based vans and pick-ups were discontinued. Based on the current Vanguard/Ensign it could be ordered with either the old, but still current, 85mm x 92mm 2088cc (its compression ratio now a heady 7.7:1 but still 68bhp) Vanguard engine or the smaller 76mm-bore 1670cc Ensign version. Gearbox was a four-on-the-floor with synchro on all but bottom, but you could specify a three-speed to go with the larger engine. A bench seat – they called it a divan – was standard and so was the chromium front bumper, but you'd have to find your own for the rear if you wanted one once you'd had the body made. Wheels, with complementary chromium hubcaps, were 16in and the tyres 6.00s.

The compact 948 c.c. O.H.V. power unit of the Standard 6 cwt. Van and Pick-up which develops 33 b.h.p. at 4,500 r.p.m. All the main components are readily accessible and include Solex carburettor, Lucas ventilated type dynamo, thermostatically controlled cooling with pump circulation and four-bladed fan. Air cleaner and silencer. Mechanical and suction controlled advance and retard mechanism, mechanical petrol pump, four speed gearbox with synchromesh on 2nd, 3rd and top gears.

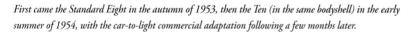

First came the Standard Eight in the autumn of 1953, then the Ten (in the same bodyshell) in the early summer of 1954, with the car-to-light commercial adaptation following a few months later.

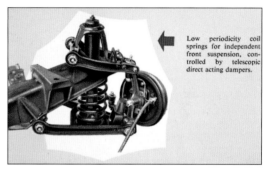

Low periodicity coil springs for independent front suspension, controlled by telescopic direct acting dampers.

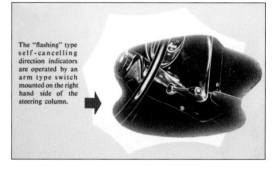

The "flashing" type self-cancelling direction indicators are operated by an arm type switch mounted on the right hand side of the steering column.

Just over 5ft clear behind the cab or 6½ft with the tailgate down gave the pick-up a useful load area. Tyres were chunky 5.90s on 13in rims. The manufacturer was happy to suggest 65mph as a reasonable top speed but, as the engine was turning over at 4650rpm and it'd happily go past 5000, this model would do a bit more. When you needed to stop there were Girling hydraulic drum brakes with twin-leading-shoe fronts. The makers also quoted 30-to-40mpg and the higher figure was readily obtainable – or even exceeded – providing you went easy with your right foot.

Standard Tens were amazingly capable little cars and, although some of their contemporaries such as Morris 1000s and Austin A35s are better remembered, I'll go out on a limb and say that in many respects the Ten was the better vehicle – and that goes for the light commercial as well. Fully loaded, with goods stuffed into the space for the passenger seat, the van would accommodate 88 cubic feet, but if you had that spare seat and a passenger there was 72 behind you both. The basic price of just under £420 (including tax) meant primer but if you wanted your van painted in the catalogued colours of dark blue or grey it was extra. The skinflints also wanted extra for a second windscreen wiper – only necessary, they must have supposed, if you also specified a second seat. Hubcaps too, as in this illustration, were an extra.

The updated version of Standard's Ten was the Pennant, and for 1958 the 6cwt van was endowed with the latter's crisper front wing styling featuring cowled headlamps. The pick-up, however, retained the older-style wings. How honest of Standard to depict a van sans hubcaps on the cover, for they were listed as extras. Extra too were any of the following factory colours: Coffee, Phantom Grey, Nimbus White, Cotswold Blue, Pale Yellow or black; but you did have the choice as to whether the finish was medium lustre or high gloss.

two pedal control for effortless transport

'Standrive' two-pedal control is available as an optional extra on these two models. 'Standrive' provides a clutchless gear change which adjusts itself to the driver's mood, by the use of the accelerator and brake pedal only. It permits leisurely changes of gear or, when desired, a rapid shift into higher or lower ratios with equal smoothness and precision. 'Standrive' gives you smoother, less fatiguing driving in all traffic conditions, and its simplicity of operation will appeal to all drivers of vehicles in conditions requiring frequent stopping and starting or involving many gear changes.

The exceptional interior capacity of the Standard 6 cwt. Delivery Van of 84 cu. ft. (2.4 cu. metres) enables a wide variety of goods to be carried. 96 cu. ft. (2.7 cu. metres) with passenger seat removed

The passenger seat can be removed to increase carrying capacity. The rear door opening of the Standard 6 cwt. is wider than any other van in the same class

Delivery Van

Low loading height and wide opening rear doors of the Standard 6 cwt. Delivery Van make loading or unloading an easy task

Maximum capacity with minimum running cost — the ideal combination for a small trader

The tailboard of the Standard 6 cwt. Pick-up Truck can be lowered for easy loading

Barrels, milk cans and other awkward loads can be packed easily owing to the accessibility of the carrying platform

Pick up Truck.

Versatility is the great feature of both the Standard 6 cwt. Delivery Van and the Standard 6 cwt. Pick-up Truck. These tough, efficient little vehicles have been designed to carry out a variety of jobs both for the farmer or country estate owner as well as for the small business men or city trader. Unitary chassis and body construction gives both vehicles a sturdiness which enables them to tackle all kinds of loads within their carrying capacity, while front independent suspension and semi-elliptic springs at rear, controlled by lever arm piston-type dampers, enable them to give an easy ride over all kinds of surfaces. Added to this their economical running and well-equipped driving compartments, make them really first-class investments for the man who wants to solve his transport problems for a moderate outlay.

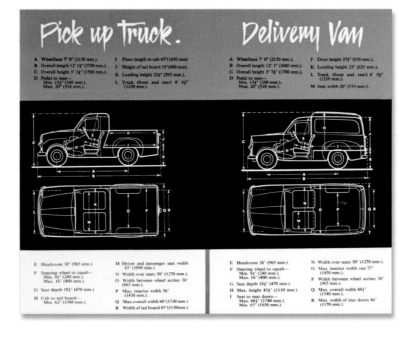

Pick up Truck.

A Wheelbase 7' 0" (2130 mm.).
B Overall length 12' 1½" (3700 mm.).
C Overall height 5' 1½" (1560 mm.).
D Pedal to seat—
   Min. 13½" (340 mm.).
   Max. 20" (510 mm.).
I Floor length to cab 65"(1650 mm)
J Height of tail board 19"(480 mm.)
K Loading height 23½" (595 mm.).
L Track (front and rear) 4' 0½" (1230 mm.).

Delivery Van

A Wheelbase 7' 0" (2130 mm.).
B Overall length 12' 1" (3680 mm.).
C Overall height 5' 7½" (1700 mm.).
D Pedal to seat—
   Min. 13½" (340 mm.).
   Max. 20" (510 mm.).
J Door height 37½" (950 mm.).
K Loading height 25" (635 mm.).
L Track (front and rear) 4' 0½" (1230 mm.).
M Seat width 20" (510 mm.).

E Headroom 38" (965 mm.).
F Steering wheel to squab—
   Min. 9½" (240 mm.).
   Max. 16" (400 mm.).
G Seat depth 18½" (470 mm.).
H Cab to tail board—
   Min. 62" (1580 mm.).
M Driver and passenger seat width 43" (1090 mm.).
N Width over seats 50" (1270 mm.).
O Width between wheel arches 38" (965 mm.).
P Max. interior width 56" (1430 mm.).
Q Max.overall width 60" (1530 mm.).
R Width of tail board 45"(1150mm.)

E Headroom 38" (965 mm.).
F Steering wheel to squab—
   Min. 9½" (240 mm.).
   Max. 16" (400 mm.).
G Seat depth 18½" (470 mm.).
H Max. height 43½" (1110 mm.).
I Seat to rear doors—
   Max. 68½" (1740 mm.).
   Min. 65" (1650 mm.).
N Width over seats 50" (1270 mm.).
O Max. interior width van 57" (1450 mm.).
P Width between wheel arches 38" (965 mm.).
Q Max. overall width 60½" (1540 mm.).
R Max. width of rear doors 46" (1170 mm.).

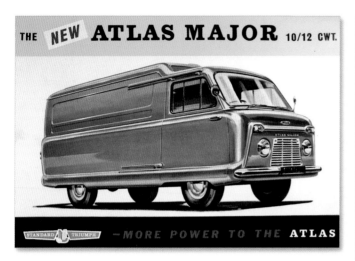

The forward-control Atlas was Standard's first commercial designed and built from scratch. But while other manufacturers of similar vehicles considered an engine of about 1½-litres the right size, the Atlas was given a powerplant of less than 1-litre. Despite an endurance run, fully loaded, from Cape Town to Gibraltar via the Sahara at an average speed of 22mph to help publicise its late 1958 launch, when it got into the hands of the public the Atlas' performance was considered to be pretty pathetic. Rather than immediately rectify the misjudgement, more than a year passed before the Atlas was, in effect, relaunched as the Major – the same vehicle but now with the 1670cc Ensign engine that could easily have been fitted in the first place.

INSIDE STORY of the biggest load carrier on seven feet!

The ATLAS MAJOR packs a load of 180 cu. ft.—all on a 7 ft. wheelbase. This is a greater capacity than any other vehicle with a similar payload. The main goods compartment is 92″ long, 63″ wide, 55″ high. There's additional space beside the driver when no passenger is carried.

A large rear door, nearly 4 ft. by 3 ft. 6 in., and a low floor height make packing heavy or awkward goods a simple matter. And the average man will not be cramped working inside. A side-loading door can also be fitted.

HINGED OR SLIDING — you choose

Hinged cab doors are normally fitted on the ATLAS MAJOR. Sliding doors are available at a small extra charge. A hinged side-loading door can also be fitted.

The ATLAS MAJOR is easily adapted for special purposes. Shelves, extra windows, can be incorporated without weakening the body.

It may have been late on the forward-control scene but Standard was not shy of announcing its pick-up had, "No equal for quick and versatile loading." The firm was also rather proud of the three-position tailboard, although why you would usefully need it to be other than down or up I can't think. The manufacturer remembered to incorporate strengthening panels to the rear of the cab but, considering the English climate, sockets for tilt hoops could have been provided. Whether van or pick-up, optional extras were heater, heavy-duty shock absorbers and/or tyres and, of course, the damn passenger seat. Anything other than primer was also in this category, and the options were Cornflower Blue, Pearl Grey, Jamaican Yellow or Coffee.

An Atlas with a hinged side door

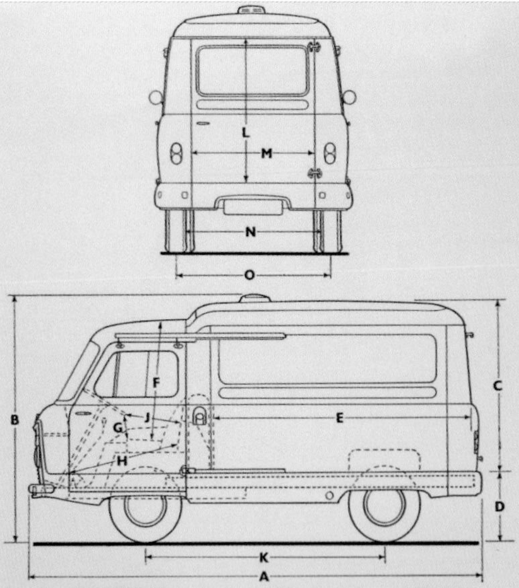
L
M
N
O
B
C
D
E
F
G
H
J
K
A

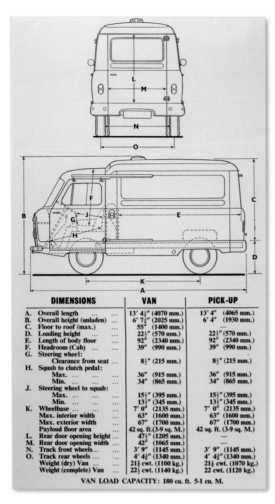

DIMENSIONS	VAN	PICK-UP
A. Overall length	13′ 4¼″ (4070 mm.)	13′ 4″ (4065 mm.)
B. Overall height (unladen) ...	6′ 7¾″ (2025 mm.)	6′ 4″ (1930 mm.)
C. Floor to roof (max.) ...	55″ (1400 mm.)	—
D. Loading height	22½″ (570 mm.)	22½″ (570 mm.)
E. Length of body floor ...	92″ (2340 mm.)	92″ (2340 mm.)
F. Headroom (Cab)	39″ (990 mm.)	39″ (990 mm.)
G. Steering wheel:		
Clearance from seat ...	8½″ (215 mm.)	8½″ (215 mm.)
H. Squab to clutch pedal:		
Max.	36″ (915 mm.)	36″ (915 mm.)
Min.	34″ (865 mm.)	34″ (865 mm.)
J. Steering wheel to squab:		
Max.	15½″ (395 mm.)	15½″ (395 mm.)
Min.	13½″ (345 mm.)	13½″ (345 mm.)
K. Wheelbase	7′ 0″ (2135 mm.)	7′ 0″ (2135 mm.)
Max. interior width ...	63″ (1600 mm.)	63″ (1600 mm.)
Max. exterior width ...	67″ (1700 mm.)	67″ (1700 mm.)
Payload floor area ...	42 sq. ft.(3·9 sq. M.)	42 sq. ft. (3·9 sq. M.)
L. Rear door opening height ...	47½″ (1205 mm.)	—
M. Rear door opening width ...	42″ (1065 mm.)	—
N. Track front wheels... ...	3′ 9″ (1145 mm.)	3′ 9″ (1145 mm.)
O. Track rear wheels	4′ 4¾″ (1340 mm.)	4′ 4¾″ (1340 mm.)
Weight (dry) Van	21⅝ cwt. (1100 kg.)	21⅛ cwt. (1070 kg.)
Weight (complete) Van ...	22½ cwt. (1140 kg.)	22 cwt. (1120 kg.)

VAN LOAD CAPACITY: 180 cu. ft. 5·1 cu. M.

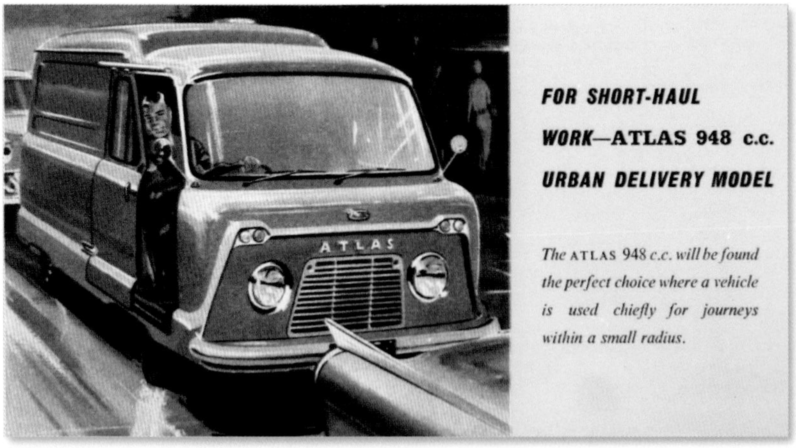
ATLAS
FOR SHORT-HAUL
WORK—ATLAS 948 c.c.
URBAN DELIVERY MODEL
The ATLAS 948 c.c. will be found the perfect choice where a vehicle is used chiefly for journeys within a small radius.

Rather quietly dropping the original small-engined model, Standard gave it another name that suggested it had all been planned in the first place.

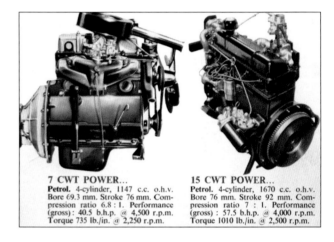

7 CWT POWER...
Petrol. 4-cylinder, 1147 c.c. o.h.v. Bore 69.3 mm. Stroke 76 mm. Compression ratio 6.8 : 1. Performance (gross): 40.5 b.h.p. @ 4,500 r.p.m. Torque 735 lb./in. @ 2,250 r.p.m.

15 CWT POWER...
Petrol. 4-cylinder, 1670 c.c. o.h.v. Bore 76 mm. Stroke 92 mm. Compression ratio 7 : 1. Performance (gross): 57.5 b.h.p. @ 4,000 r.p.m. Torque 1010 lb./in. @ 2,500 r.p.m.

STANDARD
TRIUMPH
presents the
NEW
STANDARD 15
A product of the Leyland Motors Group

The era of takeovers and buyouts was there for all to see, with three apparently unrelated manufacturers named on the cover of the 1962 brochure for the New Standard 15 – nothing more than a re-named Atlas, its moniker obviously no longer considered suitable or marketable.

Whichever engine was fitted, the Atlas had a four-speed gearbox with synchro on top three gears and a floor change with long lever that almost fell to hand just below the steering wheel.

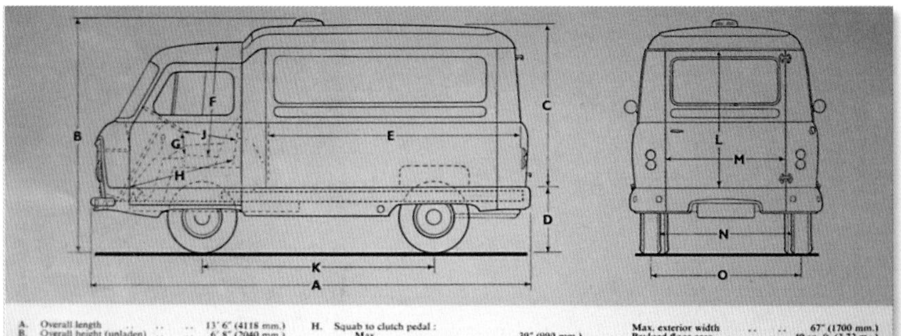
A
B
C
D
E
F
G
H
J
K
L
M
N
O

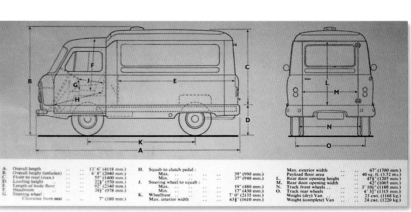

A.	Overall length	13′ 6″ (4118 mm.)
B.	Overall height (unladen)	6′ 8″ (2040 mm.)
C.	Floor to roof (max.)	55″ (1400 mm.)
D.	Loading height	22½″ (570 mm.)
E.	Length of body floor	92″ (2340 mm.)
F.	Headroom	38½″ (978 mm.)
G.	Steering wheel :	
	Clearance from seat	7″ (180 mm.)
H.	Squab to clutch pedal :	
	Max.	39″ (990 mm.)
	Min.	37″ (940 mm.)
J.	Steering wheel to squab :	
	Max.	19″ (480 mm.)
	Min.	17″ (430 mm.)
K.	Wheelbase	7′ 0″ (2135 mm.)
	Max. interior width	63½″ (1610 mm.)
	Max. exterior width	67″ (1700 mm.)
	Payload floor area	40 sq. ft. (3.72 m².)
L.	Rear door opening height ..	47½″ (1205 mm.)
M.	Rear door opening width ..	42″ (1065 mm.)
N.	Track front wheels	3′ 10½″ (1180 mm.)
O.	Track rear wheels	4′ 3¾″ (1315 mm.)
	Weight (dry) Van	23 cwt. (1168 kg.)
	Weight (complete) Van	24 cwt. (1220 kg.)

Also launched in the autumn of 1962 was the flagship 20cwt.

An extra 5in on the 20's wheelbase translated into an extra 16in of floor length due to increased body overhang at the rear; a quick way to identify one from the other was by the pair of small indented panels to the rear of the 20's cab. The sliding door option had been abandoned with the Atlas name and on both models they were hinged. Up until this point all Atlas vans, as well as the 15, had 13x6.40 wheels and tyres, but the 20 had 15in wheels fitted with 6.70 light truck tyres.

Service Time Slashed

A brilliant feature unique to Standard-Triumph forward control vehicles is the ability to remove engine, gearbox and front suspension as one unit for major overhauls. Service time is thus reduced to a minimum and the hours saved spent in revenue earning. Access to all major components is unlimited since the front end unit may be easily wheeled to the most convenient working position.

Standard 20 Pick up.

1st class Cab Comfort

Great attention has been paid to driver comfort in the layout of the Standard 20 cab. Well-upholstered, adjustable seating, sensibly positioned controls and panoramic visibility defy driver fatigue. The engine cover, easily and quickly detachable for minor servicing, is insulated against heat and noise. A boon for deliveries, the lack of obstruction enables easy access to the driving seat via either of the wide doors.

This feature had been incorporated in the design of the original Atlas.

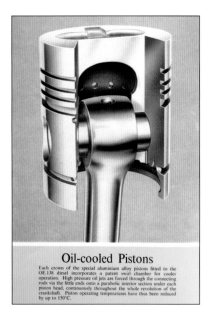

Oil-cooled Pistons

Each crown of the special aluminium alloy pistons fitted to the OE.138 diesel incorporates a patent swirl chamber for cooler operation. High pressure oil jets are forced through the connecting rods via the little ends onto a parabolic interior section under each piston head, continuously throughout the whole revolution of the crankshaft. Piston operating temperatures have thus been reduced by up to 150°C.

Wet Liners for Long Life

Centrifugally chill cast, nickel-chrome iron cylinder liners are a feature of the Standard 20 petrol engine. Fitted in direct contact with the coolant and readily replaceable, they contribute to the engine's gift of eternal youth. Connecting rods are of 60 ton steel with floating gudgeon pins secured by circlips. A robust 3-bearing crankshaft with precision lead indium bearings adds weight to this engine's claim of virtual indestructibility.

LIVE CENTRE SUSPENSION

The independent front suspension incorporates a transverse leaf spring mounted on the chassis side members. This gives firm, precise cornering with anti-roll bar characteristics.

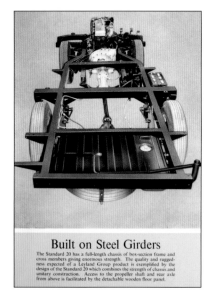

Built on Steel Girders

The Standard 20 has a full-length chassis of box-section frame and cross members giving enormous strength. The quality and ruggedness expected of a Leyland Group product is exemplified by the design of the Standard 20 which combines the strength of chassis and unitary construction. Access to the propeller shaft and rear axle from above is facilitated by the detachable wooden floor panel.

20 CWT POWER...
Petrol. 4-cylinder, 2138 c.c. o.h.v. Bore 86 mm. Stroke 92 mm. Compression ratio 7-: 1. Performance (gross): 71 b.h.p. @ 3,900 r.p.m. Torque 1435 lb./in. @ 2,000 r.p.m.

20 CWT POWER...
Diesel. 4-cyl., 2260 c.c. o.h.v. Bore 84.14 mm. Stroke 101.6 mm. Compression ratio 21.5:1. Performance (gross): 54 b.h.p. @ 3,000 r.p.m. Torque 1210 lb./in. @ 2,000 r.p.m.

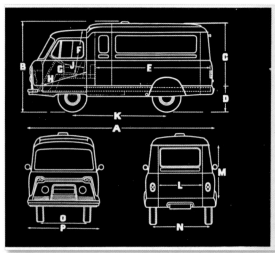

A.	Overall length	14' 10" (4520 mm.)
B.	Overall height (unladen)	6' 10" (2080 mm.)
C.	Floor to roof (max.)	55" (1400 mm.)
D.	Loading height	26" (660 mm.)
E.	Length of body floor	108" (2740 mm.)
F.	Headroom	38½" (978 mm.)
G.	Steering wheel:	
	Clearance from seat	7" (180 mm.)
H.	Squab to clutch pedal:	
	Max.	39" (990 mm.)
	Min.	37" (940 mm.)
J.	Steering wheel to squab:	
	Max.	19" (480 mm.)
	Min.	17" (430 mm.)
K.	Wheelbase	7' 5" (2260 mm.)
	Payload floor area	47.25 sq. ft. (4.4 m².)
L.	Rear door opening width	39½" (1005 mm.)
M.	Rear door opening height	47" (1195 mm.)
N.	Track rear wheels	4' 6" (1370 mm.)
O.	Track front wheels	3' 9¼" (1150 mm.)
P.	Max. exterior width	67" (1700 mm.)
	Max. interior width	63½" (1610 mm.)

If you liked driving a diesel you'd have to buy a 20 because the 15 didn't have this option.

The new
TRIUMPH COURIER
good looks without
the 'goods' look
STANDARD TRIUMPH
A member of the Leyland Motors Group

If things had been different, Standard Triumph's replacement for the Standard Ten and Pennant could have been the Standard Herald. But marketing staff were concerned that Standard conjured up austerity whilst Triumph was more uplifting, so Triumph Herald it was. The Michelotti-styled saloon went on sale in 1959 followed by coupé, convertible and estate with the Courier van last, early in 1962.

A brand-new box-section cruciform backbone chassis and transverse-leaf swing axle rear suspension, but a goodly proportion of the remaining mechanical components were hand-me-downs from the Standard Tens and Pennants.

"The Courier is made to be enjoyed as you would enjoy a private car," the sales spiel read, and right it was too, as this section of the interior was identical to the Herald's. Not sure the driving seat, "Fully adjustable to 72 positions," looked over-comfortable but compared with some of its peers it was reasonably sumptuous. Safety considerations were getting a look in, as the, "Steering column and facia edge are designed to yield on serious impact."

COURIER AGILITY
The Courier can turn about in half a tennis court. And make rings inside a 22 yard cricket pitch (if it starts just outside one wicket and ends up just outside the other, it'll do three). In a more serious vein, it can make a 3-point turn in a road only 14 feet wide.

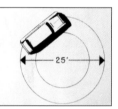

The Triumph's rack-and-pinion steering allowed for a very small turning circle. But some of you reading this will click your tongues at the memory of the front wheels scrubbing and straining if the poor thing was put on full lock, whilst manoeuvering at low speed.

Load her up!
One big door goes up and stays up, right out of everyone's way. Load in left, load in right. Nothing's in the way loading the new Triumph Courier. Low floor (with detachable wooden top for fragile loads). Bags of room. Easy loading. A pleasure to work with.

THE FOUR DIMENSIONS THAT MATTER	
Maximum load length	62 ins.
Maximum load height	34 ins.
Maximum load width	46 ins.
Maximum load volume	45 cubic feet
(Payload: 5 cwt)	

The Herald range had removable (bolted-up) body panels, including the roof and sills, which simplified the construction of different styles upon the same chassis. The Courier van was basically an estate with filler panels instead of rear windows and decking instead of rear seats. One-piece bonnet gave good access but had its drawbacks in old age – but that was hardly of concern to the manufacturer.

TRIUMPH COURIER — THE BARE FACTS

Body Van body, steel panelled, rust and dust proofed. "Triplex" toughened safety glass windscreen. Forward hinged doors with push button handles. Winding windows and pivoting ventilators. One roof-hinged goods door at rear. Driver's and passenger's seats with P.V.C. leathercloth upholstery, washable headlining in cab.
Large easily read instrument dial with speedometer, fuel gauge, ignition. oil pressure and main beam warning lights.

Locks All doors lock externally with key. Bonnet has external release catches.

General Equipment (Interior) Ashtray, sun visor, interior driving mirror, horn button in steering wheel centre, light to underside of facia rail with integral and courtesy switches to both doors, steering column dip switch hand operated, interior light above rear door, anchor points for safety harness, chrome door pulls. (Exterior) Headlamps flush fitting sealed units with pre-focus bulbs, parking lamps incorporating self-cancelling direction indicators, rear parking lights incorporating stop lights, twin rear direction indicator lamps, two screen wipers, two chrome "spring-back" wing mirrors, chrome nave plates, overriders front and rear.

Engine 4-cylinder, 1147 cc. o.h.v. Bore 69·3 mm. Stroke 76 mm. and compression ratio 8 : 1 (or 7 : 1 for use with low octane fuel).
Clutch, single dry plate, 6¼" dia.
4-speed gearbox, synchromesh on 2nd, 3rd and top.

Ratios
	Top	3rd	2nd	1st & Rev.
	1·0	1·394	2·158	3·746

Performance
Gross : 43 B.H.P. at 4,500 r.p.m.
Torque : 775 lb./in. at 2,250 r.p.m.

ENGINE SPEEDS
Road Speed	Top	3rd	2nd	1st & Rev.
10 m.p.h.	610	850	1315	2290
10 km.p.h.	380	530	820	1425
Road speed at 1,000 r.p.m. in top 16·3 m.p.h. approx.

Capacities
Fuel Tank ...	9 galls.	41 litres
Engine Sump ...	7 pints	4 litres
Gearbox ...	1½ pints	0·85 litres
Rear Axle ...	1 pint	0·53 litres
Cooling System ...	7½ pints	4·25 litres

General Dimensions
Wheelbase ...	7 ft. 7½ in.	2320 mm.
Track—front ...	4 ft.	1220 mm.
—rear ...	4 ft.	1220 mm.

Ground Clearance
(static laden) ...	6¾ in.	170 mm.
Turning Circle ...	25 ft.	7·7 metres
Height (unladen) ...	4 ft. 4 in.	1320 mm.
Width ...	5 ft.	1525 mm.
Length ...	12 ft. 9 in.	3890 mm.

Weight Dry (excluding
extra equipment) ...	15½ cwt.	794 kg.
Complete (including
fuel, tools, etc.) ...	16¼ cwt.	825 kg.
Gross (fully laden
with 2 up) ...	24 cwt.	1220 kg.
Length of load floor	62 in.	1575 mm.
Load floor to roof ...	34 in.	864 mm.
Width of load floor
(max.) ...	46 in.	1168 mm.

Rear door opening:
Height ...	28½ in.	724 mm.
Width ...	40 in.	1016 mm.
Loading height ...	21½ in.	546 mm.
Payload ...	5 cwt.	254 kg.
Payload volume ...	45 cu. ft.	1·246 cu. metres

Suspension Independent front suspension, coiled springs controlled by telescopic type dampers. Swing axle type independent rear suspension with transverse leaf spring and radius rods.

Leyland Motors Group presents
The New STANDARD 7-cwt

First light vehicles with Leyland 'Seal of Quality'

The Standard 7-cwt comes in two forms ; the large capacity van and the easily accessible pick-up

SEE INSIDE PAGES FOR FULL STORY...

THE INSIDE STORY!

Biggest load-space of any 7-cwt

At the same time as the Triumph Courier van came onto the market Leyland released the updated Standard van and pick-up. Even disregarding the Standard's larger capacity, I know which one I'd have – absolutely no contest.

Interesting! The load space was given as 96 cubic feet including passenger seat space or 82 behind, while back in 1954 the gross space was given as 88 cubic feet for what was ostensibly the same bodyshell on the same 7ft wheelbase. There were some anomalies in the two sets of internal measurements as well, but I'll leave it someone with access to both a 1954 and a post-1958 model to solve one of this book's Trivial Pursuit queries.

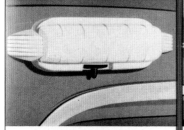

Light on the load

An interior light is one of the refinements that contributes to operational efficiency in the Standard 7-cwt. Details like this mean quicker, easier working.

'Extras' built-in

A new silver grille for the Standard 7-cwt. Full-width chromium bumpers, front and rear, chromium wing mirrors and nave plates are production fittings.

Even an ashtray

For all the modest price, there's nothing 'utility' about the Standard 7-cwt van and pick-up. For the owner-driver they offer the comfort of a saloon car.

Big, big brakes

A total swept braking area of 118 sq. in. gives the Standard 7-cwt maximum stopping power, under all driving conditions, however great the load.

Luxury touch

New white steering wheel. Very smart. Easy-to-read instruments. Very sensible. Full-width parcel shelf. Very practical. Everything designed for driving ease.

Roof ventilator

A production fitting. The Standard 7-cwt can carry different loads every day, with no 'perfumed' carry-over. Better for perishable goods, too.

Back in those days it was almost de rigueur for the van driver to have a fag on, but nowadays it's banned – at least if the vehicle is used for work; so why do modern vans have ashtrays? Along the same lines, you might ponder upon the fact that most current commercials are capable of 100mph-plus when the maximum speed limit is 70 or less in some countries…

MORE POWER!

Herald muscles for the new Standard 7-cwt

"Herald muscles," translated to 43bhp at 4500rpm but the 1147cc engine would rev past 5000rpm with no ill effects, and your 7cwt van or pick-up would be travelling at around 75mph with the standard 4.55:1 back axle ratio and 5.90x13in tyres.

TROJAN

Trojan had discontinued vehicle production during the war, and it was not until the end of the 1940s that it re-entered the field solely as a manufacturer of commercials with the Trojan 15, which, as its title denoted, would carry 15cwt.

Almost since the birth of the automobile there have been uncountable attempts to build the ideal basic, sturdy yet economical car that would suit the everyman; and one such vehicle was the brainchild of Leslie Hounsfield in the years leading up to the First World War.

By 1914 there was a prototype with a four-cylinder two-stroke engine to show for his efforts, but government work thereafter took precedence and it was not until several years later that a further half-a-dozen-or-so had been constructed at Hounsfield's Croydon, South London, premises. The finalised version eventually went on display at the 1922 Olympia Motor Show.

Basic the car most certainly was, and quirky too. But, fortuitously for Hounsfield, Leyland – which had a surfeit of workers and space at its Kingston on Thames factory – came to an arrangement whereby the big company would undertake manufacture. The result was that by end of the '20s, when Leyland had decided its facilities were better employed wholly upon the production of its own lorries and increasingly successful Lion and Lioness passenger vehicles, over 17,000 Trojan cars and light vans had been made to Hounsfield's designs.

With its under-the-floor two-stroke motor (started

by a hand lever), two-speed epicyclic gears driving a solid rear axle by chain, rear-wheel-only braking and solid rubber tyres it was a miracle that anybody wanted to own one, but the Brooke Bond tea company thought well enough of them to become long term customers of Trojan vans. Its allegiance certainly can't have been because of the Trojan's straight-line performance (which was pitiful), nor to it being outrageously cheap. For instance, in 1927 its chassis price was more than Ford's ubiquitous Model T that outperformed it on every count, other the Trojan's rather pointless ability to grind slowly up impossibly-steep unmade roads due to its low-speed torque and solid rear axle.

Mr Hounsfield was happy enough to continue manufacturing the Trojan at an enlarged Croydon works but must have thought better of it and left his brainchild and company for pastures new. Various desultory attempts were made to modernise the passenger car range and few sold, but vans found sufficient customers for production to continue throughout the '30s.

Understandably, the government did not see Trojan commercials (or some kind of military vehicle based upon the same chassis) as a means to win the war, so the company was put to work producing such things as airborne containers, petrol bowsers and simple bomb and battery trolleys.

Two-stroke-powered vans spearheaded Trojan's post-war revival as a light commercial manufacturer but it was fighting a rear-guard action with what many people – apparently apart from Brooke Bond – regarded as increasingly dated and with a somewhat cranky power plant.

A battery-electric version was introduced to broaden appeal before the manufacturer saw the light of day and called upon Perkins for one of its diesels.

By the mid-'50s, however, there were increasing numbers of freshly-designed, up-to-the minute, small-to-medium commercials on the market and Trojan had to do more than put a new heart in an old dog, even though the company was busy with a new agricultural division that would make such machines as the Airator and Bale-master.

In 1958 a commercial chassis was designed and

built at the behest of Marley Tiles, which was developed into an entirely new (and I have to say entirely ugly) range of forward-control 20cwt and 25cwt vans and passenger vehicles, powered by either three- or four-cylinder Perkins diesels.

I'm pretty certain that even Brooke Bond abandoned Trojan with this one, and in 1959 the company was acquired by the Agg family who, amongst other business interests, held the UK franchise for Lambretta. Under Agg ownership the Trojan commercials were phased out by 1961 and in their place, from 1960 to '65, the Croydon factory built in the region of

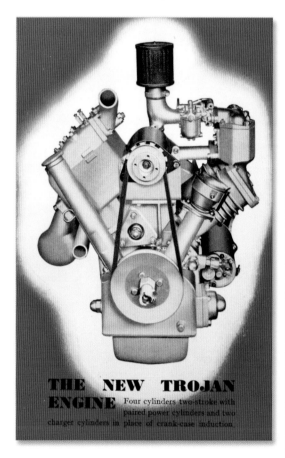

Trojan's unique so-called "supercharged" two-stroke motor had a pair of water-cooled combustion cylinders with a combined capacity of 1186cc and a bore and stroke of 65.5mm x 88mm, which were fed via a pair of air-cooled compression cylinders displacing 1293cc with a bore and stroke of 92.6mm x 88mm. I'd love to be able to write down some impressive horsepower figures but sadly I can't; and anyway, the manufacturer was more concerned with torque at minimal engine speed, so you have the following: 24bhp at 2000rpm and 70lb/ft at 1000rpm. Sadly, the thing used fuel in uneconomic quantities and, even more importantly, customers felt happier with something a little more conventional – so before long, the manufacturer looked elsewhere for motive power.

6,000 Heinkel bubble cars under licence, marketed as the Trojan 200.

The 200 would be the last road vehicle to carry the Trojan name but a myriad of other products that hinted at the old brand emanated from the South London premises, including the Trokart (go kart), the Trobike (small motorcycle) and the Toractor (garden tractor). There were various other machines, too, such as the three-wheeled Monotractor that was made in large numbers and exported to third-world countries.

Under Peter Agg's leadership the company went on to produce Elva sports cars, then McLaren-Elva and the hugely successful McLaren racing cars, as well as becoming a major manufacturer of cable car systems (to name but one other non-automotive venture).

Rather bizarrely, there was to be a final Trojan four-wheeler, and in 1974 the ever-entrepreneurial Agg built and fielded the Trojan T103-Cosworth Formula One car that contested just the one season, with tenth place in the Belgian GP its best result.

At the time of writing Trojan still exists as an independent company, although the factory was sold in the 1970s.

The 15's capacity was 165 cubic feet – and yes, this manufacturer insisted on cheating by including the space beside the driver.

TROJAN DIESEL

at the

International Commercial Motor Transport Exhibition

Earls Court
Sept. 24 - Oct. 2

.. the FIRST one-ton chassis with DIESEL power!

With the Trojan Diesel, first one-ton chassis with Diesel power, outstanding performance is an everyday experience. You can count on 40-45 m.p.g.—only 1⅓d a mile. There's economy for you! And that economy is backed by over two year's experience of faithful service in the hands of a multitude of fleet users and others. There's a variety of bodies on the sturdy Trojan chassis to meet every requirement. Ask for details on Stand 69

on
STAND
69
MAIN HALL

TROJAN LTD., CROYDON, SURREY

The Trojan van was certainly no beauty queen but was a far more practical proposition once it was equipped with a conventional engine in the form of the Perkins P3 diesel during 1953. There was also an ugly (actually fairly grotesque) PSV or small coach with this chassis and engine, which looked like a prop for a low-budget comedy film.

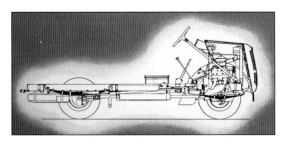

Chassis layout was absolutely conventional, with beam axles on semi-elliptic springs, hydraulic brakes all round and steel-disc 16in wheels shod with 6.50-section tyres. Ground clearance was an ample 9in and the sales literature made reference to the large number of Trojans being exported to Australia, thanks to the likelihood of poor road conditions and driving over boulders protruding about 6in above ground...

Experiencing some sales resistance on account of its unconventional engine, Trojan went for electricity to power an alternative version of its 15cwt van. "The Trojan Electrovan can maintain a sustained maximum speed on the level of 18mph," its brochure told us, which meant that, combined with a 25-mile maximum range, it was suitable for town and suburban use only.

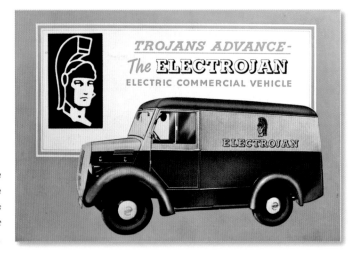

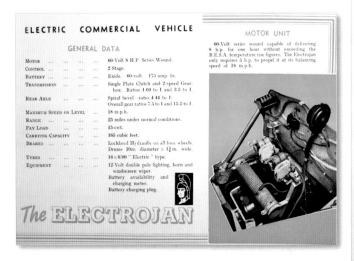

ELECTRIC COMMERCIAL VEHICLE

The new Electrojan in normal service over a long period with a well-known operator has been most favourably commented on, the driver stating that it is smooth and comfortable to drive and extremely manoeuvrable and easy to handle in traffic. The following is a typical week's work :

TESTS

	Mileage	Stops made
Monday ...	9	43
Tuesday ...	14	41
Wednesday ...	12	21
Thursday ...	13	36
Friday ...	15	39
TOTAL ...	63	180

RANGE

With a standard battery of 175 ampère hours the normal range is 25 miles, the mileage depending upon general operating conditions. Under favourably level ground operation the range would be higher.

Trojans for work!

Trojan brought this unlovely selection to the market in 1959. They did, however, have independent suspension that endowed them with, the manufacturer pointed out, "Smooth riding and superb road-holding." All the better to carry the, "Wallpaper, tea, tiles, sausages and ice cream," in comfort.

This van had a 9ft 4in and 350 cubic feet capacity, whilst the 20cwt version had a wheelbase of 7ft 10in and a capacity of 300 cubic feet. Each had 16in wheels shod with 6.50-section tyres.

The long-stroke, 88.9mm bore and 127mm stroke, 2.36-litre Perkins P3 developed 41bhp at 2400rpm and its maximum torque of 101lb/ft at 1200rpm. It was coupled to a four-speed gearbox and the final drive ratio was 4.55:1. For some models the Perkins 3.33-litre, 63bhp, four-cylinder 208 was an option.

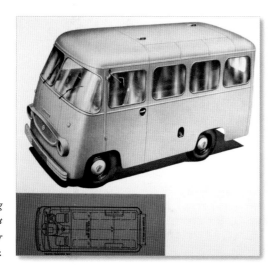

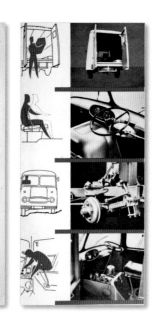

Another ugly duckling from Trojan – the 20cwt personnel wagon for 12 or 13 passengers and driver.

CAMPER VANS

When the potential for converting forward-control vans – such as the Bedford CA and Austin 152 – into self-propelled caravans was realised, exploited and taken on by the public, a whole new industry began.

The concept was nothing new, however, and almost certainly the first motor caravans to be manufactured for sale in Britain were made by Eccles in the early 1920s. Based at Stirchley, Birmingham, the firm manufactured both towed and motorised caravans – the latter catalogued as available on either a Ford Model T or a heavier Chevrolet truck chassis. Although quite a number were made, the company found that trailer caravans were far more popular, and by the '30s its motorised versions were discontinued.

One or two other small companies tried their hands at the same thing around this time, but their efforts came to nothing and the concept lay dormant until the 1950s.

It is an all-but-forgotten professional photographer of mid-European extraction by the name of Peter Pitt who may well have been instrumental in the resurrection and subsequent widespread popularity of campers.

Pitt had turned a Volkswagen van into a motorhome for use in conjunction with his business, and after frequently being asked where such a thing might be obtained he decided to offer similar conversions to others on a commercial basis. He was very unhappy with the taxation situation regarding such vehicles, however, and legend has it that he singlehandedly brought about a change in the regulations.

His belief was that not only should motor caravans be taxed as private cars, but also that they should enjoy the absence of commercial vehicle speed restrictions. Furthermore, like trailer caravans, they should be exempted from purchase tax.

At the time commercial vehicles were disallowed from entering the Windsor Great Park and so, to create something of a *cause célèbre*, he took his motor caravan there.

As he had hoped, apprehension and prosecution followed; but although the details of what then took place are somewhat obscure, in the future taxation was relaxed and motor caravans could be driven at the same speeds as a private car – if the owners dared. So, providing this version of events is true, motor caravan owners and manufacturers alike owe Peter Pitt a debt of thanks.

Pitt conversions had a distinctive rearrangeable open-plan layout, and although many were based on Volkswagen vans you'd have had a more spacious version by selecting one of the British forward-controls offered. In 1961 his company merged with Canterbury Sidecars and, thereafter based at Romford, Essex, sold as Canterbury Pitt Conversions.

CALTHORPE

If you have five minutes to spare, as well as a computer, you might try typing, "home on wheels 1957," into your search engine. By this means you will be able to view a charming 2½-minute colour film made by British Pathé featuring the actress Dora Bryan and her budgerigar Cecil Gibson on a day out with Great Britain's first post-war coach-built motor caravan, chauffeured by its designer Maurice Calthorpe.

Mr Calthorpe's Home Cruiser was built upon a Bedford CA chassis and, as demonstrated by a stand-in for Dora, even boasted a bath – as well as an elevating roof that was another first for its creator.

Just a handful of these vehicles were made before

Maurice realised that it was far simpler and cost-effective to have his Home Cruisers constructed within the existing shell of a regular light van, and thus was born his second generation that utilised vehicles in the Austin, Bedford, Commer, Ford, Morris and Standard ranges.

Innovative its domed folding roof may have been, but the increased headroom it provided was quite restrictive, and long after it had been overtaken by much more spacious versions offered by other manufacturers the Calthorpe proudly adhered to its early claim to fame. Nevertheless, buyers were found in sufficient numbers to support a goodly-sized stand at Earls Court's Motor Shows of the early 1960s.

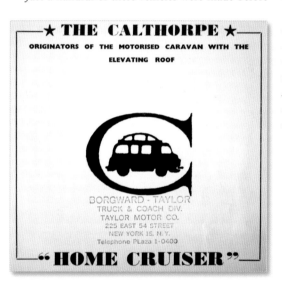

Sales material had a rather homemade look, and although this example made its way across the Atlantic, were any sales made by the New York dealership?

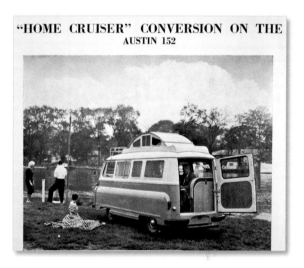

The interior layout of this version was strictly a four berth with no provision for the "pipe cot".

Beds aplenty in the Austin Home Cruiser – two doubles and an optional upper single. The latter did duty as a backrest by day.

ALL METAL ELEVATING ROOF IN LOWERED POSITION

ELEVATING ROOF IN RAISED POSITION.
PROVIDES COMFORTABLE STANDING ROOM WITH OPENING
WINDOWS AT BOTH SIDES.

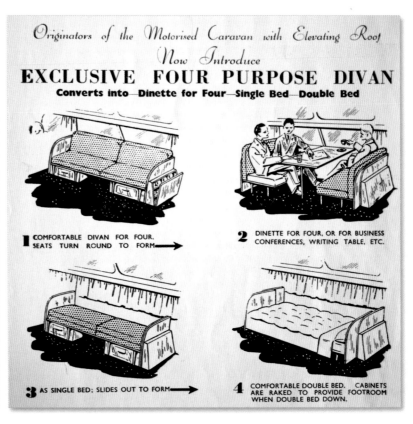

Originators of the Motorised Caravan with Elevating Roof
Now Introduce

EXCLUSIVE FOUR PURPOSE DIVAN

Converts into—Dinette for Four—Single Bed—Double Bed

1 COMFORTABLE DIVAN FOR FOUR.
SEATS TURN ROUND TO FORM ➤

2 DINETTE FOR FOUR, OR FOR BUSINESS
CONFERENCES, WRITING TABLE, ETC.

3 AS SINGLE BED; SLIDES OUT TO FORM ➤

4 COMFORTABLE DOUBLE BED. CABINETS
ARE RAKED TO PROVIDE FOOTROOM
WHEN DOUBLE BED DOWN.

After abandoning its initial coach-built Home Cruiser, Calthorpe offered a more compact version, still on a Bedford CA but utilising factory bodywork. The patented roof was said to, "Elevate in five seconds by one simple movement," and had sliding windows on both sides. Other advertised features included multi-purpose seating that converted into divan beds, a dinette for four with front bench seat reversed, six forward-facing seats with dinette seats in forward position as well as, "Complete caravan facilities," and all, "cabinets finished in light oak with mahogany surrounds."

FRONT BENCH SEAT FOLDS DOWN TO PROVIDE COMFORTABLE
INTERIOR SPRUNG DOUBLE BED. DINETTE IN REAR MAKES A
SECOND DOUBLE BED OR SEPARATE BEDS.

"The Calthorpe Home Cruiser is ideal for racing and sporting meetings, and all special events, where very often it is difficult to obtain accommodation," read the publicity. "It also affords a good vantage point for viewing an event in comfort." What event might be about to take place here, however, with the curtains drawn in bright daylight? The steering wheel could get in the way too!

COMMER

Commer was unique among the manufacturers covered in this book in that it made and marketed its own motor caravan. It was based on the passenger version of the Commer FC.

The basic model was the Special, with fixed roof and more occasional use in mind, but for the serious traveller who also wanted more room, the more expensive extending-roof model was the one for you.

Accommodation and transport worries
a thing of the past with the luxurious
COMMER 2-4 BERTH CARAVAN (petrol or diesel)

The perfect holiday home!

The FC caravan had the same mechanical specification as its stablemates, including the choice of petrol or diesel engines.

An amusing piece of artwork that shows off the concertina roof with contrasting fabric, the Marley flooring and some of the interior fittings. It also tells us that the enthusiastic chappie unpacking the picnic case is wearing two left shoes, and either the artist is trying to fool us as to exactly how spacious the interior is or the chappie has a petite lady friend. First we'd like to know whether she is wearing heels or is a ballerina on points – but either way this conservatively adds 3in to her height. Presuming the top of her head to be level with the roof in its retracted position, this would mean she is precisely 4 ft 3¾ in high.

At meal times, the dining table — normally stowed on side of body — is set up between the reversed front double seat and the rear seats, one of which is box-supported and fixed; the other of tubular construction and movable. The table, being free-standing, can also be used outside.

By simple manipulation the seating can be quickly transformed into an attractive lounge. The front double seat remains reversed and the removable half of the rear seat is moved alongside it, facing rearwards, and set back slightly to allow ease of entry; an arrangement which makes full and comfortable use of the space available.

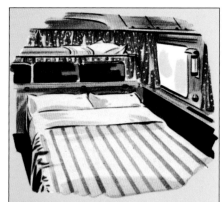

Ingeniously constructed seats are quickly positioned to form a comfortable double bed. A transverse single berth is mounted above the seats in the driver's compartment, whilst a fourth berth is fitted in the elevated roof. Blankets and linen are stored in one of the two wardrobes at rear of caravan.

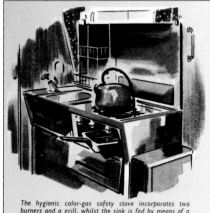

The hygienic calor-gas safety stove incorporates two burners and a grill, whilst the sink is fed by means of a hand-operated pump tap, which draws water from containers securely stowed in cupboards beneath the sink. When not in use, both stove and sink are concealed by hinged covers.

Commer offered an alternative and cheaper version of its own, with fixed roof for those who needed less accommodation – but it was still fully fitted. The awning stretched between the open rear doors gave a modicum of full headroom, but to little real purpose. On all of its FC caravans and light buses, paintwork in one of the factory colours was included in the price.

COTSWOLD

Ken Stephens had been in the business of selling caravans in Gloucestershire for a number of years when he became involved with the manufacture of motor caravans. Trading as Kingscote and Stephens of London Road, Gloucester, the company was a distributor for Berkeley cars, as well as Austin, Riley and Jaguar dealers.

Announced in the spring of 1961, its initial offering, named appropriately the Cotswold Motor Caravan, utilised the Austin 152 Omnivan as its base.

To overcome the inherent problem of headroom in any such conversion that was normally addressed with a folding roof, Stephens' Cotswold pre-empted

motor homes of more recent years in that it had a fixed high top.

The roof's practicality couldn't outweigh the ugliness of this protuberance, which was of moulded GRP, and the Cotswold failed to attract as many customers as had been hoped.

Within very few years the firm had turned to rather sumptuous coach-built motor caravans, which in the late-'60s were constructed on such chassis as the Transit, BMC 250JU, or the Austin FG for the flagship of the range – which, despite a necessarily rather steep price, found ready though diminishing sales until production was brought to a halt in the mid-'70s.

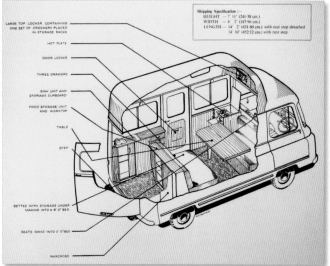

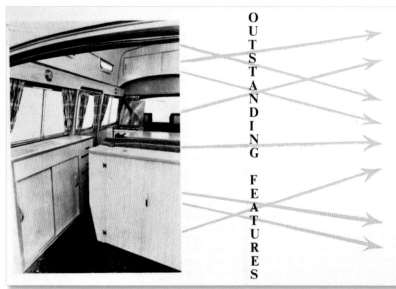

O
U
T
S
T
A
N
D
I
N
G

F
E
A
T
U
R
E
S

★ Planned by **EXPERTS** with many years of experience in both the Trailer Caravan and Motor Trade.

★ **COMPLETELY WEATHERPROOF.**

★ Light yet sturdy glass fibre fixed roof.

★ Excellent ventilation—caravan type side opening vents.

★ Commodious storage space—China Locker, complete with crockery for 4 persons, Wardrobe, four cupboards and cutlery drawers.

★ All interior surfaces are washable, furniture and walls are plastic-faced and upholstery is covered in P.V.C.

★ Calor Gas—Hot Plate and Grill and Regulator. Three 12v. Electric Lights are provided and a 12½ gallon water tank with exterior filler. Provision has been made for a Chemical Toilet.

★ Three or four berth.

★ Will tow with ease another 'van or boat.

★ Side door with automatic step and back door reinforced step designed to take a towing hitch. The rear step is detachable, if required.

Cotswold Series C

HERE, indeed, is a LUXURY coachbuilt Motor Caravan—based on the well-known Austin 152 chassis; the construction and interior layout incorporates all features that the discerning caravanner would seek in a Motor Caravan—and more

THE DE LUXE COTSWOLD · OUTSTANDING DESIGN · COMPREHENSIVELY EQUIPPED

It should have been a best-seller but wasn't so, and in a bid to win sales from other manufacturers the Cotswold bowed to the accepted folding roof concept.

NOW available with Folding Roof

To meet the requirements of the caravanner who prefers the more streamlined appearance when 'on the road' and for the caravanner whose garaging space is limited for height the . . . .

COTSWOLD MOTOR CARAVAN
the perfect HOLIDAY HOME for the family

is now available with the ████ FOLDING ROOF as an alternative to the glass fibre fixed roof.

The Folding Roof is constructed with a glass fibre top - with a ventilator incorporated - the 'bellows' sides are of striped plastic material.

THE INTERIOR LAYOUT is identical to the fixed roof model, with all outstanding features that have proved so popular.

SHIPPING SPECIFICATION:
HEIGHT
  roof raised - 8' 10" (269.24 cm)
  roof lowered - 7' 5" (226.05 cm)
WIDTH - 6' 2" (187.96 cm)
LENGTH - 14' 2" (431.80 cm) with rear step detached
  14' 10" (452.12 cm) with rear step

Designed and exclusively marketed by KINGSCOTE & STEPHENS LTD.
LONDON ROAD   GLOUCESTER   Telephone 21778

All export enquiries to THE AUSTIN MOTOR EXPORT CORPORATION LTD., Longbridge, Birmingham, England.

With its Series C, Kingscote and Stephens made a particularly good-looking vehicle considering it utilised the rather clumpy front and doors of the Austin 152 that formed its base.

It was also spacious for the day, as well as being beautifully appointed.

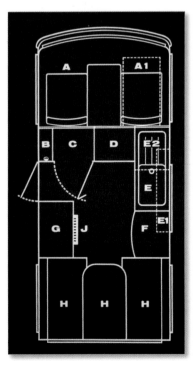

HERE IS THE LAYOUT — — — —

A.   **Cab-seating for driver and passenger** (5 ft. bed, optional extra.)
A.1. **Crockery in fitted locker.**
B.   **Locker for carrier and access to** $12\frac{1}{2}$ **gallon water tank.**
C.   **Toilet Compartment with chemical closet, washbasin, mirror, towel rail, etc.**
D.   **Gas Cooker with oven**—Formica working surface folds up to form division with cab.
E.   **Continuation of "D" as kitchen area with sink and drainer, space for refrigerator under drainer. Formica working surface; sink cover folds up to form division with cab.**

E.1. **Wall Locker.**
E.2. **Locker for Calor Gas.**
F.   **Chest of 3 large drawers and Cocktail Cabinet.**
G.   **Wardrobe with ample hanging space, 4 shelves and a shoe rack.**
H.   **Dinette — converts to luxurious double bed by night—table stores in wardrobe when not required.**
J.   **Gas Fire.**

SHIPPING SPECIFICATION—

HEIGHT —	8' 3"	(251·46 cm)
WIDTH —	6' 4½"	(194·31 cm)
LENGTH —	15' 1"	(459·74 cm)
WEIGHT —	34 cwt.	(1,727 kilos)

KENEX

Originally in the business of producing specialist bodywork for fire tenders, mobile shops and suchlike, Kenex of Dover in Kent branched out into converting light commercials into motor caravans as the 1950s drew to a close.

Before long its Carefree range of motor caravans became available on the Bedford CA, Ford Thames, BMC J4 and Standard Atlas, but from thereon the company's existence was all too brief. Shortly after the 1962 commercial motor show, Kenex was taken over by Martin Walter; production ceased early in November.

The April 1960 brochure.

Well-planned fittings give an elegant, roomy and convenient interior to the Kenex Caravan.

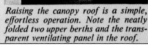

Raising the canopy roof is a simple, effortless operation. Note the neatly folded two upper berths and the transparent ventilating panel in the roof.

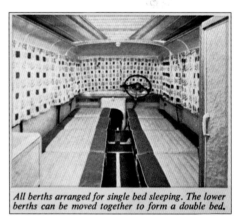

All berths arranged for single bed sleeping. The lower berths can be moved together to form a double bed.

Whether De Luxe or Standard the interior layout was very much the same, with what the manufacturer described as, "Easily cleaned plastic wood faced wood grained hardboard panelling," much in evidence.

'Carefree' Standard Caravan with roof canopy erected and enlarged windows in the rear doors. Model '102' illustrated.

STANDARD MODEL

The standard model is generally similar to the de Luxe except that the following items are omitted: Glass fibre tail fins, spare wheel flap, rear body skirts; glass fibre exterior sun visor; chrome plated front and rear bumpers and hub embellishers. Full-width rear bumper extra.

KENEX COACHWORK LTD
STANDARD COLOUR RANGE 1962
IN
BELCO 300
TRANSPORT FINISH

Manufactured by
IMPERIAL CHEMICAL INDUSTRIES LTD.
PAINTS DIVISION

Distributed by
BROWN BROTHERS LIMITED

LARCH GREEN 91	OXFORD BLUE 113	DARK ADMIRALTY GREY 105	CARNATION RED 224
LEAF GREEN 35	LARKSPUR BLUE 55	OLD IVORY 54	BLACK 122
LIME GREEN 608	SMOKE GREY 492	STRAW 45	DOVER WHITE 3049

"Vans to be converted should be ordered from Vauxhall Motors Limited to the specification of the CAL/CAS 10/12cwt van in primer when Kenex paint finishes are requested," stipulated the brochure.

STANDARD TRIUMPH

STANDARD ATLAS *Kenex* RANGE

A material such as GRP made it a simple matter for Kenex to follow the contours of the Atlas roof with its folding version. But oh dear: has someone found a maggot in their apple?

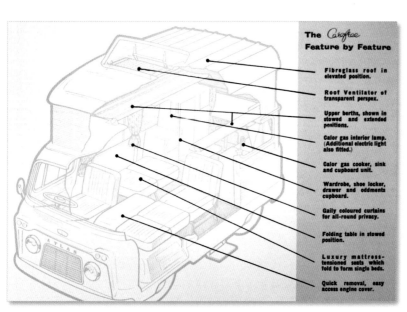

The *Carefree* Feature by Feature

Fibreglass roof in elevated position.

Roof Ventilator of transparent perspex.

Upper berths, shown in stowed and extended positions.

Calor gas interior lamp. (Additional electric light also fitted.)

Calor gas cooker, sink and cupboard unit.

Wardrobe, shoe locker, drawer and oddments cupboard.

Gaily coloured curtains for all-round privacy.

Folding table in stowed position.

Luxury mattress-tensioned seats which fold to form single beds.

Quick removal, easy access engine cover.

A particular feature of the "Carefree" is the elevating fibreglass roof, erected in seconds by spring loaded lifting gear to provide 6' 4" headroom. Ingenious use of space gives complete freedom of movement within the vehicle.

As well as the Carefree De Luxe on the cover, the autumn 1961 brochure listed the Carefree Standard and economy two-berth Siesta.

The Mk II Carefree De Luxe was easily distinguished from the earlier model by its different rear lamp treatment and side mouldings, as well as the addition of roof lights.

MARTIN WALTER

Of all the companies engaged in the conversion of vans to motor caravans, Martin Walter had by far and away the longest lineage, with roots stretching back to the 1770s when a firm of the same name made horse harnesses and then, as business prospered, expanded into building carriages.

By the early years of the twentieth century Martin Walter was based in Folkestone, Kent where, with diminishing demand for horse-drawn vehicles, it had moved into the motor trade. Then, before long, the acquisition of a local coachbuilder prompted Martin Walter to put its name to this trade.

During the 1920s the firm was responsible for equipping many of the better classes of English and Continental chassis with bodies that ranged from formal to sporting – one of the latter being built for a Bentley that ran at Le Mans in 1926.

In the early 1930s Martin Walter developed a Germanic style of convertible, which was built on a number of chassis including Daimler, Lanchester and Hillman. But the largest contract – for what were now known as Wingham cabriolets – was placed by Vauxhall. So successful were they that during 1937 a lucrative sale of this side of the business was negotiated with Abbey Coachworks, which promptly changed the name to Wingham Martin Walter.

Meanwhile Martin Walter itself was kept busy with other work that included a simple system to convert a van into a station wagon, which began to be marketed towards the end of the '30s as the Utilecon, with Ford being an early customer.

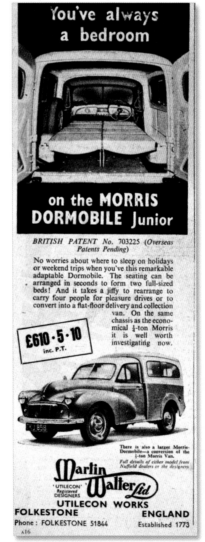

The name that was to become synonymous with motor caravans was in use before Martin Walter embarked upon full conversions. But they'd have been hard pressed to fit a cooker, sink and other accoutrements into this 1955 Junior edition.

What is more, the firm never had cause to regret the sale of the cabriolet business as, come the Second World War, it was fully employed making specialist vehicles – emerging after the hostilities to enjoy a great demand for station wagon conversions, whilst of Winghams no more was heard.

Although these Utilecon conversions enjoyed a few years of popularity, when Bedford launched its CA in 1952 another opportunity presented itself: Martin Walter was quick to offer a simple conversion featuring its Dormatic seating that could be re-arranged to form beds.

The obvious next step was to develop and manufacture full "living" conversions, and in 1957 the CA-based Dormobile motor caravan was on the market. Within a short time, Martin Walter conver-

The first of Martin Walter's fully-fitted-out Dormobiles had a distinctive porthole on each side. This is the two-berth model with smaller elevating roof.

sions were available on other makers' similarly-sized vans, and gradually the word Dormobile became generic for a motor home – the company eventually changing its name to just that.

By far and away the largest British manufacturer of motor caravans, Dormobile turned out many thousands. Its best years were during the 1960s, but throughout the '70s it was also very busy. Sales slowed at the end of the decade, by the mid-'80s motor caravans had ceased production, and ten years later the company was no more.

The Dormobile name was, however, purchased from the official receiver. It is now owned by the SHB Group that, as far as I know, are once again producing motor caravans with lifting roofs – just like the old CAs and other campers made by Martin Walter in the '50s.

THE NEW
BEDFORD
DORMOBILE
CARAVAN

The four-berth Dormobile had a larger hinging panel with Perspex ventilator, which allowed a pair of folding stretcher-type beds to be employed in the roof space. The firm's design of elevating roof, although not the earliest, was the first to go into large-scale production, and was to remain unaltered except in detail.

Here is the Bedford Dormobile Caravan (4-berth model) with the roof canopy folded down. The roof rack illustrated is an optional extra.

A four-berth model ready for the road and fitted with the optional roof rack. Chromium-plated fittings were an optional extra, along with such luxuries as a radio.

Ready for bed in the four-berth model; in a two-berth the lower sleeping arrangements were identical.

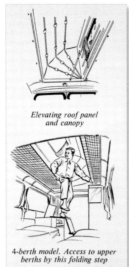

Elevating roof panel and canopy

4-berth model. Access to upper berths by this folding step

Obligatory family cups of tea being poured by a rather elegant lady who looks a little more Vogue *than mummy.*

Seats arranged to form "dinette"

Position of "two-burner" gas cooker

Roomy wardrobe with hanging hooks

THE "DORMOBILE" CARAVAN TENT

Specially designed for use with the DORMOBILE CARAVAN, as shown in adjoining illustrations, this roomy tent can be used with the DORMOBILE, UTILECON, UTILABRAKE, WORKOBUS and similar vehicles. Made of special lightweight waterproof material, ensuring easy erection and stowage. It can be left in situ, as illustrated, so that the vehicle can be used independently, or used in conjunction with the vehicle to form an extra sleeping compartment, or dining or sitting room. It also makes an excellent garden or beach tent.

Listed as an option, the tent was used here in conjunction with a two-berth Dormobile.

The autumn 1960 brochure offered the standard Dormobile on both the 90in and 102in-wheelbase Bedford CA, while the new Romany was on the longer chassis only.

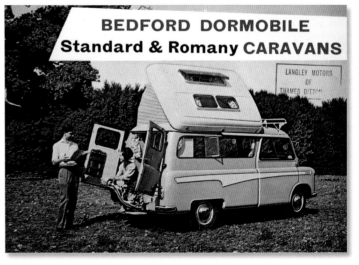

BEDFORD DORMOBILE
Standard & Romany CARAVANS

LANGLEY MOTORS OF THAMES DITTON

A four-berth Standard 102 Dormobile fitted with optional roof rack, chromium bumpers and hubcaps.

And now, the Romany . . .

Martin Walter's new de-luxe Dormobile Caravan, incorporating many additional luxury refinements of specification and equipment. Turn over for full details.

"Everything that the most critical caravanner could desire," pronounced the sales literature of the Romany. This one had been dressed up with the optional rear quarter fins with integral lamp clusters, chromium headlamp cowls and bumpers, along with a roof rack. Included as standard was a wider folding roof that gave very nearly 8ft of headroom through the living area, as well as allowing wider top bunks.

Here you see the optional refrigerator and lower berths arranged as a double, whilst the lower photo shows the optional and rather demurely described, "Elsan closet with decency curtain in position," hygienically placed right beside the fridge, having been pulled out from its storage cabinet underneath!

No fridge in this photo of the interior seating arranged around the folding table, and the optional Elsan is out of sight in its cupboard with padded top. Cooker to left foreground and wardrobe to right with water container are clearly seen.

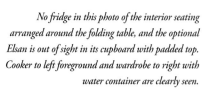

Exterior	90	102
Overall length	13′ 5″	14′ 5″
Overall width	5′ 10″	5′ 10″
Overall height (unladen)		
Roof down	6′ 7″	6′ 7″
Roof up	10′ 3″	10′ 3″

Kerb Weight		
2 berth	1 ton 5 cwt.	1 ton 5¼ cwt.
4 berth	1 ton 5¼ cwt.	1 ton 5½ cwt.

Interior		
Length:		
windscreen to rear doors	10′ 2″	11′ 2″
behind driver	6′ 4″	7′ 4″
Width:		
Panel to Panel	4′ 11″	4′ 11″
Height:		
Roof up	7′ 10″	7′ 10″
Roof down	4′ 4″	4′ 4″
Roof aperture Dimensions	5′ 9″ × 3′ 8″	

Standard colours for '62 were Lime Green, Carnation Red, Castle Grey or Mandarin Blue (all with Dormobile White flash) or Almond, Castle Grey, Georgian Cream or Dormobile White with Carnation Red flash.

Bedford Dormobile Romany Caravans

This illustration shows the de-Luxe model, on the 102 in. long wheelbase Bedford, finished in Lime Green and Dormobile White. There are ten different versions of three basic models, at prices from £695 to £875.
The vehicles described herein are the joint products of VAUXHALL MOTORS Ltd., Luton, and MARTIN WALTER Ltd., Folkestone.

It's the dawn of the emancipated '60s and it looks as though the rear door storage compartment is being used for dad's beer bottles rather than cups and plates as in the previous year's sales material; but for now he's content to enjoy a cuppa with his son. This is the same long-wheelbase Romany, finished in Lime Green and Dormobile White, as on the '62 season brochure cover.

In wet weather, or when touring, children can read or play without disturbing the driver or front passenger. The rear seats can be adapted for sitting at the table when the vehicle is on the road. Or they and the table can be folded away to give a clear floor area.

This attractive glass fibre roof extension with built-in roof rack and exterior sun visor is included in the specification of the Romany de-Luxe on the 102 in. wheelbase. It is also available as optional equipment on the long wheelbase Romany Super.

This illustration shows the useful glovebox (A) which is set into the new satin-finished wood grain plastic veneered facia, and the handy map pocket (B) fitted to the insulated engine cover on the de-Luxe model. Fresh-air ventilation controls (E) and (F) and fresh-air inlets (G) and (H)—to which optional fresh-air heaters can be fitted—can be seen at each side. There are additional parcel trays (C) and (D) on the front wheel arches.

Here's every caravanning necessity built in. Plastic trays clip onto the rear door bottle racks. A plastic waste bag hangs by the two-burner bottled gas stove. Undersink cupboards have ventilated sliding doors. Cradles beneath the floor can carry gas cylinders and a chemical toilet. The folding rear step makes access easy.

This hinged seat can be used when working at the sink or cooker, can be folded completely away, or can be further extended to form a step to the upper berths on four-berth models. Unbreakable, translucent glass-fibre water containers give a visual indication of their contents.

Through ventilation without draughts is possible with the new hinged rear door glass louvres, controlled by neat levers on the door interiors, which are fitted to de-Luxe models.

Sockets were provided in the floor to secure the legs of a folding table that allowed settings for four, but to be honest the seating looked a little awkward. Crockery was now stored in special racks under the draining board and the cutlery lived in a small drawer above the sink cupboard's sliding doors (seen on left). Upholstery was either Red or Blue Duracour.

A year later the colour schemes had become more adventurous and our family from the 1962 brochure now own a brand-new De Luxe finished in Imperial Crimson and Dormobile White (Red or Grey trim went with this combination). Other stock finishes were Castle Grey/Imperial Crimson/Red trim, Jasmine Yellow/Dormobile White/Green trim, Oxford Blue/Dormobile White/Blue trim, Avion Blue/Dormobile White/Blue trim, Lime Green/Dormobile White/Green trim, Sylvan Green/Dormobile White/Green trim, Sun Beige/Imperial Crimson/Red trim, Imperial Crimson/Dormobile White/Grey trim or Standard Fawn/Dormobile White/Red trim.

Their daughter was now old enough to enjoy a cup of tea but their dog appeared as disinterested as ever.

Upholstery was either in Grey, Blue, Green or Red Vynide.

The long wheelbase model of the Dormobile Romany Super, with exterior finish in Avion Blue and Dormobile White.

The Dormobile Romany Standard on the short wheelbase chassis, finished in Castle Grey.

Here's a Romany four-berth Super in Avion Blue with Dormobile White flash. All models were equipped with a three-speed gearbox but you could have a four-speed if you spent an extra £12. They were all petrol-powered too, unless you wanted to splash out £125 more for a diesel.

Only the Romany two-berth Standard came on the short 90in wheelbase. The economy conversion price for the CAL model of just £205 against £345 to £425 for others in the Romany range meant it came without duo-tone paint and other ornamentation.

Although it started with Bedford CA conversions, Martin Walter soon added other brands to its repertoire. The Dormobile A152 was fully endorsed by its maker and available through any Austin dealer.

With the A152 Dormobile you had just the one wheelbase of 90in but it did have side and rear doors. You also had nothing extra to pay for the benefit of a four-speed gearbox – Austin fitted it as standard.

Gosh – a member of the Royal Family for tea? If so, it's a good thing they had the Austin Dormobile, as its dining table and chairs could be arranged rather more conveniently for such occasions than those in the Bedford version.

Seats were in the normal touring position. Gas to power the cooker and a light above was stored in either one or two Calor cylinders beneath the floor.

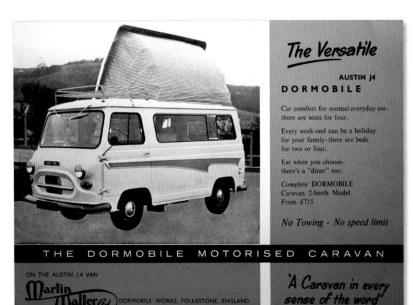

The Versatile
_____

AUSTIN J4
DORMOBILE

Car comfort for normal everyday use –
there are seats for four.

Every week-end can be a holiday
for your family - there are beds
for two or four.

Eat when you choose –
there's a "diner" too.

Complete DORMOBILE
Caravan 2-berth Model
From £715

No Towing - No speed limit

THE DORMOBILE MOTORISED CARAVAN

ON THE AUSTIN J.4 VAN
Martin Walter Ltd DORMOBILE WORKS, FOLKESTONE, ENGLAND

'A Caravan in every sense of the word'

The Austin A152 was replaced by the J4 in 1960 and Martin Walter lost no time in bringing a Dormobile version to the market. Colour schemes were from the Austin range or Martin Walter's own. If one opted for the latter, Standard models were one colour whereas De Luxe vehicles were two-tone with very much the same choice as that for the Bedford; in addition there was Iris Blue/Dormobile White/Blue trim, Foam White/Imperial Crimson/Red trim, British Racing Green/Dormobile White/Red trim or Antelope/Dormobile White/Red trim.

Only De Luxe models had the elevating roof, whether two- or four-berth. It was wise to go the extra £90-or-so for one of these, otherwise use of the interior was restricted by the roof height of just 4ft 4in with the two-berth Standard edition.

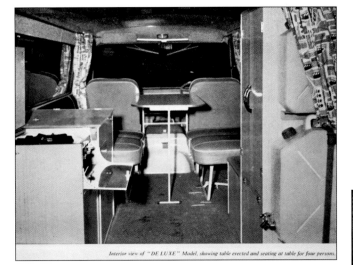

Interior view of "DE LUXE" Model, showing table erected and seating at table for four persons.

Here's the De Luxe four-berth in dining mode with the driver and passenger seats in their normal position, whilst night time would see the seats folded down and combined with the dining chairs to make a pair of single beds. Table stowage was the same as other Dormobiles – folded and clipped to the side of the body. The De Luxe had two gas rings with underfloor Calor storage, whilst the Standard had but one burner with Calor bottle in the van.

A voyeur's eye view of a Dormobile's upper sleeping compartment, but he's out of luck – it's just a couple of fully-dressed young ladies in the brochure photos, so there's no naughty nighties.

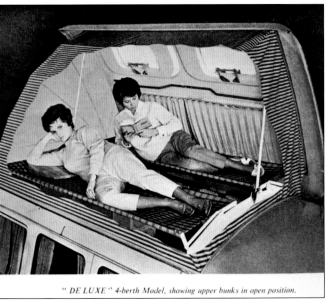

"DE LUXE" 4-berth Model, showing upper bunks in open position.

Ford's Thames 15cwt came in for the Martin Walter treatment too. Were the girls used for their brochures wives, girlfriends or employees, or were they professional models?

"Seating for six – for touring," read the caption. Colour schemes, as usual, were either the manufacturer's or from Martin Walter's extensive range. The porthole harked back to early Bedford Dormobiles.

Teatime yet again – table and chairs were arranged crosswise by the side door in the Thames Dormobile.

No need to disturb the front seats, as two full-length beds were made from those behind them. This was the four-berth, but the two-berth worked in just the same way.

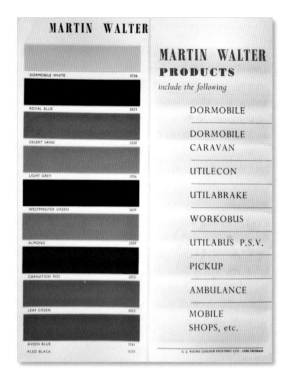

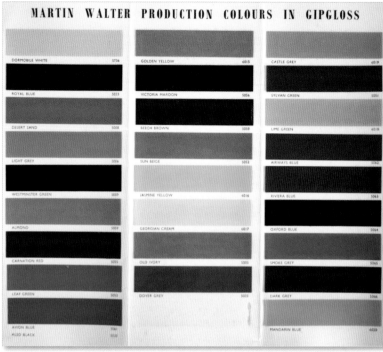

Including this brochure is a bit of a cheat, as it wasn't published until February 1966. However, I thought you'd like to see how Martin Walter dealt with the first of its Transit conversions – perhaps even the prototype, as it was wearing a 1965 Kent registration.

Rather than draw your attention to the sumptuous fit-out and two happy little chaps, I'll comment upon the nanny state of affairs that disallows such images in today's advertising. A child pouring scalding-hot tea into a cup, even though it is on a saucer, balanced on his knee? No, no, no – just sit kids down in front of the TV and learn all about life that way.

There, look – he survived, and is handing his dad the fruits of his endeavours. By the looks on the two little chaps' faces, they might have been up to a bit of mischief – so I do hope they didn't put something naughty into his cuppa.

"It's child's play to erect – a simple push on two telescopic members and the roof canopy is up, ready for use." With it erected there was a full 7 ft of headroom, and come bedtime the two pull-out top bunks plus the two made up from folded seating accommodated four adults.

A	106.0 ins.	269.24 c.m.	G	25.0 ins.	63.5 c.m.
B	29.5 ins.	79.92 c.m.	H	57.45 ins.	146.1 c.m.
C	182.0 ins.	462.30 c.m.	J	48.3 ins.	122.0 c.m.
D	85.0 ins.	215.9 c.m.	K	54.8 ins.	139.0 c.m.
E	77.2 ins.	196.1 c.m.	L	72.0 ins.	182.9 c.m.
F	62.5 ins.	158.8 c.m.	M	24.0 ins.	61.0 c.m.

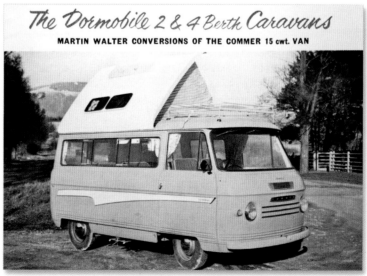

Even though Commer made its own motor caravans it was quite happy to supply vehicles to Martin Walter for its own conversions – which seemed very fair.

PARALANIAN

The Paralanian reputedly came about when a downturn in sales at the Bradford, Yorkshire, Austin dealership Central Garage during the Suez crisis prompted the owners to give their body shop some alternative work. With the possibility of future small production runs in mind, designs for an ice cream van and a motor caravan were formulated, and prototypes constructed using the current Austin 152 as a basis.

It wasn't just any old job, but one that was the last word in luxury and practicability. So why on earth call it the Paralanian? Simple: Central Garage was situated in Parry Lane.

Coach-built upon an ash frame and double-skinned with a mixture of metal and what was termed plastic, its maker pulled no punches when extolling its virtues. "We offer you a high class flat, with *all* the amenities, but possessing the mobility and handiness of a private motorcar. It is fitted and furnished in good taste and in an inviting manner, with ample head room and floor space and stowage for *all* your goods and chattels."

With prose such as this, one could imagine queues of customers eager to switch from bricks and mortar until, even in those more spartan times, they found that all their goods and chattels could not in fact be accommodated by a Paralanian. But the Trade Descriptions Act was several years up the road, along with some changes in the usage and meaning of the English language – as the continuing sales blurb exemplifies. "Cool in summer, warm in winter, homely and friendly, we commend it to you for gay adventure, in every off duty moment."

Wild claims notwithstanding, the Paralanian went on to be made in MkII and then, in 1961, MkIII versions – the latter styled in a retrospective but rather charming fashion in that it somewhat resembled an early 1950s' caravan on four wheels, with the cab of an Austin 152 tucked into the front. A touch quirky it may have been, but most agree that it was the most attractive of the series.

Even after the workshops that made the Paralanian were closed down when Central Garage was taken over by Lookers a few years later, production was recommenced elsewhere. Now based on the Austin J4 (or alternatively the Commer P-type), it was made by Spen Coachbuilders of Heckmondwike, Yorkshire, which was by then a subsidiary of the Transport Holding Company.

At around this time the original designer of the MkIII decided that he too would make a Paralanian, and employed tradesmen who had worked at Central Garage to boot. Thus Bradford-based European Caravans was born and a mildly restyled MkIII, built upon either the Austin J4 or Commer P-type, was marketed as the Tourstar.

By the early '70s the MkIII in its various guises was gone.

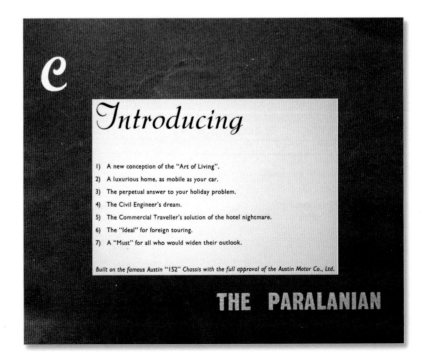

C

Introducing

1) A new conception of the "Art of Living".

2) A luxurious home, as mobile as your car.

3) The perpetual answer to your holiday problem.

4) The Civil Engineer's dream.

5) The Commercial Traveller's solution of the hotel nightmare.

6) The "Ideal" for foreign touring.

7) A "Must" for all who would widen their outlook.

Built on the famous Austin "152" Chassis with the full approval of the Austin Motor Co., Ltd.

THE PARALANIAN

The first of the Paralanians was described by its makers to be, "Of pleasing lines," but it was somewhat redolent of an ambulance, mobile shop or other such vehicle – and this was the De Luxe with chromium side flashes, as well as Rimbellishers.

"Still elegant even when viewed from the rear," they said, but if anything its utility look was more pronounced from this angle.

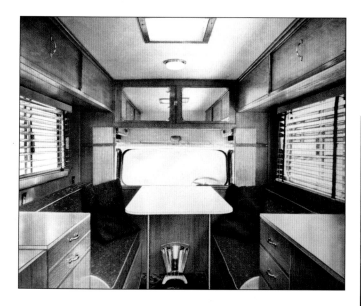

The interior, however, exuded quality and pride of workmanship that reflected a price tag of £1050 for the Standard model or £200 more for the De Luxe illustrated here. Hand-polished veneers covered the custom-made cabinetwork, while the floor was covered in Axminster carpet (linoleum for the Standard version) and the upholstery was of, "First quality Moquette." The brochure also pointed out that the driving compartment (beyond the dining table in this photo) had special seats, also trimmed with Moquette, which could be used as emergency bunks. The folding bulkhead behind the driver was only fitted as standard to the De Luxe, as was the little floor-standing gas convector heater.

The tall cupboard to the right of the rear door housed a chemical toilet, and a sink with tap was to its right. On the left was a gas cooker complete with oven. There was also, as you can see, a comprehensive range of cupboards and drawers.